Stamp Taxes

Stamp Taxes

Kevin Griffin CTA

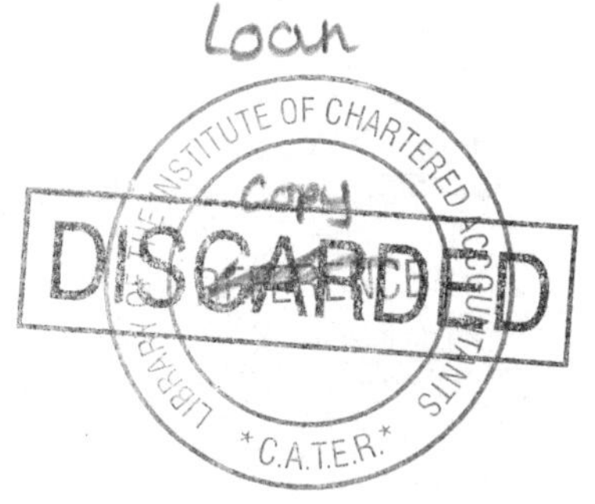

Bloomsbury Professional

Bloomsbury Professional Ltd, Maxwelton House, 41–43 Boltro Road, Haywards Heath, West Sussex, RH16 1BJ

A CIP Catalogue record for this book is available from the British Library.

ISBN: 978 1 84766 562 1

Typeset by Phoenix Typesetting, Chatham, Kent
Printed and bound in Great Britain by Hobbs the Printers Ltd, Totton, Hampshire

Preface

While I was responsible for the stamp taxes group of one of the 'big four' firms, we were frequently surprised by the nervousness induced in colleagues and clients alike by stamp tax questions. This, of course, kept us fully employed, but we did sometimes wish we could leave the relatively straightforward matters to others and have more time for the really difficult issues.

Without doubt, stamp taxes are different from other taxes, and indeed from each other. However, once the fundamentals have been understood, they are like other taxes in that they comprise a mixture of the relatively simple and the horribly complicated. The aims of this book are to help the tax-literate non-specialist:

- understand the basic ideas and concepts,
- deal confidently with straightforward matters, and
- recognise when specialist input is needed.

To this end, examples, checklists and tables have been included, together with cross-references to legislation, tax cases and HMRC guidance wherever they are expected to be helpful. HMRC material is generally available on their website, and web addresses are given where possible.

Whatever the reader's purpose in consulting this volume, it is suggested that he or she read Chapter 1 first – it is mercifully brief – as a kind of orientation exercise before using the contents, index or table of statutes to research particular points.

I am grateful to Mark McLaughlin and his colleagues at Bloomsbury Professional for guidance and suggestions as I prepared the book. I am also grateful to my wife, Sue, for patiently feigning interest as I chewed over the best way to express this or that point, and for not complaining too loudly when I took the laptop on holiday. Any errors or omissions are entirely down to me.

Kevin Griffin
October 2010

Contents

Table of Statutes

[*References are to paragraph number and appendices*]

Table of Statutory Instruments etc

[*References are to paragraph number*]

Table of EC Materials

[*References are to paragraph number*]

EC Council Regulation 2157/2001 of 8 October 2001 on the Statute for a European company 10.5

Markets in Financial Instruments Directive, Directive 2004/39/EC 10.23

Table of Cases

[*References are to paragraph number*]

Associated British Engineering Ltd v IRC [1941] 1 KB 15, [1940] 4 All ER 278, 164 LT 335, KBD ... 11.31
Attorney General v Cohen [1936] 2 KB 246, [1936] 1 All ER 583, KBD 2.36
Faber (Oscar) v IRC [1936] 1 All ER 617, 155 LT 228, KBD ... 8.21
Glenrothes Development Corporation v IRC [1994] STC 74, 1994 SLT 1310, Ct of Sess (IH) ... 8.34
HSBC & Vidacos v HMRC (Case C-569/07) [2010] STC 58, [2009] All ER (D) 03 (Oct), ECJ ... 10.27
IRC v Maple & Co (Paris) Ltd [1908] AC 22, 24 TLR 140, 97 LT 814, HL ... 8.21
LM Tenancies 1 plc v Inland Revenue Commissioners [1996] STC 880, [1996] 46 EG 155, [1996] 2 EGLR 119, ChD ... 8.36, 11.18
Prudential Assurance Co Ltd v IRC [1992] STC 863, [1993] 1 WLR 211, [1993] 1 All ER 211, ChD ... 2.24 7.25
Underground Electric Railways Co of London Ltd v IRC [1906] AC 21, 75 LJKB 117, 93 LT 819, HL; [1905] 1 KB 174 ... 8.37
Underground Electric Railways Co of London Ltd v IRC [1914] 3 KB 210, KBD ... 8.37
Wood Preservation Ltd v Prior [1968] 2 All ER 849, [1968] TR 37, 47 ATC 49, ChD ... 9.11

List of Abbreviations

CFD	contract for differences
CTA 2010	Corporation Tax Act 2010
DOTAS	disclosure of tax avoidance schemes
FA [year]	Finance Act [year]
HMRC	Her Majesty's Revenue and Customs
ICTA 1988	Income and Corporation Taxes Act 1988
LLP	limited liability partnership
LTR	land transaction return
MiFID	Markets in Financial Instruments Directive
NPV	net present value
OEIC	open ended investment company
PIK	payment in kind
PIP	property investment partnership
RI	recognised intermediary
RSL	registered social landlord
SA 1891	Stamp Act 1891
SDLT	Stamp Duty Land Tax
SDLTM	Stamp Duty Land Tax Manual
SDRT	Stamp Duty Reserve Tax
SP	Statement of Practice
SPV	special purpose vehicle/company
SRN	scheme reference number
STM	Stamp Taxes Manual
TNPV	total net present value
UTRN	unique transaction reference number

Chapter 1

Introduction to Stamp Taxes

THREE TAXES

1.1 Almost all tax which people call 'stamp duty' is really one of the two more modern taxes, Stamp Duty Reserve Tax (SDRT) and Stamp Duty Land Tax (SDLT).

SDLT accounts for the overwhelming majority of revenue raised by this group of taxes. It is also the tax most likely to impact ordinary commercial and private transactions. Its application to ordinary house purchases is fairly straightforward. In relation to commercial transactions and even some house purchases, it can be an inordinately complex tax. Therefore, the greater part of this book is devoted to SDLT.

SDRT is mostly administered and paid by professionals in the financial services industry, often operating on the basis of rules and arrangements negotiated directly with HMRC. These rules and arrangements are beyond the scope of this book, which contains only a fairly brief outline of SDRT, concentrating on the impact of the tax on transactions in unquoted securities.

1.2 Each of the taxes has its own legislative code, with relatively little interaction between SDLT and the other taxes. There is more interaction between stamp duty and SDRT because, for many transactions, they are alternatives. The following table indicates where to find the main legislation governing each tax. The principal charging provisions are in bold, while other important provisions are shown in normal type. Especially in the case of stamp duty, there are numerous other provisions in various *Finance Acts* and other legislation. These are referred to in the text of this book where appropriate. For SDRT and SDLT, most changes since original enactment of the main provisions have proceeded by amendment; if an up–to-date copy of the main law is available, it is not normally necessary to consult subsequent *Finance Acts*, unless investigating the effective date of a change or dealing with a transaction governed by transitional provisions.

Tax	Legislation
Stamp duty	***FA 1999, Sch 13*** *FA 1999, ss 109–123, Schs 12, 14–19* *FA 1986, ss 64–85* *Stamp Act 1891*; *FA 1930, s 42*; *FA 1967, s 27* *FA 2003, s 125*
SDRT	***FA 1986, ss 86–99*** *Stamp Duty Reserve Tax Regulations 1986, SI 1986/1711* *FA 1999, ss 116–122, Sch 19*
SDLT	***FA 2003, ss 42–124, Schs 3–19*** *Stamp Duty Land Tax (Administration) Regulations 2003, SI 2003/2837* *Stamp Duty Land Tax (Electronic Communications) Regulations 2005, SI 2005/844* *FA 2004, ss 306–319*; *SI 2004/1864*; *SI 2004/1865*; *SI 2005/1868*

1.3 There are three reasons why practitioners and taxpayers need some knowledge of the rules relating to stamp duty itself:

1. because non-stock market share transactions are still generally dealt with under stamp duty, failure to deal with this tax may leave unrecognised SDRT liabilities outstanding (see **10.11**);
2. some other transactions finalised on or after 1 December 2003 may still give rise to stamp duty charges because of actions taken before that date (see **2.40** and **11.29**); and
3. many of the principles and ideas in the other two taxes are derived from equivalent provisions under stamp duty and are most easily understood in that context.

It is therefore suggested that at least a brief study of the chapters on stamp duty would be worthwhile, even if the reader is dealing exclusively with transactions which may be subject only to one of the other taxes.

1.4 The names given to SDRT and SDLT are potentially misleading. They have 'stamp' in their name only because they collect tax which used to be collected through stamp duty. Unlike stamp duty, SDRT and SDLT are chargeable on transactions or agreements no matter how, where or even whether documented; no stamps are involved. They are compulsory, self-assessment taxes, with enforcement provisions similar to those which apply to corporation tax and income tax; SDLT, in particular, has draconian anti-avoidance rules.

1.5 In contrast, stamp duty is often referred to as a voluntary tax because, with few exceptions (such as the charge on issue of bearer instruments, **8.53**), there is no direct obligation to pay. The only payment enforcement mechanism comes from the fact that a document which should be stamped cannot be used for UK official purposes, such as registration of title, evidence in a civil court, or for cancelling an SDRT charge, until it has been stamped. Stamping after the due date will generally lead to charging of interest and penalties, so if a document is to be stamped, it is best to deal with this promptly. However, where a document, despite being within the charge to stamp duty, is unlikely to be needed for any relevant UK purpose, the decision may validly be taken not to pay the stamp duty and to leave the document unstamped. Under current rules, this is only likely for some transfers of interests in partnerships which hold stock or marketable securities, or where the transfer relates to non-UK securities – it is highly unlikely that a stampable transfer of UK registered securities may safely be left unstamped. Historically, many other documents were left unstamped, as explained at **11.29**.

1.6 All three taxes are administered by HMRC, who publish two manuals on their website, setting out their views and practices on the taxes:

- The Stamp Taxes Manual, which can be downloaded from www.hmrc.gov.uk/so/manual.htm, deals with stamp duty and SDRT. In this book, references to this manual are in the form 'STM1.234'. The manual is available only as a downloadable PDF file with limited interactive functionality. It has not been comprehensively updated since the introduction of SDLT. It therefore contains much redundant material and is incorrect in many places. Nonetheless, looked at with this knowledge, it does give a lot of useful information. It is an essential reference when dealing with the current completion or unwinding of 'old' transactions, dealt with in Chapter 11.
- The second manual is the Stamp Duty Land Tax Manual, available at www.hmrc.gov.uk/manuals/sdltmanual/index.htm. This is published only as an online interactive document. It is widely referred to in this book, references being in the form 'SDLTM12345'.

1.7 HMRC provide online tools for calculation of SDLT, especially useful in relation to leases, and a facility for online completion and submission of SDLT returns. Further details of these are set out below in the chapters on SDLT. Use of the online submission facility is not yet compulsory, but it may become so in due course. A project is underway in Scotland to integrate online completion of SDLT returns with the Registers of Scotland's Automated Registration of Title to Land (see **6.13**). This is a first step towards a long-term Government goal of having routine SDLT collection and administration dealt with by the Land Registries, leaving HMRC to deal with technical, policy and policing issues.

HMRC also provide a wide array of other useful information and guidance in the stamp tax section of their website (www.hmrc.gov.uk/so). The volume is so great that it is not always easy to find specific items, but references are given in this book where appropriate. A slight worry is that HMRC have recently taken to 'tidying up' this information, including removal of 'out of date' items. As a result, information which is visible today may disappear tomorrow.

A BRIEF HISTORY OF STAMP DUTY

1.8 Stamp duty was introduced over 300 years ago, copying a Dutch tax. Like income tax, it was intended to be a temporary measure to finance a war. Unlike income tax, it did not require annual renewal. A hundred years later, Pitt the Younger described stamp duty as a tax 'easily raised, widely diffused, pressing little on any particular class'. In other words, the thought was that those who paid the tax would scarcely notice – so it may, perhaps, be thought of as the original stealth tax. Unfortunately, the American colonists had noticed a few years previously – the 'Boston Tea Party', an event widely regarded as marking the start of the American War of Independence, was in fact a protest against the imposition of UK stamp duty on documents in the American Colonies. Pitt also commented that stamp duty was 'safely and expeditiously collected at a small expense'. Government statistics show that stamp duty is by far the cheapest tax to collect, although this may be because the taxpayer and his advisers have to do most of the work in calculating and administering the tax.

1.9 Stamp duty has always been a tax on documents. As the name indicates, payment is evidenced by fixing or embossing stamps on the relevant document; in general, if no document is created, there is no stamp duty. Its range has varied enormously over three centuries. Those whose memories stretch back to the mid-twentieth century may remember the practice of signing receipts across a 2d (0.8p) stamp in order to ensure their legal validity – an example of a postage stamp being used for fiscal purposes. Until 1971, bank cheques were also subject to a 2d stamp duty, and the issue of a new chequebook by the bank led to an immediate deduction from one's bank account.

During the latter half of the twentieth century, the scope of stamp duty was steadily reduced until it applied only to transactions in shares and securities, land and buildings, and intangible assets such as partnership interests, intellectual property and goodwill. In 1986, SDRT was introduced in response to market developments which allowed transfer of beneficial ownership of securities without a document. As explained at **10.1**, it was at one stage proposed to abolish stamp taxes on shares and securities. However, that proposal was abandoned and the new Government of 1997 began to increase stamp duty rates on assets other than shares and securities. However, the yield to the Exchequer did not increase as expected, because avoidance of the tax on larger transactions became the norm. To counter this, stamp duty on property transactions was replaced by SDLT from 1 December 2003.

1.10 The original intention seems to have been for documents to be stamped no later than the time they were finally executed and, to this end, the Government sold stamps and pre-stamped paper to 'authorised dealers' such as law firms, who would then use them on documents or sell them on to the end user. The Government sold the stamps at a discount to face value, allowing the dealer to make a profit upon onward sale. This was, therefore, an early example of the privatised collection of tax. William Wordsworth was perhaps the most famous individual involved in this process – he was Distributor of Stamps for the county of Westmoreland. It was possible until very recently to buy blank stock transfer forms pre-stamped with a £5 stamp (the rate then applicable to many transfers otherwise than on sale), although sadly no discount was given!

Adhesive stamps were open to abuse (*Stamp Act 1891, s 9* still imposes penalties for fraudulent removal of adhesive stamps from a document with intent to re-use), and eventually the predecessors of HMRC became directly responsible for all stamping of documents at a number of Stamp Offices situated in major cities. The section of HMRC responsible for stamp taxes is still generally referred to as 'the Stamp Office'. Stamp Offices had stamping presses, allowing them to emboss appropriate value stamps on documents whilst keeping track of the value embossed, for audit purposes. The Stamp Offices provided an 'over the counter' service for routine stamping and even, by arrangement, for 'adjudication' (see **8.45**). Stamp Office public counters have now been closed and most of the machines decommissioned. Documents requiring physical stamping are sent to the Birmingham or Edinburgh Stamp Office, and specific arrangements have to be agreed in advance for those transactions where, for commercial or perhaps overseas tax or regulatory reasons, stamping of documents on the day of execution is required.

1.11 Stamp duty is generally chargeable on the document which formally transfers the asset in question – the conveyance. In relation to shares and securities, a mere contract to transfer will not normally be liable, as this will not itself transfer the assets. When stamp duty was chargeable on other assets such as goodwill, the contract was usually the document liable to stamp duty, because no separate transfer document is needed to complete the transaction. This led to a practice of completing transactions without a written contract (for example, a written offer to sell, completed by the purchaser paying the consideration). In the absence of a written contract, there was no document on which stamp duty could be charged (see **11.30**).

1.12 As mentioned above, in most cases there is no direct obligation to pay stamp duty or have a document stamped, but an unstamped document cannot be used for certain purposes. Where documents were executed outside the UK, it was the case for a long time that no interest and penalties accrued, provided the document was stamped within 30 days of first being brought into the UK. In the case of large transactions, if there was no current need for the document to be stamped, it became standard practice to execute and retain it offshore (often in the Channel Islands or the Isle of Man) and many such unstamped documents remain there to this day. In an attempt to reduce the attractiveness of this practice, the rules were changed in 1999 to charge interest from 30 days after execution, no matter where this took place. Another common mitigation technique was simply to avoid executing a conveyance (generally referred to as resting on, or in, contract). For example, legal title to the asset might be held by a special purpose vehicle/company (SPV) for the benefit of the beneficial owner. The current beneficial owner would contract to sell to a purchaser. The purchaser would make payment, thus gaining beneficial ownership, and the owner would transfer the SPV to the purchaser. In the absence of a conveyance, no stamp duty arose. There were many disputes between taxpayers and the Stamp Office over whether other documents created in this process could be treated as conveyances. To discourage the practice, the rules were changed in 2002 to treat contracts for transfer of land for more than £10 million as conveyances.

1.13 Numerous other ingenious methods were devised to mitigate stamp duty, and the Government began consultations on modernising the tax, concentrating on property transactions. However, it quickly became clear that it would be very difficult to create a tax which was relatively simple and certain, yet dealt fairly with the wide range of modern property transactions. Consultations ended abruptly, and SDLT was introduced in *Finance Act 2003*, replacing stamp duty on transactions in UK land and buildings with effect from 1 December 2003. At the same time, the scope of stamp duty itself was restricted to transactions in stock and marketable securities and interests in certain partnerships which hold stock or marketable securities. The inadequacy of the consultation process is reflected in the complexity of SDLT, the uncertainty over its application to many transactions, and the amendments made to the legislation, by regulations even before the tax came into effect and then in every subsequent *Finance Act*. The new rules appear to have had the desired effect, raising the stamp tax take from property transactions from £5 billion in 2003–04 to £10 billion in 2007–08. However economic factors then intervened and by 2009–10 the total had fallen below the 2003–04 level, largely as a result of reduced numbers of transactions.

Chapter 2

SDLT – General Rules

INTRODUCTION

2.1 Stamp Duty Land Tax (SDLT) replaced stamp duty on transactions involving UK land and buildings from 1 December 2003. However, it would be a mistake to assume that SDLT is merely an updated version of stamp duty. Many transactions which would not have been within the stamp duty net – including informal arrangements and some unilateral actions which might not conventionally be described as transactions – do give rise to SDLT liabilities and obligations. Even where there is no liability, there may be reporting obligations, with penalties for failure to comply. For this reason, this book often refers to 'SDLT obligations', meaning both liability to pay tax and obligation to notify a transaction or make a return. So wide ranging are these obligations, it is essential to consider the possible impact of SDLT on almost any change relating to the occupation of, or ownership of rights over, UK land and buildings.

2.2 Almost all transactions in UK land and buildings completed from 1 December 2003, even if commenced earlier, are within the scope of SDLT. Some 'old' transactions remain within the ambit of stamp duty, or perhaps potentially fall within both regimes (see **2.40**). In stark contrast with stamp duty, SDLT is a true 'self-assessment' tax. The obligation to report liability and make payment falls on the purchaser. The tax is triggered by entering into or performing 'land transactions' (as defined in the legislation), no matter how or even whether documented. Some, but not all, of the reliefs previously available under stamp duty are available under SDLT. There are enforcement powers and specific anti-avoidance rules similar to those that apply to other taxes, plus far-reaching general anti-avoidance provisions. SDLT is within the *FA 2004* regime for disclosure of tax avoidance schemes, but it has its own set of criteria to determine whether disclosure is required.

2.3 The initial rates of SDLT for purchase of freeholds and existing leases were the same as they were for stamp duty, so the typical home-buyer saw little or no practical change when the tax was introduced. *FA 2010* introduced, with effect from 6 April 2011, a new 5% rate for residential property costing more than £1 million. Anti-avoidance provisions and the absence of some reliefs mean that many commercial transactions suffer a greater tax burden than they would have incurred under stamp duty, even though there has been no change in rates. The regime for the grant, variation or surrender of leases is sufficiently complex to warrant a separate chapter in this book (**Chapter 4**). In most cases involving a lease at rent, the SDLT charge is substantially higher than would have arisen under stamp duty, up to ten times as much in extreme cases.

2.4 Obligations in relation to SDLT may extend beyond the time of the original transaction. In some circumstances, reliefs may be withdrawn or liabilities increased as a result of subsequent events as innocuous as a rent review or the refinancing of a group company. Constant monitoring of potential liabilities is therefore necessary. The tax applies irrespective of country of establishment or residence of the taxpayer, and it is possible that a non-UK entity, unaware of the rules, may unknowingly trigger an SDLT charge. An example would be where UK land is transferred in the course of a merger of overseas companies by operation of (overseas) law – normally free of stamp duty under the old regime, but subject to SDLT under current rules.

2.5 With the introduction of SDLT, stamp duty was abolished on transfers of all other assets apart from stock and marketable securities and, in some circumstances, interests in partnerships which hold such stock or securities.

GENERAL SCHEME OF SDLT

Importance of definitions

2.6 The SDLT rules rely on a number of concepts and expressions which are defined in *FA 2003*. It is important to apply these definitions and not to rely on the general meaning of the relevant words. The table below details statutory and HMRC SDLT Manual references for definitions of key terms; there is also a useful list of statutory references in *FA 2003, s 122*. Some of the definitions are interdependent, so it is necessary to see the whole picture before it makes sense; the definitions and the following paragraphs may require several readings! These paragraphs give a general outline of the tax and the defined expressions are shown, in the next few paragraphs only, in **bold**. Subsequent paragraphs and chapters examine the interpretation and application of the expressions in more detail.

Term	***FA 2003 section/Schedule***	**SDLTM para**
Acquisition	*s 43(3)*	00270
Chargeable interest	*s 48*	00280

Term	***FA 2003 section/Schedule***	**SDLTM para**
Consideration	*s 52; Sch 4*	03600
Conveyance	*s 44(10)(b)*	08100
Effective date	*s 119; s 44(4)*	07600
Exempt interest	*s 48(2)–(3A)*	00320
Land transaction	*s 43(1)*	00260
Linked transactions	*s 108*	30100
Major interest	*s 117*	04130
Purchaser	*s 43(3)–(4); Sch 17A, para 15A*	07200
Substantial amount/ substantially all	*s 44(7)*	07950
Substantial performance	*s 44(5)–(7)*	07700 et seq

The charge

2.7 SDLT is charged on **land transactions**, whether effected by a document or not. Neither the places of residence of the parties, nor the place where any documents are executed, are relevant to the charge. The tax is under the control of HM Revenue & Customs (HMRC), and that departmental name is used here despite the fact that much of the legislation still refers to the Commissioners of Inland Revenue (*FA 2003, s 42*). A **land transaction** for these purposes means the **acquisition** of a **chargeable interest**. **Acquisition** may include not only a normal land sale and purchase, but also the creation, surrender, release or variation of a **chargeable interest**. The **acquisition** may occur under the terms of a court order, a statutory provision or by operation of law. A complex and indirect definition makes clear the intention that any party whose interest in land benefits under the transaction is to be regarded as the **purchaser**. Poor wording of the legislation originally led to uncertainty when leases were varied, so supplementary rules were introduced to deal specifically with this (see **2.18**). A person will only be treated as a **purchaser** if he has either given **consideration** for, or is a party to, the transaction. It can thus be seen that the new charge catches a wider range of transactions than the old stamp duty regime.

Timing

2.8 In general, SDLT obligations arise 30 days after the **effective date** of the transaction (*FA 2003, ss 76(1), 86(1)*). At the latest, the **effective date** is the date of completion. Completion is not defined, except in relation to Scotland where it means settlement or, for a lease, signing or constitution by any means. The word, therefore, bears its normal legal meaning, broadly summarised as the final action required to give the transaction full legal effect. However, in many cases, the **effective date** is triggered by **substantial performance** of the transaction before completion.

Substantial performance

2.9 **Substantial performance** is defined using a combination of terms such as 'possession' and 'occupation', which are themselves not clearly defined, together with measurement of the proportion of any consideration actually paid. In any dispute as to whether an agreement has been **substantially performed**, expert legal advice may be required as to the meaning of terms. However, in general, a contract is **substantially performed** where either the purchaser takes possession of **substantially all** of the property passing under the contract, or **substantially all** of the consideration is paid or provided. HMRC have indicated that they will regard 90% or more as **substantially all**, but SDLTM07950 indicates they will not consider themselves tied to this figure if they detect an attempt to exploit it for avoidance. *Any* payment of rent under the terms of a lease will be regarded as **substantial performance** of the lease, as will the purchaser becoming entitled to receipt of *any* rent etc from a tenant.

This gives rise to a potential issue – Standard Terms & Conditions for land transactions may entitle the purchaser to rent from a tenant or sub-tenant earlier than the time of payment for the property, which may trigger early substantial performance. It is worthwhile to review the terms and conditions carefully, to avoid such problems.

Formal completion

2.10 If a contract for a **land transaction** is entered into and is completed by a formal **conveyance** not later than the time of **substantial performance**, the contract and **conveyance** are treated as a single **land transaction**, taking effect at the date of completion (*FA 2003, s 44(3)*). Submission of a return and payment of the tax will be due 30 days from that date. Where, however, the contract is entered into and **substantially performed** before completion, the contract itself is treated as a **land transaction**, the effective date being that of **substantial performance** (*s 44(4)*). The return and tax payment are due 30 days from that date. If such a transaction is later completed by a formal **conveyance**, that **conveyance** will be a separate **land transaction** (in some circumstances, but not always, requiring submission of a further return), but SDLT will only be payable to the extent that the tax payable on the **conveyance** is greater than the tax paid on **substantial performance** of the contract – there should be no overall 'double charge' (*s 44(8)*). However, care is needed where reduced or zero SDLT is paid at the time of **substantial performance** because of a relief or exemption – in some circumstances, the later completion can trigger further liability because conditions for the relief or exemption are not satisfied at that time. The circumstances in which two or more returns may be required for the same transaction are explored in more detail at **6.15** et seq.

What is chargeable

2.11 The terms **conveyance** and transfer are used interchangeably, and include any instrument. Accordingly, they cover the grant of a lease as well as a transfer of land. A transaction is chargeable unless it is specifically covered by an exemption. **Chargeable interests** include estates, interests, rights and powers over UK land, as well as the benefit of any obligation, restriction or other condition that would affect the value of any such estate, interest, right or power. However, licences to occupy, mortgages and similar security interests, and certain equivalent Scottish property interests, are excluded. The extension of the definition to include obligations and restrictions will mean, for example, that a payment to the owner of a neighbouring plot of land, for a restrictive covenant or wayleave, may give rise to a charge. For some purposes, it matters whether an interest is a **major interest**. This term covers interests generally referred to as freeholds, leaseholds and other tenancies, together with equivalent interests in Scotland.

2.12 The grant of an option to acquire an interest in land is specifically identified as a **chargeable transaction**. The transfer or exercise of an option is a separate transaction from the grant, but the two may be **linked transactions** for determining the amount of tax due. This is intended to counter attempts to take advantage of lower rates of SDLT by splitting a purchase into two steps. An option is not, itself, a **major interest**, although this fact is of little practical significance unless it is a component in an exchange.

2.13 If interests in land (at least one being a **major interest**) are exchanged, each transfer is separately chargeable; see **2.29**.

OCCASIONS OF CHARGE

Chargeable transactions

2.14 SDLT is chargeable on a chargeable land transaction – that is, any acquisition of a chargeable interest unless the transaction is itself exempt from charge. Any interest in UK land and buildings is chargeable unless it is specifically identified as exempt (see **2.16**). Examples of chargeable interests include freeholds, leases, sporting rights, the benefits of restrictive covenants, and equivalent interests under Scottish law – but this list is not exhaustive. The following give rise to the acquisition of a chargeable interest:

- transfer of all or part of a freehold or leasehold interest in UK property;
- grant of a lease out of a freehold or superior leasehold interest in UK property;
- surrender of a lease to the landlord;
- variation of a lease where that variation is treated as a surrender and re-grant in law, or where the variation includes a reduction in rent or a reduction in term; and
- grant, transfer, variation or surrender of an interest in UK property other than a freehold or lease – for example, sporting or mineral rights, right of light, right of passage, etc.

2.15 In relation to leases (and arrangements treated as leases for SDLT purposes), certain events, which are not in law any of the above, are nonetheless deemed to be one of this list. The most common is probably an increase in rent which, even if in accordance with the terms of the lease, may be deemed to be the grant of a further lease. These matters are considered in **Chapter 4**.

Exempt interests

2.16 The following limited list of interests is regarded as exempt, so that no SDLT liability or obligation arises on their creation, transfer, variation or surrender (*FA 2003, s 48(2)*). All other interests are chargeable:

- a security interest – that is, an interest or right (other than a rentcharge, feu duty or similar) held for the purpose of securing payment of money or performance of other obligations. This has been expanded to include the interest held by a financial institution as a result of an 'alternative property finance' transaction (see *FA 2003, s 73B*);
- a licence to use or occupy land. HMRC have made clear their view that this only applies to an interest which is a licence in both name and substance. They will resist attempts to 'dress up' as a licence an interest which is in substance greater than that, and care is required in relying on this exemption;
- a tenancy at will (not applicable to Scotland). Informal occupation arrangements sometimes begin as a tenancy at will but over time may develop into some other form of tenancy which is not exempt and which therefore may give rise to SDLT obligations, see **4.9**; and
- except in Scotland, certain somewhat archaic rights which might otherwise be regarded as including interests in land – an advowson (the

right to appoint a clergyman to a benefice), a franchise (the right to hold a fair or market) and a manor (a right of certain kinds of jurisdiction over a specified area or estate).

Exempt transactions

2.17 Even if the land interest is not exempt, the transaction may be so – see **3.7** for details.

THE PURCHASER IS CHARGEABLE

2.18 SDLT obligations fall on the purchaser, identified in the legislation as the person who acquires the chargeable interest, or whose existing interest is enlarged or enhanced. The identity of the purchaser is obvious in straightforward transfers and grants of leases, but less obvious in some other cases. In particular:

- if a chargeable interest is transferred or granted to trustees of a settlement, the trustees are jointly purchasers (*FA 2003, Sch 16, para 4*);
- if an existing chargeable interest is transferred to bare trustees or nominees, the beneficial owner is the purchaser (*Sch 16, para 3(1)*);
- if a lease is granted to bare trustees, those trustees are (jointly, if more than one) purchasers of the whole interest (*Sch 16, para 3(3)*);
- if a lease is surrendered or the term shortened, the landlord is the purchaser (*FA 2003, s 43(3)(b), Sch 17A, para 15A(2)*);
- if the rent under a lease is reduced, the tenant is the purchaser (*Sch 17A, para 15A(1)*); and
- if any chargeable interest other than a lease (eg an easement) is varied, whoever benefits is the purchaser (*FA 2003, s 43(3)(c)*). This is an enigmatic definition, since it is normally the essence of a commercial transaction that both parties benefit, but it should probably be read as the person whose interest in land is enhanced.

However, a person cannot be a purchaser unless he gives consideration or is a party to the transaction.

Example 2.1 – identifying the purchaser

Peter owns the freehold of property F, and Rachel owns the freehold of property G which abuts F.

Peter pays the HCA* £100,000 for removal of a restrictive covenant preventing use of F for carrying on a manufacturing business. Peter is the purchaser.

Rachel agrees to pay Peter £500 per annum for the right to bring maintenance vehicles through the car park of Peter's property F to service the rear of Rachel's building on her property G. Rachel is the purchaser.

Peter and Rachel agree to exchange small parts of their respective properties to create better shaped plots, allowing construction of better buildings on both. Peter is purchaser in respect of the parcel of land he gains, and Rachel is purchaser in respect of the parcel she gains – that is, there are two chargeable transactions, even though no money changes hands.

* The Housing and Communities Agency is a UK Government body which has inherited the benefit of restrictive covenants originally imposed on land by other, now defunct, agencies, such as the Commission for the New Towns.

CONSIDERATION

Measuring consideration – valuation

2.19 The basic definition is 'any consideration in money or money's worth, given directly or indirectly by the purchaser or a person connected with him' (*FA 2003, Sch 4, para 1(1)*). The full face value of consideration must be taken into account – no discount is given for the fact that the consideration may be postponed, payable in instalments etc (*Sch 4, para 3*). However, where consideration *is* postponed, it is sometimes possible to apply for postponement ('deferment' in the legislation) of the corresponding SDLT (see **6.32**). In some circumstances where instalments are payable over many years, the consideration is taken to be the amount payable in 12 years (see **2.26**). Non-sterling consideration is valued at the London closing exchange rate for the effective date of the transaction; consideration which is not in the form of money or debt must be valued at its market value at the effective date. However some forms of consideration are ignored in some transactions (see **2.24**, **2.31** and **3.7**); in some cases, actual consideration is replaced or supplemented by deemed consideration (see **2.27**). When a lease at rent is in point, there are specific computational rules (see **4.43–4.56**).

Contingency, uncertainty and attribution

2.20 If payment of any part of the consideration is contingent on some future event, it is assumed that the amount will be payable and SDLT must be paid accordingly (*FA 2003, s 51*).

If the amount of consideration is uncertain or has not been finally ascertained by the time payment and submission of the SDLT return are due, a reasonable estimate must be used.

When two or more related transactions are entered into, or there is a composite transaction for acquisition of various assets, the overall consideration must be apportioned between the assets on a just and reasonable basis (*FA 2003, Sch 4, para 4*).

Once the figures are finally known, if the final SDLT amount is higher than originally entered on the return, an amended return must then be submitted and the further SDLT paid. If the final figures show that too much SDLT has been paid, the surplus SDLT may be reclaimed (*FA 2003, s 80*). The stamp duty concepts of unascertainable and contingent consideration (see **8.35, 8.37**) do not apply to SDLT. There is one exception to the treatment of contingent consideration set out above, and that relates to 'right to buy' transactions (see **3.38**).

Example 2.2 – measuring consideration

Lissa agrees to transfer a plot of land M to Norman. In return, Norman agrees to pay Lissa £150,000 cash, payable in ten annual instalments of £15,000, commencing immediately, and to have his family company Quickbuild Ltd build Lissa a new house on a different plot of land P, which Lissa also owns. Norman is subject to SDLT on the acquisition of M, and the consideration is £150,000 plus the market value of the building work to be undertaken by Quickbuild Ltd. Although Lissa gets a new house out of the arrangement, this is built on land she already owns, so she has no SDLT obligations.

VAT

2.21 If the consideration is subject to VAT, this must be included in the amount on which SDLT is charged. If the purchaser is able to recover VAT suffered as input tax, this means that SDLT is charged on a greater amount than the cost. At current VAT rates, the maximum effective rate of SDLT on non-residential property is 4.7%, rising to 4.8% from 1 January 2011. If the land is not subject to VAT at the effective date of the transaction, but may become so through exercise of the 'option to tax', VAT is not taken into account, provided the option to tax is not exercised until after the effective date (*FA 2003, Sch 4, para 2*).

Example 2.3 – SDLT on VAT

On 1 December 2010 Big Manufacturer Ltd (B) buys a plot of land from Land Trader Ltd (L) for £600,000 excluding VAT, intending to build a new factory. L has exercised the VAT 'option to tax' the land and charges VAT, but B is able to recover this fully through its own VAT returns and is able to negotiate to pay the VAT to L on the same day it recovers it from HMRC. So, commercially, the real cost of the land is simply £600,000. SDLT is chargeable at 4% on the VAT inclusive price of £705,000. This is £28,200, which is 4.7% of £600,000.

Debt as consideration

2.22 If property is transferred in satisfaction (or in return for the release) of a debt due to the purchaser or in return for the purchaser assuming responsibility for a debt, the amount of debt (including any interest due but unpaid) counts as consideration. However, if the amount of debt exceeds the market value of the property, the consideration is limited to that market value (*FA 2003, Sch 4, para 8*).

2.23 The position may be less clear where there is a debt secured on the property before the transfer, which remains in place after. In principle, it could be possible for the property to be transferred without the purchaser taking on responsibility for payment of the debt, in which case the debt should not be taken into account as consideration for the transfer.

Example 2.4 – debt as consideration?

Parent has purchased a house with the aid of a loan secured on the house. The house is occupied by Student. Parent transfers the house to Student for no consideration and retains full and sole responsibility for the loan. The amount of the loan should not be taken into account as consideration for SDLT purposes.

With a view to prevention of avoidance, it is provided that the amount of debt secured on the property *will* be taken into account as consideration if the rights or liabilities of any party to the transaction in relation to the debt are changed in connection with the transaction (*FA 2003, Sch 4, para 8(1A)*). In the example, arrangements between Parent and the lender would require very careful drafting to ensure that Parent's rights and obligations in relation to the loan remain unchanged when the property is transferred – and it may prove difficult to persuade a lender to accept the necessary drafting.

Carrying out works on land

2.24 This is a widely misunderstood and, in practice, very limited exclusion from chargeable consideration. If consideration given for a chargeable transaction includes works of construction, repair or improvement, their value is excluded from chargeable consideration if the following conditions are met (*FA 2003, Sch 4, para 10*):

- the works are carried out after the effective date of the transaction;
- the works are carried out on the land being acquired or on other land already held by the purchaser or someone connected with him; and
- it is not a condition that the works are carried out by the vendor or someone connected with him.

Example 2.5 – works which do not count as consideration

Chemical Co Ltd (C) agrees to sell land to Housebuilder Ltd (H). The land is contaminated and C is under an obligation to carry out decontamination works within one year. In consideration for the transfer, H pays £500,000 and agrees to engage an unrelated company to carry out the required decontamination works at an expected cost of £1 million. The works do not commence until after completion of the transfer. The value of the decontamination works does not count as consideration for the transfer of the land, and H pays SDLT only on the £500,000 cash consideration.

Example 2.6 – works which are consideration

Beryl (B) agrees to buy a plot of land from Landbank Ltd (L) for £200,000 (its true market value) and, on the same day, engages Quickbuild Ltd (Q) to construct a house on the plot at a cost of £300,000. L and Q are associated with each other but unconnected with B. The provision relating to carrying out of works has no application in this scenario. The £300,000 is being paid for construction of the house and is not consideration for the transfer of the plot of land. Instead, it is necessary to consider the case of *Prudential Assurance Co Ltd v IRC* [1992] STC 863. HMRC set out their view (in SP 3/98) of the impact of this case on stamp duty liability in this kind of transaction. HMRC intend to apply the same principles to SDLT liability. Provided the land purchase and building contracts are genuinely independent of each other,

SDLT will be charged only on the price paid for the land. However, if there is, in reality, only one transaction – for example, if in truth L will only sell the land if B also agrees to engage Q to build the house – HMRC will seek SDLT based on the overall price for the land and completed building. In the present example, HMRC are likely to be difficult to convince that this is anything other than a single transaction, with SDLT due on £500,000.

Services as consideration

2.25 Where services are provided as consideration, they are valued at the amount which would have been paid in the open market for such services. In general, this is likely to be more than the cost to the purchaser of providing the services, since an open market provider would expect to make a profit (*FA 2003, Sch 4, para 11*).

Payment in instalments

2.26 If consideration is payable in instalments, the effective date of the transaction is likely to be triggered by something other than payment of consideration (for example, occupying the property or even formal completion). Once the effective date arrives, SDLT is payable on the whole consideration, no matter when that consideration is payable. In certain circumstances, it is possible to apply to defer payment of some of the SDLT, as mentioned at **2.19** (see **6.32** for details).

However, where the consideration comprises or includes an annuity capable of lasting for at least 12 years, the consideration is taken to be 12 years' instalments. For these purposes, any consideration payable periodically is an annuity. If the yearly amounts vary, the highest 12 separate years are taken into account (although increases in line with the Retail Price Index are ignored). If this treatment applies, it is not possible to apply for deferment of any of the SDLT, and there is no adjustment to reflect actual consideration if the total payable proves to be more or less than the 12 years' payments initially assessed.

Example 2.7 – annuities

On 1 July 2011, Pru sells her house to ER plc in return for:

(1) a lump sum of £100,000, plus

(2) a rent-free tenancy of the house for life (valued at £40,000), plus

(3) an annuity for life, initially at £15,000 pa, increasing to £20,000 pa after four years and increasing in line with RPI thereafter.

The consideration on which ER must pay SDLT is the sum of (1) and (2) plus 12 times the £20,000 annuity – £380,000 in total. For these purposes, since the annuity is for life, it is assumed Pru will live at least until 30 June 2027, so that at least 12 instalments at £20,000 will be payable, but the subsequent RPI increases are ignored. The SDLT is due by 31 July 2011, with no facility to defer and no adjustment if Pru dies before or after 30 June 2027.

Substitution of market value

2.27 SDLT is generally chargeable by reference to the value of the actual consideration, but in some circumstances this is substituted by the market value of the property acquired. One example is where property is transferred in payment of a debt exceeding the value of the property (see **2.22**); another is where properties are exchanged (see **2.29**).

Perhaps the main relevance of market value is when a property is transferred to a company which is connected with the transferor. When this happens, the consideration is to be taken as not less than the market value of the interest transferred (plus any rent where the transaction is the grant of a lease) (*FA 2003, s 53*). For these purposes, 'connected' is as defined in *Corporation Tax Act 2010 (CTA 2010), s 1122* (previously *Income and Corporation Taxes Act 1988 (ICTA 1988), s 839*). If the actual consideration is greater than market value, SDLT is chargeable by reference to the actual consideration, unless a relief or exemption is available.

The market value rule does not apply in the case of some transfers to trustees. Nor does it apply where the transfer is a distribution out of the assets of a company. However, an anti-avoidance rule re-applies the market value rule if group relief has been claimed on the property (or a superior interest, if the property is a lease) within the previous three years (*FA 2003, s 54*).

2.28 There are two noteworthy points which often cause confusion. First, there is no general relief available where the transfer to a connected company occurs in the course of incorporation of a business by a sole trader or unincorporated partnership (apart from a very specific relief on transfer from an unincorporated partnership to a limited liability partnership; see **3.44**). Other tax reliefs are available to ease the process of incorporation but, where the business has substantial property assets, the SDLT cost acts as a significant disincentive. This was the cause of heated parliamentary debate when SDLT was introduced, but the Government of the day was not prepared to introduce a relief.

Secondly, where a lease at rent is granted to a connected company, there is no requirement to substitute a market rent. Rather, if the rent is less than a market rate, the lease itself will have a capital value (ie at arm's length, a lease at that rent would also attract a premium). SDLT is chargeable on the actual rent plus the capital value as if paid as a premium.

Exchanges and partitions

2.29 Where interests in property are exchanged, this is treated as two land transactions. Assuming at least one of the interests transferred is a major interest (see **2.6** and **2.11**), the consideration for each acquisition is the value of the property acquired and *not* the value of the property given in consideration (*FA 2003, s 47*).

Example 2.8 – exchanges

Erica agrees to transfer a plot of land, X, to Hosta, in exchange for Hosta transferring plot of land Z to Erica. It is agreed that the open market value of X is £200,000 and that of Z is £180,000. The parties agree to ignore the difference in value for commercial purposes. Erica will pay SDLT on the acquisition of Z, based on £180,000, being the market value of Z, and not on the value given in consideration. Hosta will pay SDLT on the acquisition of X, based on £200,000, being the market value of X, and not on the value given in consideration.

2.30 If none of the interests is a major interest (that is, the interests are limited to options or matters such as sporting rights, wayleaves, etc), the consideration for each acquisition is simply the amount of any further consideration given apart from the interest in land itself.

Example 2.9 – exchanges, not major interests

Juniper Ltd owns fishing rights over a stretch of Minnow River. Unrelated company Gorse Ltd owns shooting rights over Sparrow Moor. The companies agree to exchange their rights, with Juniper paying Gorse £300,000 cash, being the agreed difference in values. Juniper will pay SDLT based on consideration of £300,000. Gorse will not pay SDLT, as the deemed consideration for its acquisition of the fishing rights will be nil.

2.31 Where two or more persons hold a property jointly, whether as joint tenants or as tenants in common, they are generally treated for SDLT purposes as owning separate and distinct (but undefined) parts of the property. A property held in this way may be partitioned, so that each person takes a specific part. If this happens, the interest which each gives up is not treated as consideration for the part of which he becomes sole owner. The only consideration for SDLT purposes will be any payment or other valuable consideration which one may give to another, perhaps to compensate for differing values of the parts taken by each (*FA 2003, Sch 4, para 6*).

Example 2.10 – partition of jointly held property

Brothers Bill and Ben own a plot of land worth £1 million, divided into two paddocks, as joint tenants. They agree to partition it so that Bill owns paddock A and Ben owns paddock B. They agree that paddock A is worth £100,000 more than paddock B, but Bill is short of cash and they agree he will give Ben only £20,000 in compensation for his loss of value. For SDLT purposes, Bill is treated as giving consideration of £20,000 (and, since this is below the relevant threshold, Bill has no SDLT liability or notification obligations); Ben is treated as giving no consideration. Neither the market value of the overall plot nor the difference in values of the divided plots is relevant. Market values could be relevant where transfers involve a company which is connected to other owners (see **2.27**).

PFI transactions

2.32 Transactions in which a private sector company performs services, often including provision of premises, for a public sector organisation, are widely referred to as Private Finance Initiative (PFI) transactions. Such transactions often involve transfers and leases of property. There is a specific provision allowing many forms of consideration to be ignored in qualifying transactions. This is dealt with at **3.11**.

Sundry liabilities not treated as consideration

2.33 The following liabilities and obligations taken on by a purchaser do not count as consideration:

- an indemnity given to the vendor in respect of liability to a third party arising from breach of an obligation relating to the land (*FA 2003, Sch 4, para 16*);
- an agreement to bear any inheritance tax liability arising from the transfer (*para 16A*);

- an agreement to bear any capital gains tax liability arising from the transfer if it is not (or is treated as not being) a bargain at arm's length (*para 16B*); and
- certain specified costs borne by a leaseholder in connection with enfranchisement (*para 16C*).

RATES OF SDLT

2.34 The rate at which SDLT is charged on consideration other than rent depends on the amount of the consideration. However, the rates are not progressive (like personal income tax); rather, the whole consideration is chargeable at the rate determined by the amount of the consideration. The current rates plus the increase due in 2011 are listed below (*FA 2003, s 55*). On grant (or deemed grant) of a lease at rent, special rules apply for calculation of the SDLT on the rent (see **4.41** et seq).

Consideration (£)	Residential property#	Non-residential# or mixed property
Not exceeding £125,000	0%	–
Not exceeding £150,000	0%, only for property in a designated Disadvantaged Area	0%*
Exceeding £125,000/£150,000 but not exceeding £250,000	1%, but 0% for first-time buyers if effective date before 25 March 2012	1%
£250,001 to £500,000	3%	3%
£500,001 to £1,000,000	4%	4%
Exceeding £1,000,000	4% until 5 April 2011, 5% thereafter	4%

* 1% in the case of grant of a lease of non-residential or mixed property with a yearly rent of £1,000 or more attributable to the non-residential part (see **4.46**).
# See next paragraph

Residential property

2.35 Residential property means property used as a dwelling (or in the process of being built or adapted for this purpose) and includes associated gardens, grounds, outbuildings and other rights which subsist for the benefit of the property – for example, access rights across adjacent property (*FA 2003, s 116*). The status of a house or flat is usually obvious. The legislation provides a list of other categories of building which are treated as residential property, but then removes many examples from the list, as set out below.

Since the virtual abolition of Disadvantaged Areas Relief, the distinction has not been very important, as most properties of uncertain status are likely to have changed hands for more than £150,000, so the SDLT rate will not have depended on the status as residential or otherwise. However, the distinction may become more important with the increased top rate for residential property. Where six or more dwellings are the subject of a single transaction, they are treated as wholly non-residential property (*s 116(7)*).

Residential	**Non-residential**
Residential accommodation for school pupils	Home or other institution providing residential accommodation for children
Residential accommodation for students	Hall of residence for students in higher or further education
Residential accommodation for members of the armed forces	–
An institution which is the sole or main residence for at least 90% of its residents	Home or other institution providing residential accommodation with personal care to those in need of such care by reason of age, disablement, drug/alcohol dependence or mental illness
–	Hospital, hospice, prison or similar, hotel/inn or similar

Linked transactions

2.36 If two or more transactions are linked, the consideration for all of the linked transactions is aggregated to determine the rate of SDLT. Transactions are linked if they form part of a single scheme, arrangement or series of transactions between the same vendor and purchaser or, in either case, persons connected with them (*FA 2003, s 108*). Connected persons are as defined in *CTA 2010, s 1122* (previously *ICTA 1988, s 839*). Whether transactions are linked is a question of fact, but transactions between the same vendor and purchaser which occur at similar times are likely to be presumed to be linked unless there is evidence to the contrary. In *Attorney General v Cohen* [1936] 2 KB 246, [1936] 1 All ER 583, several purchases of properties by the same purchaser from the same vendor at auction were held not to be part of a series of transactions, because each property was the subject of a separate bidding process.

Example 2.11 – linked transactions

Over coffee, Tanya agrees to buy two houses, located in different towns, from Gerald – the first for £160,000, and the second for £200,000. Different solicitors are engaged to deal with the two purchases. The first is completed on 10 January 2011 without prior substantial performance, but the second is delayed, while old Land Registry entries are investigated, and does not complete until 15 June 2011.

The two transactions are linked, because they were agreed in principle between the same people as part of an overall deal. Aggregation of the consideration gives £360,000, which falls in the 3% SDLT band, so each acquisition is chargeable at 3%. SDLT of £4,800 is due on the first purchase and £6,000 on the second. See **6.17** and Example 6.4 for the practical implications of this in relation to submission of SDLT returns and payment of tax.

Example 2.12 – transactions not linked

Gerald attends an auction where he successfully bids for two houses in the same street, which are sold as separate lots. Gerald pays £110,000 for one and £115,000 for the other. After the auction, he discovers the vendor is the same for both houses. The transactions are not linked, because each purchase was agreed totally independently of the other; no SDLT is payable on either purchase, as the consideration for each is below the relevant threshold.

TIMING OF OBLIGATIONS

2.37 In general, payment of any SDLT must be made and SDLT returns must be submitted within 30 days of the effective date of the transaction. The processes for making a return and payment, together with details of the circumstances in which further returns may be needed, are set out in **Chapter 6**.

The effective date

2.38 There is more than one statutory attempt to define the effective date, covering separate specific circumstances, but they all seek to achieve the same overall result (*FA 2003, ss 119, 44(4)*). In essence, the effective date for a transaction is the earlier of:

- the date of legal completion – that is, the date of execution of the conveyance, lease or other document giving the transaction final legal effect, and
- the date on which the transaction is 'substantially performed'. This date depends on the nature of the transaction and is the earlier of the following:

- the date on which a substantial amount of any consideration is paid. If the consideration includes payment of rent, this is the earlier of the date on which the first payment of rent is made and the date on which a substantial amount of any other consideration is paid. For consideration other than rent, a 'substantial amount' means substantially the whole. Although not set out in the statute, HMRC considers that 90% or more is substantially the whole, but reserves the right to argue for a smaller proportion if they believe avoidance of SDLT is involved; and
- the date on which the purchaser takes possession of the whole or substantially the whole of the property. 'Possession' is not comprehensively defined, but is considered further below.

Possession

2.39 The term 'possession' has a long legal history and cannot readily be comprehensively defined. The following explanation sets out the view which HMRC are understood to take. The purchaser takes possession of the property when he first occupies or uses it, or becomes entitled to occupy or use it. This is not restricted to the time when the purchaser finally moves in, but may include, for example, having the right to enter the property for the purpose of fitting out. However, a person also has possession if he receives rents or other profits from the land, or has the right to receive them. It does not matter whether any of these occurs under the terms of the contract governing the transaction, or under some other arrangement such as a temporary licence or lease. However, if the purchaser already has possession of the property under an interest before entering into a land transaction to acquire a different interest in the same property, the prior possession will not itself cause the later transaction to be substantially performed (SDLTM07900).

Example 2.13 – occupation under previous interest

William occupies an office building under a lease which has 25 years to run. The current rent is £100,000 per year, payable quarterly in advance. His landlord is Vera, who owns the freehold. William agrees to buy the freehold from Vera for £750,000, subject to satisfactory structural survey etc. The agreement provides that William will pay a deposit of £75,000 on 1 February 2011, a further instalment of £300,000 within 10 days of delivery of the structural survey, and the balance of £375,000 on final completion. The agreement also provides that the final instalment will be reduced by any rent which William pays and which relates to the period after delivery of the structural survey. William occupies and therefore has possession of the property immediately after the agreement is signed. However, he occupies under the terms of the existing lease and not as a result of entering into the agreement to buy the freehold. Therefore, the agreement is not regarded as substantially performed by reason of William's occupation. 50% of the purchase price is paid prior to completion, or possibly slightly more because of the adjustment of the final instalment to allow for rent paid; since this is less than 90%, the agreement will not be regarded as substantially performed until the remaining 50% is paid, on completion.

Example 2.14 – receipt of rents as substantial performance

The same fact pattern applies as in the previous example, except that William's property-holding company Uppercase Ltd, rather than William himself, agrees to buy the freehold from Vera. As part of the agreement, Uppercase Ltd is entitled to receive all rent payable on the property from the date the structural survey is delivered and the £300,000 is paid. The agreement will be regarded as substantially performed no later than the due date of the first rent payment after delivery of the structural survey, because at that time Uppercase Ltd will become entitled to receive rents. Of course, if completion occurs before the next rent payment is due, the agreement will be substantially performed and completed at the same time.

Transitional provisions

2.40 SDLT was introduced on 1 December 2003, and transactions commenced from that date are wholly within the SDLT rules. Where the contract was entered into on or before 30 November 2003, the transaction may be subject to stamp duty, SDLT or both, as set out below (*FA 2003, Sch 19*). *FA 2003* received Royal Assent on 10 July 2003:

(1) **Contract entered into on or before 10 July 2003**: Subject to stamp duty only, no matter when substantially performed or completed. However, if the contract is varied or assigned after 10 July 2003 or given effect as a result of the exercise of an option or similar right after that date, it is effectively treated as entered into on the date of variation/ assignment/ exercise.

(2) **Contract entered into after 10 July 2003**:

   (a) **Contract completed on or before 30 November 2003**: subject to stamp duty only;

   (b) **Contract completed after 30 November 2003**: subject to SDLT, but the contract may also have been subject to stamp duty under *FA 2002, s 115*, in which case credit is given for any stamp duty paid.

For these transactions liability to stamp duty or SDLT is not affected by when the transaction was 'substantially performed', as this phrase has no meaning in the context of stamp duty. However, this does affect the 'effective date' and therefore the date on which SDLT is payable. If the transaction is subject to SDLT but the contract was substantially performed before 1 December 2003, the effective date is the date of completion. If the contract is substantially performed after 30 November 2003, the effective date is, as normal, the earlier of substantial performance and completion.

Example 2.15 – application of transitional provisions

On 1 June 2001, Propco Ltd contracted to buy a property Q which was under construction. The vendor had previously bought the site for Q using the 'resting on contract' planning (see **11.29**), so title was held by two nominee companies. On 1 August 2003, Propco assigned the purchase contract to its parent company, Holdco. Continuing the planning, Holdco paid the purchase price to the vendor on 30 September 2003 and took a transfer of the shares in the nominee companies. As a result, the transaction had been substantially performed within the SDLT meaning of that term, but not completed and no stamp duty had been paid.

On 1 March 2011, as part of an exercise to 'tidy up' the Holdco group before a stock market listing, title to Q is transferred from the nominee companies to Holdco. This effectively completes the original purchase contract entered into in 2001.

Although the contract was entered into before 11 July 2003, it was assigned after that date and so is treated as having been entered into on the date of assignment, which is after 10 July 2003. It was completed after 30 November 2003, and so is within (2)(b) in **2.40**. The effective date is 1 March 2011 (date of completion) and SDLT is payable and a return due before 31 March 2011.

Chapter 3

SDLT Reliefs

INTRODUCTION

3.1 Some transactions are automatically exempt from obligation to notify HMRC and do not give rise to any SDLT charge. The legislation labels some (but not all) of these as 'exempt transactions'. In this book, the term 'exemption' is applied to all such cases. Even where an exemption applies, so that there is no liability to pay SDLT or submit a return, the taxpayer is still required to keep appropriate records and documents for up to six years (see **6.62**). However, it should be noted that the requirement to 'self certify' transactions as exempt, using form SDLT60, was abolished by *FA 2008, Sch 30* with effect from 12 March 2008. Land Registries should now agree to register exempt transactions on the basis of a statement by the purchaser that the transaction is exempt from SDLT.

3.2 In contrast, there are many reliefs reducing or eliminating SDLT liabilities which would otherwise arise. Such reliefs do not apply automatically (despite the fact that, in many cases, the legislation describes qualifying transactions as 'exempt from charge'), but must be claimed by submission of an SDLT return (see **6.2**, *FA 2003, s 62(3)* and SDLTM60050). The relief is claimed in the return by putting appropriate codes in boxes; the form provides no space for disclosure of further information explaining circumstances surrounding the claim. Many reliefs are hedged around with complex anti-avoidance rules, which create genuine uncertainty as to their availability.

3.3 It is often desirable to provide further information in order to ensure full disclosure and reduce the risk that HMRC may reject the claim and make a 'discovery' assessment up to six years later. As a result, it has become commonplace to submit further information by way of letter when the SDLT return is completed (see **6.48**). HMRC have acknowledged this process in informal discussion, but do not appear to have issued any formal guidance on the matter.

3.4 There are several reliefs which are subject to retrospective withdrawal ('clawback') if certain events occur, as explained below in the descriptions of the reliefs. In these cases, it is necessary to keep track of both the property and the owner(s), in order to be able to make necessary returns and payments should clawback apply. Special rules apply where the interest disposed of is a lease, on grant of which group relief (or one of a list of other reliefs) was claimed. If nothing has already happened to cause clawback of that relief, the first transfer of the lease which does not itself qualify for one of the specified list of reliefs is treated as the grant of a new lease for the remaining term of the actual lease and at the rent payable by the transferee. SDLT is chargeable on the transferee accordingly (*FA 2003, Sch 17A, para 11*). See **4.15** et seq for an explanation of this and an example.

3.5 Finally, to add to the confusion, there are two provisions which are generally regarded as reliefs but strictly are not. The first exempts certain consideration from charge. It applies automatically (like an exemption) but still requires submission of a return (like a relief). This is the so-called 'PFI relief' in *FA 2003, Sch 4, para 17* (see **3.11**). The second is usually referred to as 'sub-sale relief', but is in fact a computational provision which applies automatically to disregard all except the final step in certain series of transfers (see **3.8**).

3.6 In this chapter, reliefs with a wide application are dealt with in some detail, but those with relatively narrow or specialised application are dealt with only briefly, the most specialised being summarised in table form. Reliefs which have been abolished or virtually abolished are mentioned at the end of the chapter. A few reliefs which apply specifically to leases are dealt with in **Chapter 4** (see **4.78** et seq).

EXEMPTIONS

3.7 The main exemptions are listed in *FA 2003, s 77A* and *Sch 3*, as follows:

(1) A transaction for which there is no chargeable consideration is exempt (*FA 2003, Sch 3, para 1*). Chargeable consideration is defined in *FA 2003, Sch 4* (see **2.19**). If there is no actual consideration in money or money's worth, there will be no chargeable consideration unless *FA 2003, s 53* (purchaser is connected company; see **2.27**) or *FA 2003, Sch 15* (transfers involving partnerships; see **Chapter 5**) apply. Additionally, *FA 2003, Sch 4* provides for certain amounts to be ignored where they might otherwise be regarded as consideration, see **2.33.**

(2) The grant of a lease to a tenant by a registered social landlord (RSL) is exempt if the lease is for a period not exceeding five years and certain other conditions are satisfied (*FA 2003, Sch 3, para 2*). Detailed review of the rules affecting RSLs is beyond the scope of this book, but it seems likely in practice that any transaction which might qualify for this exemption will also be exempt under the 'de minimis consideration' rules; see (7) below.

(3) A transfer between parties to a marriage or civil partnership in connection with dissolution of the marriage or partnership or separation of the parties (whether in pursuance of a court order or by agreement) is exempt (*FA 2003, Sch 3, paras 3* and *'second 3A'*, an apparent glitch in numbering of the statute).

(4) A transfer of property to a beneficiary under a will or intestacy is exempt, provided the transferee gives no consideration other than the assumption of any debt secured on the property. If other consideration *is* given, the assumption of any secured debt does not count as consideration in calculating the SDLT charge (*FA 2003, Sch 3, first para 3A*). Similarly, a variation of a will within two years of death (for example, by way of a family deed of arrangement) is exempt, provided no consideration is given other than agreement to other variations (*FA 2003, Sch 3, para 4*).

(5) A transfer not involving the grant of a lease is exempt if the chargeable consideration (together with the consideration for any linked transactions; see **2.36**) is less than £40,000 (*FA 2003, s 77A(1.2), (1.4)*). The figure of £40,000 seems somewhat arbitrary – it is difficult to see why it should not be increased to match the threshold below which no SDLT is chargeable. Note that the consideration must be less than £40,000, not '£40,000 or less'.

(6) The grant of a lease for a term of seven years or more is exempt if the chargeable consideration other than rent is less than £40,000 and the rent is less than £1,000 per annum (*FA 2003, s 77A(1.3)*). This exemption does not specifically require aggregation of chargeable consideration of linked transactions. It may be that HMRC would argue that the need to aggregate is implied by the general provisions of *FA 2003, s 55(4)* but it is by no means clear that this would be correct.

(7) The grant of a lease for a term of less than seven years is exempt, provided the chargeable consideration does not exceed the zero rate threshold – that is, provided no tax is chargeable and no tax would be chargeable but for availability of a relief (*FA 2003, s 77A(1.5), (2)*). However, where the rent for a lease of non-residential property is £1,000 or more per annum, there is no zero rate band in respect of consideration other than rent (*FA 2003, Sch 5, para 9A*). As a result, if any consideration other than rent is given for the grant of such a lease, this exemption does not apply. The interaction between this provision and the rules relating to renewal leases can lead to the obligation to notify and pay tax on very small transactions – see Example 4.25C, (iii).

(8) The assignment or surrender of a lease which was originally granted for a term of less than seven years, where the chargeable consideration for the assignment or surrender does not exceed the zero rate threshold.

PSEUDO-RELIEFS

Sub-sale relief

3.8 As noted above, this is not a true relief; it is a computational provision which applies automatically if the conditions are satisfied. However, it is widely referred to as a relief, and so is described in this section. If:

- A agrees to transfer property to B but,
- before that contract is completed or substantially performed, B agrees to transfer the same property to C, and if either
  - B drops out so that substantial performance and completion occurs directly between A and C, or
  - the A–B contract is substantially performed and completed at the same time as, and in connection with, respective substantial performance and completion of the B–C contract,

the A to B agreement is ignored for SDLT purposes, and SDLT arises only on the A to C or B to C transfer (*FA 2003, s 45*). Because this is an automatic treatment if the transaction qualifies, there is neither need nor facility for B to make a return or claim relief or exemption. SDLT is charged on the overall total amount which C pays to A and/or B.

3.9 If there are successive transfers of rights, SDLT is chargeable only on the final step, provided substantial performance and completion of all contracts occur 'at the same time as and in connection with' each other. If B agrees to transfer to C only part of the property being acquired from A, B remains subject to SDLT on the part not transferred onwards. B will be charged SDLT on the 'appropriate proportion' of the original purchase price of the whole property. It is understood that HMRC consider that this proportion must be determined on the basis of a 'just and reasonable apportionment', as required by *FA 2003, Sch 4, para 4*.

Early in the SDLT era, a mechanism exploited sub-sale treatment to avoid or defer SDLT on substantial performance, using 'alternative contracts'. These provided for the land to be transferred to the original purchaser or a third party, the main idea being that the original purchaser would never gain an interest in land and so would not have to pay SDLT. It is not clear that the planning worked, but *FA 2003, ss 44A* and *45A* were enacted to put the matter beyond doubt and ensure the SDLT liability arose as soon as the original contract was substantially performed.

3.10 There are also specific anti-avoidance provisions within *s 45* to ensure that this treatment cannot be used in conjunction with group relief or alternative finance relief to escape SDLT liability on the final transfer. There may be other circumstances in which the final step will not give rise to SDLT, so that there will be no SDLT on the overall series of transactions. However, where any series of transactions is planned to take advantage of this 'relief', it will be important to consider the impact of the more general SDLT anti-avoidance provisions (discussed at **7.5** et seq).

Example 3.1 – sub-sales

Buildquick Ltd proposes to build a block of apartments. Richman, who has an impeccable credit record and is not connected with Buildquick, agrees to buy six apartments for a total price of £1.5 million (ie, £250,000 each). This agreement allows Buildquick to borrow from its usual bank to fund construction. Richman pays the customary 10% deposit. The agreement has not yet been completed or substantially performed, so no SDLT obligations have yet arisen.

As completion of construction approaches, Richman's agent begins marketing the apartments. Sales of the first two are agreed to unconnected individuals at £270,000 each. In each case, the purchaser pays Richman's agent a deposit of 10%. At this stage, no SDLT obligations have arisen.

The apartments are completed and the time for completion of the sales arrives. At the last minute, a buyer is found for a third apartment, at a price of £240,000. Sales of the first three apartments to Richman are substantially performed and completed at the same time as onward sales to the individual ultimate purchasers. As a result, the purchases by Richman are ignored and SDLT is chargeable only on the ultimate purchasers. Since these ultimate purchasers are not connected with each other or with Richman, SDLT is chargeable on each at the rate appropriate to the amount paid – that is, 3% on each of two purchases at £270,000 and 1% on the third purchase at £240,000. The amount paid by Richman is irrelevant.

Richman completes the purchase of the fourth and fifth apartments in his own name, with the intention of letting them out at rent. He assigns the benefit of the contract to purchase the sixth apartment to his family company Money Ltd, which is jointly controlled by himself and his two sisters. Money Ltd pays £10,000 for the benefit of the contract, and pays Buildquick the balance of the original purchase price, £225,000, to complete the purchase. The arrangements relating to the fourth, fifth and sixth apartments give rise to SDLT issues as follows:

- Although the market value of the sixth apartment is probably at least the £240,000 paid by the last-minute purchaser of the third, the total amount paid by Money Ltd is only £235,000 (£10,000 to Richman for transfer of the contract and £315,000 to Buildquick to complete). However, Richman has paid £25,000 deposit. Since Richman is connected with Money Ltd, the amount of consideration given by Richman must be added to the consideration given by Money Ltd. If the legislation is taken at face value, this could mean that Money Ltd must pay SDLT on consideration of £260,000 (£25,000 paid by Richman plus £235,000 total paid by Money Ltd), even though the total really paid by Money Ltd and Richman between them is only £250,000. In effect, if the £10,000 paid for transfer of the contract is counted, this is an element of double counting. However, in the author's view, the payment of this sum to Richman means that the amount actually paid (ie cost borne) by Richman is reduced to £15,000. The amount on which Money Ltd must pay SDLT is therefore the £15,000 borne by Richman plus the £235,000 paid by Money Ltd, which comes to £250,000 – ie the total actually paid by Money and Richman between them.

- The purchases of apartments three and four by Richman and the purchase of the sixth by Money Ltd are linked transactions (see **2.36**). The consideration must therefore be aggregated to determine the SDLT rate. The aggregate consideration is £750,000.
- The original purchase contract for six apartments was a contract for a non-residential purchase (see **2.35**). However, the sub-sale of three apartments to unconnected persons leaves residual purchases of two and one apartments respectively which therefore are residential purchases. If the aggregate consideration for these three apartments was greater than £1 million, the 5% SDLT rate would apply to such purchases taking place after 5 April 2011, subject to transitional provisions where contracts are signed before that time.

PFI relief

3.11 This is the calculation provision which looks like a hybrid exemption/relief, referred to at **3.5**. Although popularly referred to as PFI relief, *FA 2003, Sch 4, para 17* does not necessarily apply to all PFI-type transactions, nor does it necessarily remove all liability. It merely excludes certain amounts from the calculation of chargeable consideration where:

(1) there is a transfer of land (which may include the grant of a lease) from a 'qualifying body' (A) to a non-qualifying body (B), and

(2) a lease back of that land to A, and

(3) an agreement for B to provide services to, or carry out works for A, to be paid for at least in part in money.

3.12 'Qualifying bodies' include public bodies within *FA 2003, s 66* (broadly, local and central Government organisations, health authorities and other statutory bodies, but the list in *s 66* should be checked in any individual case). They also include entities operating Higher and Further Education establishments and Academies – the list in *FA 2003, Sch 4, para 17(2)* should be checked where appropriate.

3.13 Where the relief applies, the chargeable consideration for the initial transfer of land does not include the value of the lease-back or the carrying out of works or provision of services by B. The chargeable consideration for the lease-back does not include the initial transfer of land, any transfer of other land from A to B, or the payment of money by A to B. This may mean that there is no chargeable consideration for any of the land transfers; however, PFI-type transactions are often more complex than the relief appears to envisage, and each transaction must be analysed carefully to establish whether the precise conditions have been met for all consideration to be excluded from charge.

Example 3.2 – PFI relief

Anytown Unitary Authority (A) needs a new building for council offices and a public library. This is to be built on a site mostly owned by A. Buildit plc (B) owns a small piece of land adjacent to this site, which is needed for access. It is agreed that:

(1) B will transfer the freehold of the small piece of land to A;

(2) A will grant B a 25-year lease of the whole site at a peppercorn rent;

(3) B will construct the building to A's specification;

(4) B will lease the building back to A for 25 years less one day, on the basis that B will manage the building (cleaning, maintenance, security etc);

(5) A will pay B a 'unitary charge' each year for provision of the building and services; and

(6) in addition, A will transfer to B the freehold of an old library site, on which B hopes to develop luxury apartments for sale.

Items 3 and 4 do not count as chargeable consideration for the grant of the lease at 2. Items 2, 5 and 6 do not count as chargeable consideration for the grant of the lease at 4. However, the transfer at 1 is not within the relieving provisions and is potentially subject to SDLT. If A is not able to claim any other relief or exemption, it will be necessary to establish how much of the value of 2, 5 and 6 should be attributed as consideration for the transfer at 1, and SDLT will be charged on this. The natural assumption will be that the consideration is the same as the market value of the small piece of land, unless analysis of the figures suggests otherwise. Central Government bodies and some others, such as strategic health authorities, have the benefit of blanket SDLT reliefs, but reliefs available to the various local authorities are more limited and probably do not apply here.

GROUP, RECONSTRUCTION AND ACQUISITION RELIEFS

3.14 These reliefs are dealt with together because they appear together in *FA 2003, Sch 7* and many of the conditions and anti-avoidance provisions are similar. The basic operation of each relief is outlined separately below, with an account of the conditions which apply to the particular relief. This is followed by discussion of an anti-avoidance provision which is common to all three reliefs. Finally, there is a review of the circumstances in which each relief may be retrospectively withdrawn (clawed back) as a result of events after the initial transaction.

3.15 The reliefs apply to transactions involving 'companies' (*FA 2003, Sch 7, para 1*). There are no restrictions as to residence or place of incorporation of the companies, providing they can be recognised as bodies corporate. In all cases, with the possible exception of the top company of a group, they must have 'issued ordinary share capital' or its equivalent. This can cause difficulties in relation to some overseas entities, where their 'corporate' nature may be open to question or which may have no concept of shares or share capital. In any case of doubt, it is possible to ask the opinion of HMRC. However, if it is not a type of body on which they have previously opined, HMRC are likely to demand an appropriate legal opinion from a lawyer in the relevant country (paid for, inevitably, by the taxpayer).

3.16 Relief may not be due, or in some cases may be withdrawn, if there are 'arrangements' for certain events to happen – the specific events are mentioned in relation to each relief below. The legislation makes it clear that 'arrangements' may exist even though there is no legal commitment by the parties; in relation to stamp duty, HMRC gave their view that arrangements exist where it is intended that the event will happen and there is no likelihood in practice that it will not (see SP 3/98, para 6); it is understood that HMRC apply the same criteria in relation to SDLT.

Group relief

3.17 Group relief removes any SDLT charge on land transactions between companies (ie bodies corporate) which are members of the same group (*FA 2003, Sch 7, para 1*). To be members of the same group, one company must be the 75% subsidiary (direct or indirect) of the other, or each must be the 75% subsidiary of a third company. For A to be the 75% subsidiary of B, B must be:

(a) the beneficial owner of not less than 75% of the issued ordinary share capital of A;

(b) beneficially entitled to at least 75% of any profits of A available for distribution to equity holders; and (c) beneficially entitled to at least 75% of any assets of A available for distribution to equity holders on a winding up.

Where ownership is indirect, proportions are to be calculated in the normal algebraic manner under *Corporation Tax Act 2010 (CTA 2010), ss 1155–1157*. Rights of equity holders are measured in accordance with *CTA 2010, Pt 5, chapter 6* (omitting references to arrangements which might affect future rights if put into effect). If shares in a particular company are not identical as to par value and rights, or if creditors have greater rights than payment of the relevant debts, it will be necessary to consider the impact of this chapter.

Example 3.3

Fred, an individual, owns 100% of the shares of Gill Ltd and 100% of the shares of Irene Ltd. Gill Ltd owns 90% of the shares of Jack Ltd and 75% of the shares of Kerri Ltd. Irene Ltd owns the other 10% of Jack Ltd and 20% of Harry Ltd. Jack Ltd owns the remaining 80% of Harry Ltd. Fred's business partner Leo owns the remaining 25% of shares in Kerri Ltd. All shares are ordinary, same class and denomination, and there are no share options or other instruments which might change relative entitlement to dividends or asset distribution in a winding up. The structure is therefore as follows:

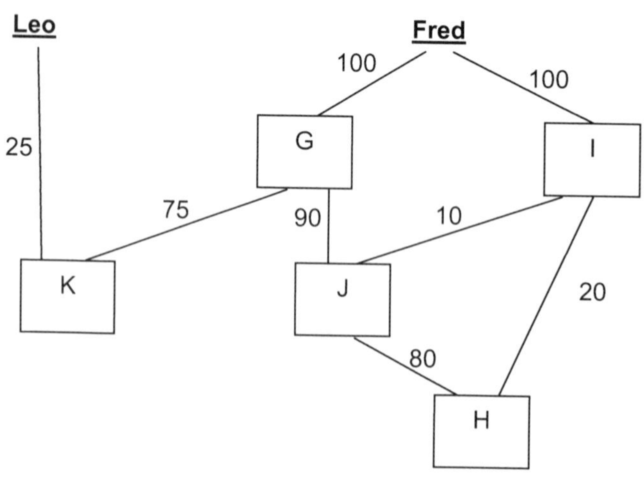

Clearly, Fred ultimately controls all of the companies, so they are associated. This has implications for the measurement of consideration for any land transactions between them (see **2.27**). However, they are not all members of the same group. J and H form a group, so transfers between them are capable of qualifying for group relief. Equally G, J and K form a group, and transfers between them may qualify for relief. However, H is not grouped with G or K. This is because G has (indirect) beneficial ownership of only 72% (90% × 80%) of H, the other 28% being owned directly and indirectly by I (and I is not grouped with any of the other companies). Note that J is separately grouped with both H, and G and K. In contrast with some direct tax provisions, it is acceptable for SDLT purposes for a company to be a member of more than one group in this way. Although H and G (or K) are not directly grouped, it appears at first glance that it should be possible to transfer land between them free of SDLT, for example by G making the transfer first to J, and then J transferring onwards to H. However, group relief is surrounded by anti avoidance provisions (see **3.22**), and it is highly likely that these would apply to such a sequence, potentially denying relief on both transfers and leading to a higher charge than would have applied to a direct transfer.

Treatment of LLP – company or partnership?

3.18 There is a conflict between possible treatments of a limited liability partnership (LLP). For most purposes, an LLP is regarded as a body corporate. On this basis, it can be the top company of a group for group relief purposes, and transfers between companies owned by the LLP may qualify for SDLT group relief. An LLP cannot be a subsidiary within a group, because it does not have issued ordinary share capital. However, the special rules governing the application of SDLT to partnerships state that any chargeable interest held by a partnership (which includes an LLP) is regarded as held not by the partnership but by the partners. Therefore, group relief should not be available for a transfer from a subsidiary company to an LLP, or from an LLP to a subsidiary company, unless perhaps the partners in the LLP are themselves members of a group. The writer has experience of HMRC advising that group relief is available for such transfers, but it is not clear whether this advice reflects HMRC's settled view and, in such cases, taxpayers would be well advised to seek clarification before relying on the availability of the relief.

Arrangements

3.19 In accordance with *FA 2003, Sch 7, para 2*, group relief is not available if, at the time of the transfer, there are 'arrangements' under which:

- at that or a later time, a person could obtain control of the purchaser but not the vendor. This condition may be breached if a third party has options to acquire or subscribe for shares of the purchaser, for example. However, if the arrangements are part of a scheme of reconstruction which itself will qualify for stamp duty relief under *FA 1986, s 75*, relief will not be denied (see SDLTM23035); or

- any part of the consideration is to be provided or received by someone other than a group member. In principle, this could lead to denial of relief where, for example, the purchaser borrows funds from a bank. In connection with the stamp duty version of this relief under *FA 1930, s 42*, HMRC stated in SP 3/98 that borrowing on normal commercial terms to fund an intra-group transfer would not normally lead to denial of relief. It is understood that HMRC apply the same principles in relation to SDLT group relief; or
- the companies are to cease to be members of the same group by reason of the purchaser leaving the group. It is not generally a problem if there are arrangements under which the vendor is to leave the group. However, arrangements even for this must not be too far advanced, or beneficial ownership of relevant shares may already be lost and the group broken before the time of the transfer.

Reconstruction relief

3.20 Reconstruction relief removes any SDLT charge on land transactions in the course of a qualifying reconstruction under which one company, A, acquires all or part of the undertaking of another, B (*FA 2003, Sch 7, para 7*). The reconstruction qualifies if:

(1) the consideration includes the issue of non-redeemable shares in A to all of the shareholders of B;

(2) there is no other consideration, except that A is permitted to assume or discharge debt of B;

(3) the shareholders of B before the transaction end up owning identical proportions (or as near as is possible) of company A; and

(4) the transaction is for bona fide commercial purposes, without a main purpose of avoiding tax.

See **3.22** for a discussion of the last of these conditions.

This relief is the SDLT equivalent of stamp duty relief under *FA 1986, s 75* (confusingly headed 'acquisitions: reliefs' in the legislation), and the stamp duty case law relating to the term 'undertaking' applies here too. The HMRC view on this is set out in STM6.198 (note, *not* SDLTM) but, broadly, there must be some form of active business originally carried on by B and subsequently continued by A – a mere transfer of assets which are passively held or subsequently used by A for a different purpose will not qualify.

Acquisition relief

3.21 Acquisition relief is the SDLT equivalent of stamp duty relief under *FA 1986, s 76*. It reduces the rate of SDLT chargeable to 0.5% where a company, A, acquires all or part of the undertaking of another, B, and relevant other conditions are met (*FA 2003, Sch 7, para 8*). The conditions are

(1) the consideration includes the issue of non-redeemable shares in A to B, or to any or all of the shareholders of B,

(2) the only other consideration (if any) comprises one or both of:

- payment of cash not exceeding 10% of the nominal value of the shares issued, and
- the assumption or discharge by A of liabilities of B,

(3) A is not associated with any company which is party to 'arrangements' with B relating to the shares issued by A, and

(4) the main activity of the undertaking consists of a trade other than property dealing or development.

Condition (3) is intended to prevent relief where the parties agree in advance that B will sell the newly issued shares to a member of A's group or other associated company, so that as far as B is concerned the sale of the undertaking is effectively for cash. However, the condition can cause difficulties in relatively innocent circumstances, where A and B are themselves associated perhaps because they are held by members of the same family, and shareholder agreements give pre-emption rights where one shareholder wishes to exit. All such transfers require careful detailed analysis to establish whether the relief applies; in general, HMRC seem reluctant to provide guidance on whether particular arrangements fall foul of this condition.

Condition (4), which was added in 2005, means that the relief can no longer apply to the transfer of a property letting business (not a trade) or a property development activity. The relief is, however, potentially useful in relation to the transfer of a trade where property forms a large proportion of the fixed assets – for example, retailing or hotel operation.

Anti-avoidance provision

3.22 Each relief is additionally subject to the condition that the transaction must be for bona fide commercial purposes, without the avoidance of tax forming a main purpose. 'Tax' here means stamp duty, SDLT, and income, corporation or capital gains tax. This condition is effectively a general anti-avoidance provision. There is no legislative guidance as to its scope, and doubt over this has led to significant uncertainty as to whether relief is due. In response to widespread disquiet, HMRC produced a 'white list' of transactions which would not normally be regarded as falling foul of this condition. The list can be found at SDLTM23040. However, the list itself is heavily caveated and gives limited comfort in the context of real commercial transactions.

Clawback of relief

3.23 Even where a transaction initially qualifies for one of these reliefs, in certain circumstances the relief may be retrospectively withdrawn, leading to crystallisation of the SDLT charge originally relieved. Because SDLT is a self-assessment tax, it is for the taxpayer to detect and disclose any situation in which a clawback arises. Where one of these reliefs has been claimed, it is therefore important to put in place arrangements to monitor ownership of the property, and of the companies involved in the original claim, for an appropriate period, which is generally three years.

Clawback of group relief

3.24 Group relief is clawed back if the purchaser, while it or a 'relevant associated company' still owns the property (or an interest derived from it), ceases to be a member of the same group as the vendor, either within three years of the effective date of the property transfer, or later but under arrangements entered into within that three-year period. A 'relevant associated company' is any other member of the group which leaves the group 'in consequence of' the purchaser leaving. This provision prevents an otherwise simple avoidance arrangement, under which the purchaser transfers the property to a wholly-owned subsidiary before leaving the vendor's group and is thus able to claim that it no longer holds any interest in the property. If the interest which the purchaser (or a relevant associated company) still holds is less than the interest originally transferred, a pro rata amount of the relief is withdrawn (*FA 2003, Sch 7, para 3*).

Example 3.4

Xerxes Ltd owns 100% of the shares of Yolande Ltd and Zeb Ltd. On 2 March 2010, Y transfers to Z a freehold property worth £800,000, and group relief from SDLT is claimed. In September 2010, Z grants a capital lease of part of the property to a third party, in return for a premium of £600,000 and a peppercorn rent. It is agreed that the value of the part thus disposed of is three-quarters of the value of the whole property. On 24 February 2011, X sells 50% of the shares of Z to another third party, in the course of setting up a joint venture. Z therefore leaves the X group while still holding an interest in the property with a value of one quarter of the value of the whole property. The SDLT payable is, therefore, one quarter of the SDLT which would have been payable on the original transfer on 2 March 2010, if group relief had not been claimed. The SDLT on the original transfer would have been 4% × £800,000 = £32,000, so the amount chargeable under the clawback is one quarter of this or £8,000.

Note the SDLT is *not* calculated as if there was a transfer of a property with a value of one quarter of the original; in the present case, such a calculation would give a liability of 1% × £200,000 = £2,000 – but, sadly, this is not how the clawback operates! However, even if SDLT rates or thresholds have subsequently changed, the clawback is still calculated on the basis of rates and thresholds which applied at the time of the original transfer.

3.25 Group relief is not clawed back where the purchaser leaves the vendor's group (*FA 2003, Sch 7, para 4*):

- as a result of the winding up of the vendor or a company above the vendor in the group;
- in the course of a reconstruction which itself qualifies for relief under *FA 1986, s 75*, as a result of which the purchaser becomes a member of the same group as the 'acquiring company'; or
- in the course of a qualifying demutualisation of an insurance company.

3.26 Group relief is not clawed back if it is the vendor which leaves the group rather than the purchaser. This allows a group to remove property which it wishes to keep from a subsidiary which is to be disposed of. However, if there is subsequently a change of control of the purchaser within three years of the original transfer, the purchaser is at that time treated as leaving the vendor's group, and clawback applies accordingly. See **3.28** for discussion of what amounts to a change of control. There are complex anti-avoidance provisions designed to ensure the 'change of control' rules apply as intended, where successive transfers of the property might otherwise lead to doubt as to their application. Although it is not clear why, the winding up of the purchaser is also treated as a change of control (*FA 2003, Sch 7, paras 4ZA, 4A*).

Clawback of reconstruction or acquisition relief

3.27 These reliefs are clawed back if, within three years of the effective date of the property transfer, or later under arrangements entered into within the three years:

- control of the acquiring company changes; and
- that company or a relevant associated company holds the property or an interest derived from it (*FA 2003, Sch 7, para 9*).

A 'relevant associated company' is a company controlled by the acquiring company immediately before the change in control, control of which changes as a consequence of the change in control of the acquiring company. If only part of the property, or a lesser interest derived from it, is held, an amount of relief is withdrawn pro rata to the relative values of the whole property and the part or interest still held. The calculation is analogous with that for withdrawal of group relief (see Example 3.4).

Change of control

3.28 In many cases, a change of control is easily identified – for example, when a majority shareholder sells the shares to a third party. However, a change of control may be very difficult to identify or define in some circumstances and, in the case of a publicly traded company, may be subject to the whim of the market. In the 2003 *Finance Bill* debates, the Government stated that normal market transactions in the shares of traded companies would not be regarded as giving rise to a change in control (see *Hansard*, Standing Committee B, 10 June 2003, col 425). However, this leaves open the possibility that the transfer of a minority shareholding in the case of a non-traded company may still give rise to a change of control, since the company would then be controlled by a different group of people.

3.29 There is no clawback of reconstruction or acquisition relief where control of the acquiring company changes for one of the following reasons:

(1) as a result of transactions in connection with divorce etc or distribution of an estate, as set out in (3) and (4) at **3.7**,

(2) as a result of a transfer of shares which itself qualifies for group relief under *FA 1930, s 42* or share acquisition relief under *FA 1986, s 77* (see **9.9** et seq), or

(3) purely as a result of a loan creditor becoming or ceasing to be treated as having control. This may happen, for example, when a loan creditor gains additional rights if the company defaults on payments under the loan.

There are anti-avoidance provisions to ensure that, where (2) above applies to prevent clawback, subsequent transactions leading to the relevant company either leaving the group or suffering a change of control within the original three-year period (or later under arrangements entered into within the period) will lead to clawback (*FA 2003, Sch 7, paras 10, 11*).

3.30 In relation to the clawback of all three reliefs, if the liable company fails to pay within six months of the due date, there are provisions (*FA 2003, Sch 7, paras 5, 12*) allowing tax to be recovered from:

- any company which was above the liable company in a group structure at any time between the original transfer and the event leading to clawback,
- a controlling director of the liable company or any other company having control of it, or
- in the case of group relief, the vendor.

Purchasers of companies should be aware of the risk of liability under these provisions and should seek appropriate protection in the form of warranties, indemnities, retentions etc.

OTHER MAJOR RELIEFS

Alternative finance reliefs

3.31 A series of reliefs has been introduced in an attempt to ensure that additional SDLT liabilities do not arise on property transactions where funding is structured in such a way as to avoid payment of interest. The need to avoid interest typically arises from specific beliefs, particularly the acceptance of Shari'ah principles; however, availability of the reliefs depends only on the nature of the transaction and participants, and not on subscription to any particular set of beliefs. The reliefs fall into two groups. The first (*FA 2003, ss 71A–73B*) relates to the purchase or ownership of property where, in other circumstances, mortgage finance might be obtained; these are dealt with in more detail below. The second (*FA 2003, Sch 61, paras 6–9*) relates to property backed investment bonds. Review of the reliefs available to those involved in the issue and management of such bonds is beyond the scope of this book; it is sufficient to note that a portfolio investor in qualifying bonds, although in fact gaining a direct interest in the underlying property, is deemed not to have such an interest for SDLT purposes (*FA 2009, Sch 61, para 2*). This does not apply if the investor, together with connected persons, has the right of management and control of the underlying property (for example, by virtue of the proportion of bonds held). Careful fact gathering and analysis may therefore be required where anything more than an obvious minority of bonds is held, and especially where family members or connected companies may hold investments in the same products. This difficulty is acknowledged in the legislation. If connected persons obtain control inadvertently, the favourable tax treatment is not lost, provided the control is not in fact exercised and holdings are reduced to remove that control once the issue has come to light (*FA 2009, Sch 61, paras 3–4*).

3.32 The reliefs relating to purchase or ownership of property envisage two forms of transaction. In the first (*s 71A*), under arrangements with the ultimate or intended owner ('Owner'), a financial institution ('Bank') purchases a freehold or leasehold property, leases it to Owner and grants Owner a right (the 'option') to require Bank to transfer the original freehold or leasehold interest to Owner. The terms of the lease and option typically ensure that Bank receives the same economic return as if it had provided mortgage finance secured on the property. If the relief applies, the lease to Owner and the final transfer to Owner under the option are relieved from SDLT. Partial transfers to Owner under the option during the course of the arrangement (for example, as a result of Owner making capital payments) are exempt from SDLT. As a result, the only SDLT payable is on the initial purchase by Bank, which is equivalent to what would happen if Owner purchased the property from a third party with the aid of conventional mortgage finance. However, if Bank buys the property from Owner, that purchase is also relieved from SDLT. In this situation, no SDLT is payable on the overall transaction, reflecting the position where a property owner obtains a loan secured on property already held.

The second form of transaction (*s 73*) envisages purchase of the property by Bank and onward sale to Owner, the onward sale typically being on instalment terms designed to replicate the economics of a repayment mortgage. If the relief applies, the onward sale to Owner is relieved from SDLT. Again, if the purchase by Bank is itself from Owner, that transaction is also eligible for relief.

There are provisions to ensure that the reliefs apply with the same overall effect where the property is located in Scotland (*ss 72, 72A*).

However, relief is denied if, at the time of the transaction, there are arrangements to transfer control of the financial institution. This is an anti-avoidance provision, to counter the possibility of a bank setting up a subsidiary to enter into the transaction, with every intention of then selling the subsidiary to the erstwhile purchaser of the property. Further anti-avoidance provisions (*s 73A*) seek to prevent the combination of these reliefs with group, reconstruction and acquisitions reliefs described above, to obtain an overall tax advantage. Beyond this, the Government appears to accept that it may be possible to exploit the reliefs to avoid SDLT and has stated that the reliefs 'will be kept under careful review'. The implied threat is that they may be withdrawn if abuse is perceived.

3.33 The interest held by Bank is an exempt interest (*s 73B*). This means any transfer to another financial institution (for example, if the bank sells its loan book) will not give rise to an SDLT charge.

Sale and leaseback relief

3.34 If A transfers a property to B (or grants a lease to B) (the Sale), and out of the interest transferred B grants a lease back to A (the Leaseback), relief from SDLT is available on the leaseback. The purpose of the relief is to facilitate transfer of properties from occupiers to investors. Absent the relief, it might be possible for the same effect to be achieved in some cases by A first granting a lease to a group company, then transferring the property, subject to this lease, to B. However, the relief allows a simpler process and resolves doubts as to whether anti-avoidance provisions might otherwise apply.

The relief does not reduce the SDLT charge on the original transfer from A to B. The relief should still be available even if, for some reason, no SDLT is payable on the original transfer, but A and B must not be members of the same group and the transfer to B must not be a sub-sale (see **3.8**). The transactions must be entered into in consideration of each other, so it would be wise to have this overtly stated in the documents. The only other consideration permitted for the original transfer is financial. Thus, the relief is not available if, for example, in consideration of the first transfer, B agrees to provide A with services or perhaps to transfer a different property to A. However, subject to possible application of general anti-avoidance rules (see **7.5**), it may be possible to structure such transactions as separate contracts for cash consideration due from A, left outstanding as a debt. The transfer from A to B could possibly then be partly in satisfaction of the debt, which is within the terms of the relief (*FA 2003, s 57A*).

First-time buyer's relief

3.35 *FA 2003, s 57AA*, introduced by *FA 2010, s 6*, provides a time-limited relief for the first purchase of a wholly residential property by a person or persons ('first-time buyer/s') who have not previously purchased a residential property. The relief is available for purchases with an effective date between 25 March 2010 and 24 March 2012 inclusive. It applies if the consideration for the purchase exceeds £125,000 but does not exceed £250,000. It therefore only applies to purchases which would otherwise be subject to SDLT at 1%. No relief is available if the price exceeds £250,000 – there is no question of partial relief. The relief also applies to appropriate acquisitions under 'alternative finance' arrangements (see **3.31**), removing the single charge to SDLT which would otherwise remain after application of the alternative finance reliefs. Strangely, the relief does not overtly specify that the first-time buyers must be one or more individuals, but this is perhaps implied by the condition that the property must be for occupation by the buyer(s) as their only or main residence. If the transaction is the grant of a lease or the acquisition of a second-hand lease, the lease must have at least 21 years to run. The relief is denied if the acquisition is linked with any others.

At the time of writing, no instructions on this relief had yet appeared in the Stamp Duty Land Tax Manual, but notes (which do no more than summarise the legislation) appear at www.hmrc.gov.uk/sdlt/calculate/reliefs-exemptions.htm#15. To claim the relief, an SDLT return must be completed and code 32 must be entered in Section 9.

Zero carbon homes relief

3.36 This relief in *FA 2003, s 58B* was introduced by *FA 2007*. It applies for a limited period of five years from 1 October 2007. Full relief from SDLT is available on the first acquisition of a dwelling which is a 'zero carbon home' and with a price not exceeding £500,000. For more expensive homes, the SDLT bill is reduced by £15,000. Zero carbon is defined by reference to zero net carbon dioxide emissions over the course of a year, and therefore effectively requires the dwelling to generate power for return to the national grid to compensate for energy used. 'First acquisition' means acquisition on or before first occupation. As initially drafted, the relief applied only to houses which were separate buildings, but it was realised that, in the immediate future at least, the only dwellings with any practical hope of being 'zero carbon' would be flats. The relief was therefore modified, with retrospective effect, to include parts of buildings. Detailed regulations provide a mechanism for assessment and certification of qualifying homes – it is considered that this could easily be combined with the normal energy efficiency assessment required for new homes under Building Regulations (*FA 2003, ss 58B, 58C; SI 2007/3437*). To claim this relief, code 30 must be entered in Section 9 of the SDLT return.

The relief only applies to the first acquisition of a new dwelling. It does not, therefore, encourage the modification of existing homes to improve their energy efficiency.

Social housing, right to buy and shared ownership

3.37 This group of reliefs applies to a limited range of acquisitions by providers of social housing and qualifying leases/sales to their tenants. The general regime dealing with providers of social housing is in a period of transition, as provisions of the *Housing and Regeneration Act 2008 (HRA 2008)* are brought into effect. This paragraph generally uses the old title of registered social landlord (RSL), but under *HRA 2008* the title is registered providers of social housing. An acquisition by a non-profit making RSL qualifies for complete relief from SDLT if:

(1) the majority of trustees/board members/management committee members are tenants, or

(2) the vendor is an RSL, a housing action trust or a qualifying local or central Government body (see list at SDLTM27500), or

(3) the transaction is partly or wholly funded with a grant or other financial assistance from the National Lottery or pursuant to one of the *Housing Acts*.

Profit-making registered providers will also be able to benefit from the relief, but only if condition (3) is satisfied (*FA 2003, s 71*, as amended by *FA 2009, s 81*).

3.38 Certain tenants are entitled to buy their homes from their public sector landlord (or from a successor body under a preserved right) at a discount to market value. The sale conditions normally include a contingent liability to repay the discount if the purchaser re-sells within a certain period. Under normal SDLT rules, this contingent further consideration should be charged to SDLT (see **2.20**). *FA 2003, Sch 9, para 1* provides that the contingent consideration does not count as consideration for SDLT purposes. This is expressed as a computational provision rather than a relief, but it is the view of HMRC that a claim to relief is required on an SDLT return, entering code 22 in Section 9 of the form. The return should be completed showing the actual consideration paid and not including the contingent amount. *FA 2003, Sch 9, para 1(3)* contains a comprehensive list of relevant 'public sector bodies', which are mainly central and local Government entities and social housing bodies.

3.39 *FA 2003, Sch 9, paras 2–12* provide a treatment which may provide partial relief from SDLT for the tenant who buys an interest in his or her home under 'shared ownership' arrangements. The normal 'shared ownership' arrangement is for the tenant to enter into a lease, paying a premium (representing part ownership of the property) and rent (for the part not purchased). The treatment is available where the tenant has a right to purchase further shares by making capital payments leading to a reduction in rent ('staircasing') and/or, where the freehold reversion is available, has the right eventually to purchase it. Where staircasing is allowed, the lease must state the minimum rent which can be payable as a result of maximum staircasing without acquiring the freehold. The rules relating to this relief are complex. The following paragraphs provide a summary, but it will be important to check the terms of the lease and the status of the parties in detail against the legislation to be sure that the relief is available.

In the absence of any special treatment, SDLT would be potentially chargeable on both the premium and the rent, and further SDLT could be chargeable on later 'staircasing' transactions. This could lead to an element of double charge, since the capital payment on the staircasing transaction would relate to the same interest in the property as the initial SDLT payment on the rent. To avoid such problems, the tenant may elect to have SDLT charged on the full value of the property at the time of the initial transaction. 'Full value' here means market value, or the discounted value where the tenant is entitled to buy at a discount. Equivalent treatment is available for 'shared ownership trust' arrangements often used in relation to blocks of apartments where individual ownership of the freehold reversion is not possible.

If this election is made, SDLT is not chargeable on the rent, nor is it chargeable on subsequent staircasing transactions and/or the eventual purchase of the freehold. Even if no election is made, staircasing transactions are not subject to SDLT, provided the total share of the property owned by the tenant does not exceed 80%. Any subsequent staircasing purchases which take the proportion owned above 80% and any purchase of the freehold reversion remain subject to SDLT. Whether the election is made or not, the normal 'linked transactions' rules are modified so that the consideration for later transactions is not aggregated with that for the original grant in determining the rate of tax on the original grant. This means the later transactions do not lead to the need to reconsider the tax charged on the original grant. However, if no election is made, the consideration for all transactions (including the grant of the original lease) is aggregated in order to determine the rate of SDLT payable on staircasing transactions which leave the tenant with more than 80% of the property and on acquisition of the freehold reversion.

Election to apply the 'full value' treatment must be made in the SDLT return, or by amendment of the return within 12 months of the due date of the return. Guidance on completion of the standard SDLT1 return form in these circumstances is at SDLTM27080. HMRC instruct that the election is made by showing the market value of the property as the consideration in Box 22, although it seems likely that this should say the 'full value' as defined above, since this is the amount by reference to which the SDLT liability will be calculated. If there is thought to be any uncertainty, the election could also be notified by letter to Birmingham Stamp Office (see **Appendix A**), quoting the UTRN of the return. Careful review of the circumstances is required because the election, once made, is irrevocable.

Example 3.5

Stanley and Oliver enter into identical 100-year shared ownership leases with the Holly Wood Housing Trust. They each pay an initial premium of £100,000 (which is considered to give them each a 50% share in their property) and rent of £5,000 per annum which is subject to yearly adjustment in line with the Consumer Price Index. They have the option to increase their ownership at the end of each year in multiples of 10% of the total value of the property. The minimum rent, which would apply if the tenant held 90% of the property, would be £500. Any acquisition which would take ownership above 90% necessarily includes acquisition of the freehold. Stanley elects to apply the 'full value' SDLT treatment; Oliver does not. After four years, they each opt to acquire a further 30% interest, paying £36,000 (based on the then market value) and reducing rent accordingly. At the end of the sixth year, they each buy a further 10% for £13,000. Finally, at the end of year eight, they each buy the remaining 10% including the freehold reversion, for £14,000. Neither qualifies for first-time buyer's relief or any other special treatment. Their SDLT positions are as follows:

	Stanley	**Oliver**
Initial purchase	Full value is £200,000, SDLT payable at 1% = £2,000. The NPV of the minimum rent is £13,827, which is below the £125,000 threshold, so no SDLT is payable on it.	Lease premium £100,000 and NPV of rent £138,276, so no SDLT on premium and £132 on rent. As this is residential property, the full zero rate band is available for the premium. The indexing of the rent is ignored for SDLT purposes, so this is treated as a flat £5,000 per annum rent.
30% addition, taking total ownership to 80%	No liability; no SDLT return required.	No liability; no SDLT return required.
10% addition	No liability; no SDLT return required.	Aggregate of capital sums paid to date (£100,000 + £36,000 + £13,000) = £149,000, so the 1% rate applies. SDLT payable on £13,000 at 1% = £130. SDLT return required.
Final 10% purchase including freehold	No liability, but SDLT return must be submitted (see SDLTM27080).	Aggregate of capital sums paid to date (£149,000 + £14,000) = £163,000, so 1% rate still applies. SDLT payable on £14,000 at 1% = £140. SDLT return required.

Overall, Stanley pays SDLT of £2,000, Oliver pays £402 but has to complete an extra SDLT return. Economically, it would not appear to be worthwhile to make an election. However, this depends on the precise facts. In particular, Oliver faces the risk of substantial increases in value or changes in SDLT rules, leading to a higher SDLT cost. Note that, if the final purchase had pushed the aggregate consideration over £250,000, the 3% SDLT rate would have applied to both of the last two purchases as they are fully linked, and it would have been necessary to complete a further SDLT return in respect of the penultimate purchase (see **2.36**).

3.40 The final relief in this section is in *FA 2003, Sch 9, paras 13–14* (introduced by *FA 2009, s 82*) and concerns 'rent to mortgage' and 'rent to loan' transactions. These are transactions where individuals initially rent a property under an assured shorthold tenancy, perhaps while saving for a deposit, and subsequently purchase an interest under a shared ownership lease or trust. The relief provides that the shorthold tenancy and the shared ownership lease/trust arrangement are not linked with each other, and that the effective date of the shared ownership transaction is determined without regard to the shorthold tenancy. This ensures that no SDLT disadvantage arises from the fact that the tenant initially occupies under a pure rental lease.

SPECIALIST AND MINOR RELIEFS

House trader relief

3.41 Full relief from SDLT is available for certain acquisitions of residential property from individuals who are buying another property. The acquisition may be made by a house building company from which the individual is buying a new dwelling, or by a property trader whose business includes buying such properties from individuals. Relief is also available for acquisition by such a company, whether or not the replacement home is new, if arrangements to sell the old home have broken down or if the individual is moving due to relocation of employment. In the latter case, it is also possible for the employer to acquire the old home free of SDLT. Finally, relief is also available where the property is acquired by an appropriate trader from personal representatives of a deceased person.

The aims of the relief are to improve liquidity in the housing market and to assist with mobility of labour. Conditions apply to ensure the property really was used as the individual's residence, and to guard against exploitation by property developers who may buy property with the intention of refurbishing or redeveloping for onward sale (*FA 2003, s 58A, Sch 6A*).

Charities relief

3.42 There are two ways in which an acquisition by a charity or charitable trust may be relieved from charge, as follows; however, relief is denied if the transaction was entered into for the purpose of avoiding SDLT:

(1) Relief is available if the whole property is to be held for 'qualifying charitable purposes'. This means either furtherance of the charity's charitable purposes or as an investment to produce profits to be used for those charitable purposes (*FA 2003, Sch 8, para 1*).

(2) Alternatively, full relief is still available if less than all, but more than 50% by value, of the property is to be held for qualifying charitable purposes, but the clawback rules are then different (*FA 2003, Sch 8, para 3*).

3.43 In either case, relief is clawed back if, either within three years of the acquisition, or later under arrangements entered into within the three-year period, a 'disqualifying event' occurs and the charity still holds the property or an interest derived from it.

If relief was obtained under (1) above, 'disqualifying event' means either the charity ceasing to be established for charitable purposes only, or the charity beginning to use the property or any interest derived from it for non-charitable purposes. If only part of the property is still held when the disqualifying event occurs, or if only part becomes used for non-charitable purposes, an appropriate proportion of the relief is withdrawn.

Alternatively, if relief was obtained under (2) above, 'disqualifying event' *additionally* includes any transfer of all or part of the land, or the grant of a lease at a premium or at a rent of less than £1,000 per year, unless that transfer or grant is made in furtherance of the charitable purposes of the charity.

Example 3.6

On 1 December 2010, the Q Charitable Trust buys freehold land for £1 million, with the intention of constructing a new operations centre for its own use on three quarters (by area) of the site and selling the other quarter to an unrelated company, R, for a previously negotiated price of £300,000. Because the property is not to be used wholly for charitable purposes, full SDLT relief of £40,000 is claimed under *FA 2003, Sch 8, para 3*, as set out under (2) above. The sale to R falls through, but on 1 May 2011, a slightly different plot is sold to another unrelated buyer, S, for £350,000. It is agreed with HMRC that the value of the plot sold is one quarter of the value of the whole site. At this point, one quarter of the relief previously granted is clawed back, and Q must complete a new SDLT return disclosing the charge and making payment. The SDLT payable is one quarter of 4% of £1 million, ie £10,000. The rate used is that which would have applied to the whole original purchase price, *not* the rate which would apply to the value of the plot disposed of alone.

Note that, if Q had intended to use the whole site for its charitable purposes at the time of acquisition and thus claimed relief under *FA 2003, Sch 8, para 1*,

as set out under (1) above, but subsequently decided to sell the plot to S, this disposal would not have led to any clawback of relief.

Construction proceeds slowly but, as a result of changes in practice at Q during the development period, the operations centre is larger than needed. On 1 November 2013, Q agrees to grant a 25-year lease of one floor to an unrelated company, T, at a premium of £800,000 and a peppercorn rent. The premium is paid and T occupies on 31 March 2014. It is agreed with HMRC that the value of the floor leased out is 40% of the value of the whole development. At this point, 40% of the relief originally granted and not yet withdrawn is now clawed back – that is 40% of £30,000 (£40,000 relief claimed less £10,000 already withdrawn), or £12,000. At this point, Q owns less than 50% of the original site. This is not a problem as, when the relief was claimed, Q intended to use more than 50% for its charitable purposes. However, given the amount finally disposed of, there may be some risk that HMRC would challenge the original intention.

Incorporation of limited liability partnership

3.44 Relief is available where partnership property is transferred to a limited liability partnership (LLP) from some other form of partnership or from the partners, on incorporation of the LLP. The relief only applies to a straightforward change of form from another kind of partnership, with no change in partners or their relative interests in the partnership. To qualify, the transfer must happen within 12 months of the date of incorporation of the LLP. In the absence of the relief, SDLT would be charged on the market value of any property transferred, because an LLP is a 'company' which would presumably be connected with the transferors of the property (see **2.27**) (*FA 2003, s 65*).

Reliefs for other specified bodies and transfers

3.45 Relief is available for acquisitions in a range of transactions by other bodies, specified either individually or by class. These are listed below; most are very specialised. Relief is usually subject to conditions, so it is essential to consult the relevant legislation and/or take expert advice before claiming the relief. In general, the relief is claimed by inserting '28' (other reliefs) at the appropriate point in the SDLT return (see **6.23**). In addition, specific relief is often provided in legislation other than *Finance Acts*, in respect of transfers in the course of Government-sponsored projects. It is, therefore, generally worth checking such legislation in these cases or, if involved early enough in the process, lobbying for such relief to be provided. Much of the legislation noted below pre-dates SDLT and originally granted stamp duty relief, but it has been amended, largely by statutory instrument under *FA 2003, s 123(3)*. There is a list of miscellaneous reliefs not in the SDLT legislation at SDLTM29600, accessible at www.hmrc.gov.uk/manuals/sdltmanual/sdltm29600.htm.

Qualifying transfer	**Legislation and notes**
Transfer on compulsory purchase facilitating development	*FA 2003, s 60*; relief applies to planning authority or other person making the compulsory purchase order
Transfer to a public authority to comply with planning obligations, for example under *Town and Country Planning Act 1990, s 106*	*FA 2003, s 61*
Between 'public bodies' (local and national Government bodies, National Health Service bodies, their wholly-owned subsidiary companies and other statutory bodies, on reorganisation*	*FA 2003, s 66* (see detailed list in legislation) References to NHS bodies are probably redundant (see below)
Between Local Constituency Associations on reorganisation of parliamentary constituencies	*FA 2003, s 67*
Acquisition by British Museum, Natural History Museum, and other specified similar bodies; certain transfers to 'heritage bodies' of property accepted in payment of tax	*FA 2003, s 69*; *National Heritage Act 1980, s 11A**
On demutualisation of an insurance company or a building society	*FA 2003, ss 63, 64* (provided the demutualisation satisfies conditions; see legislation)
On merger of building societies or transfer of business*	*Building Societies Act 1986, s 109A*
Acquisition by NHS Trusts, Foundation Trusts or equivalent bodies in the UK*	*National Health Service and Community Care Act 1990, s 61(3)(b), (3A)*; *Health and Social Care (Community Health & Standards) Act 2003, s 33(2)*; *National Health Service (Scotland) Act 1978, s 104A*
Acquisition by designated visiting armed forces or NATO headquarters*	*FA 1960, s 74A*
Transfers in the course of an amalgamation of friendly societies or transfer of friendly society business*	*Friendly Societies Acts 1974* and *1992, s 105A* in each case
Certain transfers in relation to roads, airports and lighthouses*	*Highways Act 1980, s 281A*; *Airports Act 1986, s 76A*; *Merchant Shipping Act 1995, s 221*
Certain transfers relating to inclosures and common land*	*Inclosure Act 1845, s 163A*; *Metropolitan Commons Act 1866, s 33*

* These reliefs are subject to the modified rules on subsequent disposal of a lease; see **4.15**.

Disadvantaged areas relief

3.46 This relief, in *FA 2003, s 57* and *Sch 6*, originally allowed complete relief from SDLT on transfer of property in some 2,000 specified areas of the UK which, on the basis of rather old census information, were regarded as disadvantaged. They included areas which had subsequently become desirable and valuable, in particular a number of high-profile shopping centres which were transferred into special purpose companies, allowing future transfers free of SDLT. The relief was modified by *FA 2005, s 96* and now only applies to wholly residential property where the consideration does not exceed £150,000. Since there is a general threshold of £125,000 below which SDLT is not chargeable on residential property, and there are or have been various temporary increases in this threshold, in practice disadvantaged areas relief now applies to very few transactions.

Unit trust seeding relief

3.47 This relief, originally in *FA 2003, s 64A* but now abolished, allowed transfer of property to a new unit trust in return for the issue of units, without SDLT cost. Its purpose was to allow bodies such as investment and pension funds to turn fundamentally illiquid property investments into tradable units, in order to comply with new regulations relating to the structure of their balance sheets. However, the relief was loosely drawn and allowed many owners to transfer properties to essentially privately held, non-UK unit trusts. It was then possible for effective ownership of the properties to be transferred free of stamp tax by transfer of the units. Many properties are still held in this way. The relief was withdrawn by *FA 2006*; unusually, the 2006 Budget announcement specified that the withdrawal took effect from 2pm on Budget day, in an attempt to prevent a last-minute scramble to take advantage of the relief.

Chapter 4

SDLT and Leases

INTRODUCTION

4.1 Each of the grant, variation, assignment and surrender of a lease is a 'land transaction' and therefore potentially gives rise to SDLT obligations as set out in **Chapter 2**. As with other UK land transactions, there may be obligations to make or amend SDLT returns even if no liability arises (see **6.2**). However, where leases are concerned, the general rules are substantially amended and generally made more complex. There are special rules for calculation of SDLT on rent in *FA 2003, Sch 5*, but the main technical provisions are in *Sch 17A*. This schedule was inserted after enactment of the main SDLT rules, and has itself been amended several times in an attempt to make the rules easier to apply whilst guarding against avoidance.

Obligations may arise at various times, such as when a payment is made, on first occupation, when rent amounts are agreed or changed, and even when the lease itself is formally executed. They may also arise in connection with arrangements which are not normally regarded as giving rise to a lease – for example, informal occupation or periodic tenancies – and on less formal changes, even if not documented as a variation etc. It is, therefore, important to establish clearly the nature of the transaction. The four key questions to address are the same as for other transactions; but, in relation to leases, the fourth question is likely to require the most attention:

- What SDLT obligations and liabilities may arise?
- At what time do SDLT obligations and liabilities arise?
- What reliefs are available?
- What special rules may affect this transaction?

4.2 SDLT may be chargeable on both rent and any real or deemed premium. SDLT obligations fall on the 'purchaser'. In most cases, this will be the tenant/ lessee but, where a lease is surrendered or varied to shorten the term, the landlord/lessor is the purchaser (*FA 2003, s 43, Sch 17A, para 15A*). The general rules relating to timing and notification of liability, availability of reliefs and disclosure of information apply to lease transactions. Specific rules for calculating the SDLT liability and modifications to other general rules are dealt with in detail by way of examples in the text which follows.

4.3 Sometimes, liabilities will arise at a future time on a lease granted now, or now on a lease granted years ago. It may, therefore, be important to obtain and retain the full detailed history of a lease, and of previous leases of the same premises if they are linked with the present lease (see **4.58**).

4.4 Scottish terminology and practice in relation to leases differs from that in the rest of the UK, but the legislation provides that the same rules apply to the Scottish commercial and legal equivalents to English terminology and practice.

EVENTS GIVING RISE TO SDLT OBLIGATIONS AND LIABILITIES

New lease

4.5 SDLT may arise on entering into a lease (*FA 2003, s 43(3)(a)*). It is common for the parties initially to enter into an agreement for lease, the definitive lease being executed later, after all necessary details have been settled. In Scotland, 'missives of let' may be exchanged, and these may or may not be followed by a definitive lease. The agreement or missives may be acted on before the definitive lease is executed (for example, by payment of rent or the tenant having access to the premises). The general SDLT concept of 'substantial performance' applies to an agreement for lease or missives of let (see eg *FA 2003, s 44(7)*). SDLT obligations may therefore arise when the agreement is acted on, when missives are exchanged, and when the definitive lease is executed – see **4.69**.

With one exception, an amount payable in respect of a period before a lease commences (or is treated as commencing) cannot be regarded as rent even if it is expressed as such (see SDLTM14015). Provided it really is consideration for the lease, any such amount will be treated as a premium. This may occur, for example, when negotiations between landlord and putative tenant have been delayed and the landlord is able to demand 'rent' for an earlier period before the tenant took occupation or signed the lease (see Example 4.3 for an illustration of this). More usually, the payment of such an amount, (or earlier taking possession of the property) will trigger the commencement of a notional lease, as explained at **4.69**, and the amount paid will be respected as rent for that notional lease.

The one exception arises on renewal of a lease originally entered into within the SDLT regime; see **4.65** and Example 4.25C, (iii).

New lease for seven years or more

4.6 For non-lease transactions, there is no requirement to make an SDLT return if the consideration is less than £40,000 (*FA 2003, s 77A(1)*). Where a lease for seven years or more is granted, this exemption from making a return only applies if the annual rent is also less than £1,000. This is logical for a non-residential lease involving both rent and premium because, if the annual rent is £1,000 or more, there is no 'zero rate band' for the premium and any premium will give rise to an SDLT liability (*FA 2003, Sch 4, para 9*) (see **4.46**). The requirement is less logical for a residential lease (where the zero rate band for a premium still applies) or for a non-residential lease with rent up to about £5,200 and no premium. No SDLT liability will arise even on a very long non-residential lease which is only at rent unless the yearly rent exceeds £5,200, or it is linked with one or more other such leases so that the aggregate yearly rent exceeds that figure.

Example 4.1 – rent below threshold, notifiable

On 1 January 2011, Methuselah enters into a 250-year lease as tenant on a plot of farmland at a yearly rent of £5,200, subject to revision every five years in line with movement in the Retail Price Index. The tenant has the right to terminate the lease at any time after 1 January 2031. Increases in rent in line with the Retail Price Index are ignored for SDLT purposes (see **4.37**), so this is treated as a lease at a fixed rent of £5,200 per annum. The NPV of the rent is £148,542, which is below the threshold of £150,000 so no SDLT is payable. Nonetheless, an SDLT return must be submitted within 30 days of execution or earlier substantial performance of the lease.

New lease for less than seven years

4.7 The grant of a lease for less than seven years does not have to be notified unless the consideration (rent and/or premium) exceeds the relevant zero rate band. However, in the case of a non-residential lease where the rent exceeds £1,000, the absence of a zero rate band in respect of any premium (see **4.46**) means that even a very small premium will be sufficient to make the grant of the lease notifiable.

Example 4.2 – rent below threshold, not notifiable

Moira grants Nathan a six-year lease of a house (single residence) for a premium of £30,000 and an annual rent of £10,000. The NPV of the rent is clearly below the residential threshold for rent (£125,000), and the premium is within the zero rate limit (also £125,000). Since the lease is for less than seven years and no tax is payable on either rent or premium, no SDLT return or other notification is required.

Example 4.3 – liability on small premium

On 1 March 2011, Orla agrees to grant a five-year lease of a shop to Piet for rent of £12,000 per annum, payable quarterly in advance. It is agreed that the lease will commence on 1 April 2011. However, a dispute over the detailed terms and conditions means the lease is not executed until 1 May 2011. Piet makes the first rent payment, for the period 1 April to 30 June 2011, on 1 May, and takes possession of the shop on the same day. Since nothing happens to cause the agreement to be substantially performed before the lease is executed, the lease is deemed to commence on the date of execution and not at the (earlier) alleged start date – so, for SDLT purposes this is a 4 year 11 month lease commencing on 1 May 2011. Although £1,000 of rent is expressed as being for the period 1 to 30 April 2011, rent cannot in fact relate to a period before the lease begins (see **4.5**) (the one exception to this rule arises when a lease, originally executed under SDLT, is renewed – see **4.65** and Example 4.25C, (iii)). It is HMRC's view that this amount must therefore be regarded as a premium for the lease. The lease is at a yearly rent of £12,000, and so there is no zero rate band for SDLT on the premium. The £1,000 premium is chargeable at 1%, and this £10 SDLT liability is sufficient to trigger an obligation to submit an SDLT return.

Licence to occupy and informal arrangements

4.8 A licence to occupy land is not a 'chargeable interest' (*FA 2003, s 48(2)(b)*), so no SDLT obligations arise on entering into or terminating a licence. However, HMRC warn that the nature of an interest in land is not determined by calling it a 'licence'; in any case of doubt, appropriate legal advice should be sought. A tenancy giving exclusive occupation of a property is more than a licence and is potentially subject to SDLT.

4.9 Normally, a transaction creating a tenancy is reduced to writing, but it is possible for a tenancy to be implied by the actions of the parties. No liability should arise on a tenancy at will (*FA 2003, s 48(2)(c)*), but over time this may develop into a periodic tenancy which is potentially within the charge. However, it may be that the arrangement commenced before 1 December 2003 (the date on which SDLT was introduced). In that case, no SDLT obligations should arise unless and until the arrangement is varied. It is suggested that appropriate legal advice should be taken to establish the status of any such arrangements.

4.10 HMRC's draft guidance on SDLT and partnerships originally suggested that, if a partnership informally occupied a property owned by a partner, the property should be regarded as belonging to the partnership rather than simply let to it. An article in SDLT Technical News 5 (August 2007) announced the more reasonable view that this would depend on the facts of the individual case (see **5.43**).

Lease for an indefinite term and holding over

4.11 A periodic tenancy, whether or not reduced to writing, is one example of a 'lease for an indefinite term' (*FA 2003, Sch 17A, para 4*). Such a lease is treated in the first instance as a lease for one year. If it continues beyond the end of the first year, it is treated as having been a lease for two years from the outset. At the commencement of each successive year thereafter, it is treated as having been, from the outset, a lease for one year longer than at the commencement of the previous year. It is necessary to consider what SDLT obligations arise at the beginning of each year. Commonly, particularly in relation to residential tenancies, the rent will not be high enough to produce any SDLT liability in the early years. However, as time passes and the lease 'grows' in length, SDLT obligations may arise. Although the notification requirements for leases under and over seven years are different, it is specifically provided that a periodic tenancy does not become notifiable purely as a result of passing the seven-year mark.

A tenancy at will is also specifically stated to be a periodic tenancy. This seems a bizarre provision, given that a tenancy at will is outside the charge to SDLT, as noted at **4.9**.

4.12 A tenant may remain in occupation after the end of a lease ('holding over'), continuing to pay rent, perhaps while a new lease is negotiated. The precise SDLT consequences will depend on whether the old lease was granted under the stamp duty or SDLT regimes and the terms of any new lease; see **4.64**.

Transfer of a lease or agreement for lease

4.13 In a straightforward case, the transfer of an existing lease to a new tenant (with no other change in terms and conditions) will be subject to SDLT in the same way as the transfer of any other interest in land. The new tenant will be subject to SDLT on any consideration given (a) to the outgoing tenant and (b) to the landlord (apart from ordinary rent) – for example, a lump sum paid to persuade the landlord to consent to the transfer. However, neither the rent payable under the lease nor any premium paid to the landlord by the outgoing tenant (for example, in return for the landlord agreeing to release the tenant from the lease) will figure in the new tenant's SDLT liability. Equally, the assumption of normal tenant's obligations and undertakings (such as to maintain the property) do not count as consideration (*FA 2003, Sch 17A, para 17*). There are provisions at *FA 2003, Sch 17A, para 12A* designed to ensure that assignment of an agreement for lease rather than the lease itself produces the same overall SDLT liability.

Liabilities which fall on transferee

4.14 Many cases are not straightforward, and it is always necessary for the new tenant to understand the full history of the lease, in order to determine whether the transfer, or the nature of the lease itself, may give rise to other SDLT liabilities and obligations. Additional obligations may arise in two situations. The first is where the rent was uncertain or variable when the lease was granted. If the lease is transferred to a new tenant before the SDLT liability is resolved, the new tenant inherits the obligation to make any necessary disclosures or further returns and to pay any additional SDLT once the uncertainty is resolved. See **4.37** et seq for an explanation of those obligations.

Relief claimed on original grant of lease

4.15 The second situation where the new tenant may incur unexpected liabilities is where one of a specified list of reliefs (see **4.18**) was claimed when the lease was granted (*FA 2003, Sch 17A, para 11*). If nothing has already happened to cause clawback of that relief, the first transfer of the lease which does not itself qualify for one of the specified list of reliefs is treated as the grant of a new lease for the remaining term of the actual lease and at the rent payable by the transferee. This means, for example, if there have been any rent increases between the dates of original grant and transfer, the current (higher) rent will be taken into account in calculating any SDLT payable. SDLT is also payable, in the normal way, on any premium which the new tenant pays to the landlord. HMRC consider that any amount paid by the new tenant to the outgoing tenant in respect of the transfer is also within the charge to SDLT, as would be the case for a straightforward transfer of a lease on which no relief had previously been claimed. It is logical that this should be the case, but it is by no means clear that the wording of the legislation supports this view.

4.16 SDLT is chargeable on the transferee, and not on the original lessee who claimed the relief. Therefore, strictly, this is not clawback, it is merely a modification of the normal rules for determining a purchaser's SDLT liability.

However, as the example below demonstrates, in practice the rules do lead to effective clawback of part of the relief previously claimed, even though it is the new owner/tenant who has responsibility for the resulting SDLT.

4.17 The rules are not subject to any kind of time limitation: they apply on disposal of the lease at any time in its life. Anyone acquiring a second-hand lease should check whether it will be subject to these special rules and seek protection from unexpected SDLT liabilities by way of warranties, indemnities, retentions or whatever may be thought appropriate.

4.18 The special rules apply where any of the following has been claimed on the grant of a lease:

(1) group, reconstruction or acquisition relief,

(2) sale and leaseback relief,

(3) charities relief,

(4) relief for transfers involving public bodies, or

(5) any relief brought forward from the stamp duty rules by regulations under *FA 2003, s 123(3)*.

Care must be taken in relation to the last of these, as many of the reliefs mentioned in the table at **3.45** fall into this category. However, the rules do not apply if the transfer itself qualifies for any of the reliefs in the list (not necessarily the same relief as that previously claimed), provided the transferee claims the relief in an SDLT return.

Example 4.4 – transfer of lease after relief claimed

On 1 March 2006, V plc granted a 25-year lease to its subsidiary W Ltd at a rent of £100,000 per annum, subject to five-yearly upwards-only rent reviews. Group relief was claimed. On 1 March 2011, the scheduled rent review leads to a rent increase, to £110,000. On 1 June 2012, W Ltd transfers the lease to an unrelated company X Ltd. X Ltd pays W Ltd £80,000 for the transfer and takes over all of the other terms and conditions of the lease.

X Ltd is not entitled to any relief in the list mentioned above, so the transfer is treated as the grant of a new lease for the remaining 18 years 9 months of the term, at an initial yearly rent of £110,000. This charge effectively claws back part of the relief claimed by W Ltd when the lease was first granted. In this example, it is worse than a simple clawback because it also takes account of the new, higher rent. In addition, in this example, X Ltd pays a sum to W Ltd for the transfer, and this will be subject to SDLT as if it was a premium. Since the rent under the lease is greater than £1,000 per annum, there is no 'zero rate band' for any premium (see **4.6**), and tax will be charged on the £80,000 at 1%. This particular example is worse than that. When X Ltd takes on the lease, a further rent review is due in less than five years. Therefore, the acquisition is treated as a grant of a lease for uncertain or variable rent. It will be necessary for X Ltd to review the position when the rent review occurs, submitting a further SDLT return and paying further SDLT as appropriate (see Example 4.13).

Shared ownership leases

4.19 In the context of affordable/social housing, arrangements are often made for the purchase of a part share in a dwelling. The purchaser then occupies the rest of the dwelling under a lease or tenancy. There are specific provisions (*FA 2003, Sch 9*) designed to remove or minimise any SDLT charge on such arrangements, and these are explained at **3.37** in relation to reliefs.

Variation of existing lease

4.20 The original rules dealing with variation of an existing lease were substantially rewritten in 2006. A variation may give rise to SDLT obligations, depending on:

- the precise nature of the variation, including whether, in law, it amounts to a surrender and re-grant;
- whether either party gives consideration or is deemed to give consideration;
- when the variation occurs relative to the date(s) on which the term of the original lease began or was deemed to have begun (see **4.22–4.24**); and
- whether the original lease was granted under the stamp duty or SDLT regime.

Examples of variations

Increase in rent within first five years

4.21 An increase in rent in accordance with the terms of the lease (for example, as a result of a rent review) does *not* arise from a variation. However, where such a change in the rent is possible within the first five years of the term, the rent should have been regarded as uncertain at the inception of the lease. This will have given rise to particular SDLT reporting obligations (see **4.37**).

4.22 A lease may be varied to increase the rent – that is, other than in accordance with the original terms of the lease. If this happens with effect from a date within five years of the beginning of the term, a new notional lease is normally deemed to be granted, covering the period from the effective date of the rent increase to the end of the original lease. The rent for the new notional lease is equal to the increase. This notional lease is then subject to SDLT (*FA 2003, Sch 17A, para 13*). The new notional lease may be linked with the original lease but is not necessarily so – this is a question of fact. These rules are disapplied where the variation arises from certain provisions relating to agricultural tenancies and holdings. In such cases, a variation has no immediate SDLT consequences; however, should there be a further increase after the first five years of the lease, the 'abnormal increase' calculation will be based on the original rent, as in Example 4.8.

Example 4.5 – rent increase in first five years

On 1 July 2009, Giovanni entered into a new ten-year lease of a storage and distribution depot at a yearly rent of £25,000 and no premium, with a market rent review due on 1 July 2014. An SDLT return was submitted accordingly. The lease restricted activities in the premises to storage, repackaging and distribution. Giovanni always intended in due course to carry out repairs of faulty goods returned to the depot (and had mentioned this to the landlord when taking the lease on). The landlord agrees to vary the lease to permit this, in return for an increase in rent to £28,000 from 1 January 2011. An additional lease is deemed to come into existence on that date, for a term equal to the remaining 8.5 years of the original lease and at a yearly rent of £3,000. Giovanni must decide whether any SDLT arises on this deemed additional lease and, if so, must submit a further SDLT return accordingly. Since it was always expected that the lease would be varied in this way, it seems likely that the original lease and the deemed additional lease are linked. On this basis, additional SDLT will arise on the deemed lease; see **4.61**.

Increase in rent after first five years

4.23 If the original lease was granted before 1 December 2003, or after that date but with the benefit of the implementation transition provisions (see **2.40**), it will have been subject to the stamp duty regime. A variation to increase the rent after the first five years of the term will not be subject to SDLT (*FA 2003, Sch 17A, para 17*).

Example 4.6 – original lease under stamp duty

Lucy is tenant of a 1960s office building under a 20-year lease which was granted on 1 January 2000. Rent is increased every five years in line with inflation and is currently below the market rent for an equivalent modern building. The building requires significant work to bring it up to current standards. Lucy agrees to a variation of the lease to provide for market level rent reviews at 1 January 2012 and 2016. In return, the landlord agrees to arrange and fund refurbishment of the building. Because the lease was granted under the stamp duty rules, this variation has no SDLT or stamp duty consequences.

4.24 If the original lease was granted within the SDLT regime, *any* increase in rent after the first five years, whether as a result of a rent review, variation or any other matter, leads to the need to consider whether the increase is 'abnormal' (*FA 2003, Sch 17A, para 14*). If the increase is abnormal, a new notional lease is deemed to be granted for the period from the date of the increase to the end of the original lease, and for a rent equal to the 'excess rent' calculated as set out below. If the increase is not abnormal, there are no SDLT consequences.

Is the rent increase abnormal?

4.25 The concept of abnormal rent increases only applies to rent increases after the first five years of the lease, and only to leases granted or deemed granted within the SDLT regime. The general principle is that a rent increase will be abnormal if the new rent is greater than the 'rent previously taxed' by more than 20% (measured on a straight line basis) for each complete year which has elapsed since the starting date for the rent previously taxed. The rent previously taxed is the last rent by reference to which SDLT has been charged.

4.26 A five-step calculation is necessary to determine this point precisely:

- Find the highest annual rent which has previously been taken into account in determining SDLT liabilities on the lease – this is the 'rent previously taxed', R. Note that this will not necessarily be the rent for a year starting on an anniversary of grant of the lease. In Example 4.17, if considering a rent increase in Year 6 or later, the rent previously taxed would be the rent for the 12 months from 1 June 2012, even though the lease started on 1 November 2011.
- Find the 'excess rent', E – this is the difference between R and the new annual rent. Note that this, therefore, automatically includes any previous rent increases which have not themselves given rise to an SDLT charge.
- Find the 'start date'. This is the date from which R is treated as applying. If there has previously been an abnormal rent increase, the start date is the date from which that previous increase applied. If there has not been a previous abnormal increase, but the rent was initially uncertain or variable, it is the beginning of the period within the first five years from which the assumed rent after the first five years was calculated (in Example 4.17, the 'start date' would be 1 June 2012). If there have

been one or more variations in the first five years of the lease, as set out at **4.21**, the start date is the date of the latest such variation. In all other cases, the start date is the beginning of the term of the lease.

- Find the number of complete years which have elapsed since the start date, Y. Note that part years are ignored, not taken into account.
- Compare E with R × Y/5. If E is greater, the increase is abnormal.

4.27 The HMRC website provides an online calculator at www.hmrc.gov.uk/tools/stamps/abnormalrentcalculator.htm for determining whether a rent increase is abnormal. To use the calculator, it is necessary to assemble all of the information set out above, together with the original NPV of the rent and the SDLT paid on original grant. The calculator then assesses whether the rent increase is abnormal and, if it is, provides a calculation of the additional SDLT payable. It also provides comforting 'official' confirmation of the position, potentially useful if a copy of the output is retained. It is set up as if to deal only with the first abnormal rent increase in the life of a lease; there is also a specific 'health warning' that the calculator can only be used for the most straightforward cases. For complicated cases and/or any subsequent increases, it is probably safer to perform the calculation manually as set out above.

Example 4.7 – lease under stamp duty, no abnormal rent increases

Petra is the tenant of a shop under a 30-year lease which commenced on 1 October 2003 at an initial rent of £10,000 per annum. The lease provides for ten-yearly market rent reviews. At 1 October 2013, the new market rent is agreed at £35,000 per annum. If the calculation is performed, it shows this is an 'abnormal' increase. However, the original lease was granted under the stamp duty regime, so the abnormal rent increase rules do not apply. The rent increase does not give rise to any SDLT consequences.

Example 4.8 – lease under SDLT, abnormal rent increase

Orion is tenant of a factory under a 25-year lease. The agreement for lease was entered into on 1 January 2004 and completed without prior substantial performance on 1 March 2004. The lease, which is expressed as 25 years from 1 March 2004, provides for market rent reviews every five years. The initial rent was £10,000 per annum; the rent review at 1 March 2009 increased this to £15,000, and this increase was found to not be 'abnormal' so no further SDLT return was required. At the 1 March 2014 review, the new rent is agreed as £32,000. Using the calculation process above, R is £10,000, E is (£32,000 – £10,000) = £22,000, Y is 10, and R × Y/5 is £20,000. E is greater than this, so the rent increase is abnormal. Note that, because the rent increase at 1

March 2009 was not abnormal, it is effectively ignored in this calculation. The abnormal rent increase is treated as the grant of a notional lease at 1 March 2014, for a term of 15 years (the remaining term of the real lease) and at a yearly rent of £22,000 (ie E). This notional lease is treated as linked with the real lease (**4.61**), but the special rules for successive linked leases (**4.59**) do not apply. It is therefore necessary to calculate SDLT payable on the notional lease *and* to recalculate SDLT payable on the original lease (if any) as set out in **4.62** and Example 4.23. On a strict reading, the legislation probably requires separate notification of the notional lease (presumably by submission of an SDLT return) and any additional SDLT on the original lease (by amendment of the original return). However, the output from the HMRC abnormal rent increase calculator (see next paragraph) indicates that the whole liability should be notified by a single letter to Birmingham Stamp Office (see **Appendix A**), quoting the reference number of the SDLT return used to notify the original lease.

The HMRC calculator input screen looks approximately like this:

Abnormal rent increase calculator

You can use this calculator to help you work out whether a rent increase is considered abnormal and - if it is - how much SDLT, if any, is payable. The abnormal rent rules apply to leases granted on or after 1 December 2003 so this calculator cannot be used for leases granted before that date.

This calculator can be used for only the most basic Abnormal Rent Increases and leases. More complex leases and rent increases cannot be accommodated using this tax tool

Please provide all relevant information then click the calculate button and the results will be shown. If you need help completing any of the details please refer to the abnormal rent increase calculator guidance notes.

Type of lease at start date of original lease

- Residential
- Non residential
- Mixed use

Highest 12 months consecutive rent in the first five years of the term

0.00

Date the lease was initially granted (dd/mm/yyyy)

Date the lease is due to end (dd/mm/yyyy)

Net present value (NPV) calculated when the lease was originally granted

Amount of SDLT paid, if any, on the grant of the lease

0.00

Date the rent increase becomes payable (dd/mm/yyyy)

New annual rent payable

0.00

Type of lease that will apply when new rent is payable

- Residential
- Non residential
- Mixed use

Once details from the example are entered, the output then looks like this:

Abnormal rent increase calculator - results

What you told us:
The highest 12 months consecutive rent in the first five years of the term was: £10,000.00
The original lease was granted on: 01/03/2004
The original lease is due to end on: 28/02/2029
The net present value at the grant of the lease was: £164,814.00
The amount of SDLT originally paid on the grant of the lease was: £148.00
The new rent becomes payable on: 01/03/2014
The new rent payable is: £32,000.00

Results:
The rent increase is abnormal. This means you need to notify HMRC and pay any additional SDLT where it is due.
The SDLT due on the notional lease is: £1,624.00

The additional SDLT due on the original lease is: £908.00

Total amount of SDLT due: £2,532.00

Your next steps
Please send a letter to the Compliance Team at the Birmingham Stamp Office explaining that there has been an abnormal rent increase.

If additional SDLT is payable you should include a cheque for the amount due along with your letter.

- Make your cheque out to 'HM Revenue & Customs only'.
- Write the Unique Transaction Reference Number (UTRN) of the original notification on the front.
- Please don't fold your cheque or fasten it with paper clips or staples or in any other manner.

Note that you'll need to write and pay by cheque even if you sent the original SDLT online.

Get contact details for the Birmingham Stamp Office *(on screen this is a link to the contacts page)*

Please note that the above result is based on the information you entered in the calculator. If any details you input are incorrect you should re-enter the correct details and recalculate.

HM Revenue & Customs cannot be held liable for incorrect output from this calculator. Correct information can only result from this calculator if correct details are entered.

Decrease in rent

4.28 A decrease in rent is specifically treated as an acquisition of a chargeable interest by the tenant (*FA 2003, Sch 17A, para 15A(1)*). If the tenant gives or is deemed to give consideration, this will be within the charge to SDLT. Normal compliance rules apply – if no consideration is given or if the consideration is below £40,000, there will be no need to notify HMRC; otherwise, an SDLT return will be required, even if no tax is actually payable.

Decrease in term

4.29 If a lease is varied to decrease the term, this is treated as the acquisition of a chargeable interest by the landlord (*FA 2003, Sch 17A, para 15A(2)*). If the landlord gives or is deemed to give any consideration, this will be within the charge to SDLT. However, if the tenant gives consideration, for example in order to have the term of an onerous lease reduced, this will not be subject to SDLT.

Other variations

4.30 The most common types of variation of a lease are covered by specific rules as set out in preceding paragraphs. All other variations are treated as the acquisition of a chargeable interest by the tenant only if the tenant gives (or is deemed to give) consideration in money or money's worth (*FA 2003, Sch 17A, para 15A(1A)*). Other variations are specifically excluded from the scope of SDLT (*FA 2003, s 43(3)(d)*).

Surrender

4.31 The surrender of a lease is the acquisition of a chargeable interest by the landlord (*FA 2003, s 43(3)(b)*). Therefore, if the landlord gives or is deemed to give chargeable consideration, this will be within the scope of SDLT.

Surrender and re-grant

4.32 Whether a variation of a lease amounts to a surrender and re-grant is a matter of law and, in any case of doubt, appropriate advice should be sought. However, it is generally true that a variation which does not overtly state that the old lease is surrendered is not likely to amount to a surrender and re-grant unless it varies the term or the extent of the premises demised.

Where a surrender and re-grant occurs, SDLT is chargeable in respect of rent under the new lease in the normal way. Any obligation to notify the transaction and pay SDLT falls on the tenant.

4.33 If the original lease was granted under the stamp duty regime, no credit is given for any stamp duty previously paid. For this reason, it is generally best to avoid surrender and re-grant of a lease at rent where the old lease was granted under the stamp duty regime.

4.34 However, if the original lease was granted under the SDLT regime, and if the premises under the two leases are 'the same or substantially the same', credit may be available in respect of rent for the 'overlap period'; see **4.80**.

4.35 Where rent under the new lease is variable or uncertain, it should also be noted that the overlap relief is ignored in measuring the highest 12-month rent in the first five years, in order to determine the deemed rent for Year 6 onwards. The surrender of the old lease does not count as consideration for the grant of the new, nor does the grant of the new count as consideration for the surrender of the old (*FA 2003, Sch 17A, para 16*). If the landlord gives consideration for the surrender of the old lease other than the grant of the new lease, it may be necessary for the landlord to notify the surrender as a separate transaction and pay any SDLT arising on that.

Example 4.9 – superseding lease, no credit for stamp duty

The facts are as in Example 4.6 above. However, the landlord is only prepared to fund the refurbishment if Lucy agrees to a longer lease. Therefore, on 1 January 2012, the original lease is surrendered in return for a new 15-year lease at a market rent and with five-yearly market rent reviews. SDLT is payable on this in the normal way. Because the original lease was dealt with under the stamp duty rules, no credit is available for the stamp duty already paid in respect of the 'unused' period of the old lease. The SDLT liability would be lower if the parties agreed to amend the old lease, as in the original example, and at the same time enter into a 'reversionary lease' to cover the period from expiry of the old lease (31 December 2019) to the intended end date of the new lease (see **4.36**).

Example 4.10 – superseding lease, credit for SDLT

The facts are as in Example 4.5 above. However, shortly after the July 2014 rent review (which increases the yearly rent to £35,000), Giovanni concludes that use of the premises would be enhanced if a small patch of land to the side were added to the lease. The lease is amended on 1 October 2014 to include this, with no additional rent payable. At the same time, the term of the lease is extended by five years to 30 June 2024. This extension of both term and premises is deemed to be a surrender and re-grant of the lease. It is considered that the additional land is small enough for the old and new leases to be regarded as leases of 'substantially the same' premises. SDLT is payable on the 'new' lease, which is for 9 years 9 months at a rent of £35,000 per annum, but credit is given for the £28,000 per annum rent which would have been payable under the old lease for the period to 31 June 2019. The rent (before discounting to NPV) to be taken into account in the SDLT calculation for each year of the new lease is as follows:

Period	Calculation	Deemed rent (£)
Each of 4 years to 30/9/2018	35,000 – 28,000	7,000
Year to 30/9/2019	35,000 – 21,000	14,000
Each of 4 years to 30/9/2023	–	35,000
Period to 30/6/2024	9 months at 35,000 pa	26,750

The highest deemed rent in any 12-month period in the first five years of the new lease appears to be £14,000; however, the reduction for rent under the old lease is ignored in determining this 'highest rent' figure, so the deemed rent for periods after the end of the overlap period reverts to the highest figure before relief, which is £35,000 in this case.

Reversionary leases

4.36 Varying a lease to increase the term amounts, in law, to surrender and re-grant, and is subject to SDLT accordingly, as set out above. Sometimes, an alternative is for the parties to enter into a further lease of the premises, covering the period from expiry of the current lease to the desired later expiry date. When this happens, the lease is granted before its start date. The effective date for SDLT purposes is the date of grant, not the commencement date. However, the commencement date is used in calculating the NPV of rents, so no benefit is gained from the fact that rent will not become payable under the new lease until some future date. The original and reversionary leases may be successive linked leases if the reversionary lease was contemplated when the original lease was implemented (see **4.59**). However, this is a question of fact and the leases are not necessarily linked.

Example 4.11 – reversionary lease

Gwen occupies a shop unit under a ten-year lease which expires on 30 September 2015. She wants to remain in occupation beyond this date and, on 1 December 2011, a reversionary lease is executed for a further ten years from 1 October 2015 at a rent of £20,000 per annum. Gwen must submit an SDLT return no later than 30 December 2011 and pay any SDLT due on the new lease by the same date. The NPV of the rents, calculated using 1 October 2015 as the start date, is £166,332. The lease is not linked with the old lease or any other, so the SDLT payable is 1% of £(166,332 – 150,000), which is £163.

ONGOING OBLIGATIONS

SDLT liability not finally determined when lease was granted

4.37 Sometimes, when a lease is granted, the rent for the first five years is actually or potentially variable or uncertain – for example, because the rent depends on the tenant's business results or there is a rent review scheduled within the first five years. (Note, however, that rent increases in line with the Retail Price Index are ignored.) In such cases, it is not possible finally to determine the SDLT liability until the uncertainty is resolved, potentially after the end of the first five years. Once the rent for the first five years is known, the deemed rent for the rest of the lease can be determined (see **4.48**). Any uncertainty or variability after the end of Year 5 is ignored at this stage, but will figure in deciding whether there has been an abnormal rent increase (see **4.25**). As with other UK land transactions, the return must initially be completed on the basis of a reasonable estimate. The return must then be amended once the consideration is finally determined (*FA 2003, Sch 17A, para 6*).

Example 4.12 – variable or uncertain rent

On 23 April 2011, Richard grants Harold a 25-year lease of the site for a theme park. The lease requires Harold to construct and open the theme park within two years of grant. No premium is payable. Rent is set at a base level of £10,000 per year but, from Year 4 onwards, the rent is to be 5% of the turnover of the park, if this is higher than £10,000 (additional rent based on turnover to be estimated and paid quarterly with adjustment at the year end). Reasonably conservative business projections indicate that 5% of turnover will be £8,000 in Year 4 and £12,000 in Year 5.

Before 23 May 2011, Harold must submit an SDLT return on the basis of a reasonable estimate of rent, and it seems that £10,000 for Years 1 to 4 and £12,000 for Year 5 would be justifiable. Once the rent for Years 4 and 5 is finally determined (presumably, fairly early during Year 6), Harold must consider whether a further return is required. If the actual rent exceeds the estimate used in the original return, a further return must be submitted and additional SDLT paid. If the actual rent is less than the estimate, Harold is entitled (but not required) to submit an amended return and claim repayment of any SDLT overpaid. See **6.17** for details of submission of further or amended returns.

4.38 Two specific points require care where the uncertainty arises from a rent review which is due within the first five years after the date of grant. The first is where a tenant takes possession on the basis of an agreement for lease, the final lease being granted some time later once minor details have been settled. Such a lease will often be expressed as commencing from the date on which the tenant took possession with a rent review five years from that date. For SDLT purposes, the final lease is usually treated as beginning on the date of grant (see **4.69** for an explanation of what happens to the period between taking possession or other substantial performance and execution of the final lease), and the first rent review will be due less than five years later. Hence, a lease with normal five-yearly rent reviews and no other uncertainty over rent will nonetheless often be treated as a lease with variable or uncertain rent for SDLT purposes.

Example 4.13 – rent review within five years of final execution

Tom enters into an agreement for a 12-year lease of a workshop and the agreement is substantially performed by Tom taking possession on 1 November 2010. The lease is finally executed on 20 February 2011, is expressed as ending on 31 October 2022, and provides for rent reviews at 1 November 2015 and 2020. The term of the lease is treated as commencing when it is executed on 20 February 2011, so the first rent review falls within five years of the commencement date. The lease is therefore at an uncertain or variable rent. When the first rent review is settled, it will be necessary to review the original SDLT return and calculation. If (as is likely) the SDLT liability is greater than originally disclosed, a further return must be made and the additional SDLT must be paid.

4.39 The second point arises when the date of the first rent review falls in the final quarter of the fifth year of the term. This may occur, for example, when rent is payable on traditional quarter days but the lease commences on some other date. In this situation, it may be possible to treat the first rent review as falling five years after commencement of the lease, so that the variable or uncertain rent provisions do not apply (*FA 2003, Sch 17A, para 7A*). However, in applying this rule, the precise wording of the lease will be important. The lease must provide that the first rent review is due five years after a specified date which itself falls within the three months before the commencement of the lease. It appears that, if the lease merely states 'the first rent review will be on [date within the last quarter of the first five years]', without specifically referring to a date within the three months before the lease began, the rule will apparently not apply and the lease will be treated as having variable or uncertain rent. There does not appear to be any policy reason for this restriction, so it may simply be a case of poorly worded legislation. It is not known whether HMRC will allow any flexibility in applying this rule.

Example 4.14 – rent review in final quarter of Year 5

Sales Ltd leases a shop unit from Retail Mall plc for ten years from 1 January 2011. Sales Ltd takes possession on 1 January 2011 but the lease is not finally executed until 10 February 2011. The lease provides for a rent review after five years and, to fit with Retail Mall's other leases, this is due on 25 December 2015. Sales Ltd must make an SDLT return no later than 31 January 2011. Providing the rent review clause of the lease is appropriately worded (on the lines of 'the rent review shall occur five years after 25 December 2010'), the fact that it falls before the fifth anniversary of both substantial performance of the agreement and grant of the lease itself will not cause the rent to be regarded as variable or uncertain. Note, however, that, were execution of the final lease delayed beyond 24 March 2011, the rent review would then fall more than three months before the end of the first five years of the lease. As a result, the rent would be regarded as variable or uncertain, and a further SDLT return would be needed once that review had occurred, assuming this led to a rent increase.

MAKING AND AMENDING SDLT RETURNS

4.40 SDLT returns relating to lease transactions are made and amended in just the same ways as for other UK land transactions; see **Chapter 6**. Some forms/sections of the return apply only to transactions involving leases. If the return is completed online, these sections only appear if appropriate entries are made in the early sections to indicate that leases are involved. This is set out more fully in **Chapter 6**. As with other transactions, there is generally no prescribed form for amending a return, and amendments are made by writing to SDLT Compliance at Birmingham Stamp Office (see **Appendix A**). HMRC do say that minor amendments may be notified by telephone, but written communications have the advantage of leaving a record.

CALCULATING THE LIABILITY

What is consideration?

4.41 SDLT is charged on 'chargeable consideration' which is defined for leases as for other transactions as 'any consideration in money or money's worth given … by the purchaser or a person connected with him' (*FA 2003, Sch 4, para 1*). In relation to the grant or variation of a lease, consideration may be in the form of rent and/or premium. Since the tax treatments of the two forms of consideration differ, it is important to distinguish between them (see **4.44**). In relation to both rent and premium, the usual valuation rules apply to consideration other than in cash and in sterling (see **2.19**), as do the limited exemptions where the consideration includes the carrying out of works (see **2.24**) or the transaction qualifies for 'PFI relief' (see **3.11**).

4.42 When a lease is surrendered in consideration for the grant of another lease, the surrender and grant do not count as consideration for each other (*FA 2003, Sch 17A, para 16*). The acceptance of normal tenant's obligations other than payment of rent and premium does not count as consideration when a lease is granted (*FA 2003, Sch 17A, para 10*). The acceptance of such obligations *including* payment of rent does not count as consideration for the transfer of a lease (*FA 2003, Sch 17A, para 17*).

Rent

4.43 There is no comprehensive definition of rent, so it must be taken as having its ordinary commercial meaning of consideration paid by a tenant, usually periodically, for use or occupation of the property. Where rent is payable other than in sterling cash, it must be valued in the same way as other consideration, at the effective date of the lease; see **2.19**. A single sum expressed as payable in respect of rent and other matters, without apportionment, is to be treated as entirely rent (*FA 2003, Sch 17A, para 6*). To minimise the SDLT payable, it may therefore be important to ensure that 'inclusive' rents are overtly apportioned, in the terms and conditions of the lease, between rent proper and other items such as insurance, cleaning and maintenance. However, in practice, HMRC often seem willing to accept a reasonable apportionment even where this is not explicit in the lease. The apportionment, whether explicit in the lease or negotiated with HMRC, must be on a just and reasonable basis (*FA 2003, Sch 4, para 4*).

Example 4.15

Albert leases an office suite in a larger building owned by Big Office Co Ltd on a ten-year lease, terminable by either party on one year's notice. The rent is £30,000 per annum plus a proportionate share of an insurance premium paid by Big Office and covering the whole building. The rent includes heating/air conditioning and regular cleaning, but amounts are not allocated to these in the lease. Light and power are separately metered and charged. The insurance premium is clearly identified and, since it merely passes on actual cost, is presumably 'just and reasonable', so it will not form part of the rent for SDLT purposes. Since the remaining rent is not allocated between real rent and matters such as cleaning and heating, strictly it is all rent for SDLT purposes. The parties would be well advised to insert a reasonable allocation into the lease. However, even in the absence of numbers in the lease itself, HMRC may be persuaded to accept an allocation. They may require evidence from Big Office to support amounts allocated to non-chargeable matters.

4.44 An anti-avoidance provision at *FA 2003, Sch 17A, para 18A* is designed to prevent a premium being disguised as rent, which would normally give rise to a lower SDLT liability. If the tenant pays any loan or deposit in excess of a normal 'rent deposit', the loan or deposit is to be taxed as a premium, even though it may be repayable (typically by offset against rent payments as they fall due).

New leases

4.45 When a new lease is granted or deemed to be granted, SDLT must be calculated separately on any rent and on any premium or deemed premium (*FA 2003, Sch 5*). The two components are then simply added to give the SDLT liability. As in other cases, any VAT chargeable must be included in both rent and premium. However, if VAT arises as a result of the landlord exercising the 'option to tax' *after* the effective date of the transaction, this does not have to be taken into account (*FA 2003, Sch 4, para 2*).

Loss of zero rate band on premium

4.46 The premium is subject to SDLT at normal rates up to 4% on the same 'slab' system as any other lump sum payment for an interest in land (see **2.34**), but with one important change. If a lease of non-residential property is also subject to rent of £1,000 or more per annum, the zero tax rate for a premium up to £150,000 is replaced by a 1% rate. For a mixed residential/non-residential lease, a 'just and reasonable apportionment' of amounts must be made to determine whether the rent for the non-residential portion breaches the £1,000 threshold (*FA 2003, Sch 5, para 9A*).

SDLT ON RENT

4.47 To calculate the SDLT on the rent, it is first necessary to establish the amount of rent to be taken into account for each year of the lease. If the lease is no longer than five years, the rent for SDLT purposes is simply the actual rent. As noted at **4.37**, if these amounts are not determined at the effective date of the lease, SDLT must be paid based on a reasonable estimate. A further return must be made, with payment of any additional SDLT, once the amounts are finally determined. If the final figures indicate that SDLT has been overpaid, an amendment to the return may be submitted and any overpayment reclaimed, but this is not compulsory.

Rent after fifth year

4.48 If the lease is longer than five years but the rent is fixed and at a constant rate throughout the term, again SDLT is based on the actual rent. However, this is probably unusual since most leases for more than five years are likely to provide for rent reviews. If the lease provides for the rent to change over the term for any reason, whether certainly or contingently, the following rules apply to determine the rent for SDLT purposes (*FA 2003, Sch 17A, para 7*):

(1) For the first five years, the actual rent is used.

(2) For each year after the first five, the rent is assumed to be equal to the highest rent for any consecutive 12-month period in the first five years.

This means that an abnormal 'spike' in the rent in the first five years can lead to a very large increase in SDLT payable, as the highest 12-month rent in those early years will form the basis of the deemed rent for later years (see Examples 4.17 and 4.20).

4.49 The rule applies even if the actual rent is known for periods after the first five years, so known increases after the first five years are ignored (see Example 4.16). However, once any later increase takes effect, whether or not known at the outset, it becomes necessary at that stage to consider whether the rent increase is abnormal (see **4.25**).

Example 4.16 – actual rent after Year 5 ignored

Percy grants Toni a 20-year lease of a shop at an initial rent of £10,000 per annum, commencing on 1 January 2011. The lease is executed on the start date without prior substantial performance. The lease provides for five-yearly rent reviews, with the rent increasing by at least 50% at each review, or to market rent if higher. It is therefore known that the rent will be at least £15,000, £22,500 and £33,750 per annum from the start of Years 6, 11 and 16 respectively. However, for purposes of the SDLT return at the start of the lease, the rent is treated as £10,000 per annum throughout the term of the lease. This is because the rent is £10,000 per annum for the first five years (rule 1), and the highest 12-month rent in the first five years is also £10,000 (rule 2). As the rent reviews occur, it will be necessary to consider whether they lead to abnormal increases, necessitating further SDLT returns. In fact, if the rent reviews lead simply to the compound 50% increases as set out above, none of the increases will be abnormal and no further SDLT returns will be needed.

Example 4.17 – effect of brief spike in rent in first five years

Julie grants an eight-year lease of a restaurant to Ken, commencing on 1 November 2011. The lease is executed on the start date without prior substantial performance. No premium is payable. Rent is £10,000 per quarter inc VAT but, for any quarter in which the restaurant turnover exceeds £100,000, the next quarter's rent is increased by one tenth of the excess. Over the first five years, the restaurant turnover exceeds £100,000 only in the quarters ending 31 May 2012 (when the rent for the following quarter is agreed at £11,000) and 28 February 2013 (when the rent for the following quarter is £12,300). These increases are not known when the lease is executed, and an initial return is submitted on the basis that the rent is £10,000 per quarter (£40,000 per annum) throughout. At the end of the first five years, a further return is required, with SDLT based on the following rent figures:

Year 1	£41,000	Three quarters at £10,000 plus one at £11,000
Year 2	£42,300	Three quarters at £10,000 plus one at £12,300
Each of Years 3 to 5	£40,000	Four quarters at £10,000
Each of Years 6 to 8	£43,300	This is the rent for the 12 months from 1 June 2012 to 31 May 2013, being the highest rent for any 12-month period in the first five years.

4.50 Once the rent for each year is determined (or estimated if uncertain at the outset), the net present value (NPV) of that rent over the life of the lease must be calculated, using the formula and discount rate specified in the legislation (*FA 2003, Sch 5, paras 3, 8*). Since the inception of SDLT, the discount rate has been 3.5%, but in future this may be varied by regulation. For these purposes, the length of the lease is taken as the term specified in the lease, ignoring any break clauses, other right to terminate early, or any right to extend or renew. However, if any right to extend or renew is subsequently exercised, the resulting further lease or extension may be linked with the original lease, whether successively or not; see **4.58** et seq.

4.51 In simple terms, the rent for the first 12 months is divided by 1.035 to give its discounted value, the rent for the second 12 months is divided by $(1.035)^2$, and so on to the end of the term of the lease. The discounted rent figures for all years are then totalled. If this total does not exceed the relevant threshold (currently £150,000 for non-residential or mixed property, or £125,000 for residential property: *FA 2003, Sch 5, para 2*), no SDLT is chargeable on the rent. If the NPV exceeds the relevant threshold, only the excess is chargeable at 1%. The threshold is, therefore, a form of allowance. This is in contrast with the 'slab' system which applies to a premium or other lump sum (see **2.34**).

4.52 It should not be unduly difficult to set up a spreadsheet to perform SDLT calculations for leases. However, an SDLT calculator for this purpose is provided on the HMRC website at www.hmrc.gov.uk/sdlt/calculate/calculators.htm#2. The HMRC calculator works for most cases, provided the correct information is input, and its use is recommended. However, it is purely a mechanical aid. It will not detect whether the correct information is entered, and HMRC have made it clear that they will hold the taxpayer responsible if the calculator gives incorrect answers because incorrect information has been entered. Therefore, it is important to have a full understanding of the nature of the transaction when entering information into the calculator, to guard against errors. A copy of the output (printed or electronic) should be retained in case of any future query. A minor annoyance is that the date boxes in the calculator are not set up to move the cursor to the next box as each is completed – this must be done manually using the mouse or tab key!

Example 4.18 – calculation of NPV

On 1 May 2011, Jeremy agrees to grant Kate a 10-year lease of an hotel at an annual rent of £25,000 inc VAT and for a premium of £260,000. There is an upwards-only rent review on the fifth anniversary. The lease is granted on 1 July 2011 without previously having been substantially performed. The effective date is therefore 1 July 2011, and the rent review is due on 1 July 2016. The SDLT can be calculated manually as follows:

Year	Actual rent for SDLT purposes	Discounted rent
1	£25,000	£24,154
2	£25,000	£23,337
3	£25,000	£22,548
4	£25,000	£21,786
5	£25,000	£21,049
6	£25,000	£20,337
7	£25,000	£19,649
8	£25,000	£18,985
9	£25,000	£18,343
10	£25,000	£17,722
Total discounted rent		£207,910
Less zero rate band		(£150,000)
SDLT charged at 1% on		£57,910
SDLT on rent		£579
SDLT on premium: £260,000 @ 3%		£7,800
Total SDLT (on rent and premium)		£8,379

4.53 Alternatively, the HMRC calculator may be used. This has a series of two input screens, as follows:

First screen:

Stamp Duty Land Tax on Lease Transactions Calculator

The stamp duty land tax calculator provides the amount of stamp duty land tax on lease transactions.

Mandatory fields are marked with an asterisk | Glossary

Please answer the following questions:

Effective Date of Transaction :* [ ] [ ] [ ] DD/MM/YYYY

Type of property :* ○ Residential ○ Non Residential ○ Mixed

Start again | < Back | Next >

Insertion of the effective date (see **2.6** et seq) and type of property and clicking 'next' leads to the second screen, as shown on page 80, with the information from the first screen now included. It is not clear why two screens are required, and it is a minor irritation that the cursor has to be moved between boxes manually when inserting the date and other information.

4.54 The 'Relevant Rental Figure' box only appears for non-residential or mixed property. If the cursor is positioned over this input box on the screen, a pop-up message says this means the 'average annual rent'. In fact, the figure required is as set out in *FA 2003, Sch 5, para 9A(6).* For a lease not linked with any other, the figure is the highest 12-month rent in the first five years (or the amount apportioned to the non-residential part in the case of mixed residential/non-residential property). If the lease is linked with any other leases at rent, the figure is the aggregate of such figures for all of the leases (again, apportioned to non-residential parts where appropriate). However, this figure influences the output from the calculator in only one respect, and that is to deny the benefit of the zero rate band on any premium if the rent is £1,000 or more (see **4.46**). Therefore, unless the rent clearly is under £1,000 and the premium within the zero rate band, there seems little point in spending time on this number; it should be acceptable in such cases simply to insert the same number as used in the preceding box.

Stamp Duty Land Tax on Lease Transactions Calculator

The stamp duty land tax calculator provides the amount of stamp duty land tax on lease transactions.

Mandatory fields are marked with an asterisk

Glossary

Please answer the following questions:

Effective Date of Transaction	01/07/2011
Type of property	Non Residential
Start Date as specified in lease:*	DD/MM/YYYY
End Date as specified in lease :*	DD/MM/YYYY
Total premium payable :	£
Year 1 rent :	£
Year 2 rent :	£
Year 3 rent :	£
Year 4 rent :	£
Year 5 rent :	£
If the term of the lease is more than 5 years enter the highest 12 monthly rent in the first 5 year period:	£
Relevant Rental Figure :**	£

HM Revenue & Customs cannot be held liable for incorrect output from this Calculator. Correct information can only result from this Calculator if correct details are entered.

Start again < Back Next >

Example 4.19 – use of HMRC calculator

Using numbers from Example 4.18 above, the output from the calculator is:

Stamp Duty Land Tax on Lease Transactions Calculator Glossary

The stamp duty land tax calculator provides the amount of stamp duty land tax on lease transactions.

Values Entered	
Property Type:	Non Residential
Effective Date of Transaction:	01/07/2011
Start Date as specified in lease:	01/07/2011
End Date as specified in lease:	30/06/2021
Total premium payable:	£260000
Year 1 rent:	£25000
Year 2 rent:	£25000
Year 3 rent:	£25000
Year 4 rent:	£25000
Year 5 rent:	£25000
Highest 12 monthly rent:	£25000
Relevant Rental Figure:	£25000
Term Of Lease:	10 Years
Rent for Final (partial) Year: £25000 * 0/0	£0

Results

This calculation uses the rates and thresholds which were effective from **01/01/2010**

Total Amount of Tax for this Transaction:	£8379
Net Present value:	£207915
Stamp Duty Land Tax on Rent:	£579
Stamp Duty Land Tax on Premium:	£7800

< Back Start again

4.55 Note that the calculator output shows all of the entries made on the input screens, so it is easy to check there have been no transcription errors. The slight difference in the net present value of rent is a result of rounding in the manual calculation. It has no effect on the SDLT payable because this is also rounded down to the nearest whole pound.

Example 4.20 – HMRC calculator, spike in early rentals

Facts are as Example 4.18, except that the rent for the period from 1 January to 31 December 2012 is doubled to £50,000 in recognition of expected better business from certain sporting events. This means the rent for each of Years 2 and 3 will be £37,500, but the highest rent for any consecutive 12 months in the first five years will be £50,000, being the rent for the calendar year 2012. This is, therefore, the figure to input into the final two boxes of the second screen in the HMRC calculator. The output from the calculator is as follows:

Stamp Duty Land Tax on Lease Transactions Calculator Glossary

The stamp duty land tax calculator provides the amount of stamp duty land tax on lease transactions.

Values Entered	
Property Type:	Non Residential
Effective Date of Transaction:	01/07/2011
Start Date as specified in lease:	01/07/2011
End Date as specified in lease:	30/06/2021
Total premium payable:	£260000
Year 1 rent:	£37500
Year 2 rent:	£37500
Year 3 rent:	£25000
Year 4 rent:	£25000
Year 5 rent:	£25000
Highest 12 monthly rent:	£50000
Relevant Rental Figure:	£50000
Term Of Lease:	10 Years
Rent for Final (partial) Year: £50000 * 0/0	£0

Results

This calculation uses the rates and thresholds which were effective from **01/01/2010**

Total Amount of Tax for this Transaction:	£9567
Net Present value:	£326700
Stamp Duty Land Tax on Rent:	£1767
Stamp Duty Land Tax on Premium:	£7800

HM Revenue & Customs cannot be held liable for incorrect output from this Calculator. Correct information can only result from this Calculator if correct details are entered.

< Back Start again

4.56 The hugely increased SDLT on the rental element illustrates the effect of a temporary increase in rent during the first five years, as rent for every year after the first five is assumed to be equal to the highest rent for *any* consecutive 12-month period in the first five years. Where rent is variable during the first five years, it is important to establish the precise manner of variation and the correct attribution of rent to each period, as specified by the lease (*FA 2003, Sch 17A, para 7*; see **4.68**).

Connected company rule

4.57 The normal rule applies, that if the 'purchaser' (the lessee or, in the case of a surrender, the landlord) is a company connected with the other party, the consideration is taken to be at least equal to the market value of the lease in question (*FA 2003, s 53*). Note that it does not matter whether the 'vendor' is a company, individual or other entity. Application of the rule depends only on the 'purchaser' being a company which is connected with the 'vendor'. This is subject to the same exceptions as apply to other transactions (see **2.27**). Where this rule applies to the grant of a lease, it does not lead to any deemed adjustment of the actual rent. If the rent charged under the lease is less than a full market rent, it is assumed that the lease will have a capital value. The amount of this capital value is taxed as a deemed premium.

Example 4.21 – lease to connected company

Maria grants to her family trading company, PPM Ltd, a ten-year lease of a barn on her farm, for use as a storage facility. The lease is at a flat rent of £5,000 per annum with no provision for rent reviews. The NPV of rent over the life of the lease is clearly below the £150,000 threshold. However, it is acknowledged that a current market rent would be £7,500 and a lease at the actual rent of £5,000 would command a market premium of £20,000. The lease is therefore subject to SDLT on this premium. Because the yearly rent is £1,000 or more, there is no zero rate band for the premium and this is chargeable at 1%. SDLT of £200 is payable. It is worth noting that, if the rent had been set at a market level of £7,500 so that there was no deemed premium, the NPV of the rent would still have fallen below the £150,000 threshold and no SDLT would have been payable. However, an SDLT return would still have been required; see **6.2** and **3.7**(6).

Linked transactions

4.58 Lease transactions may be 'linked' with other UK land transactions (whether or not involving other leases) if they form part of a single scheme, arrangement or series of transactions between the same vendor and purchaser or persons connected with them (*FA 2003, s 108*; see **2.36**). There are two distinct ways in which lease transactions may be linked, and each has its own implications.

Successive linked leases

4.59 If successive leases of substantially the same premises are granted, and if those leases are linked, the second and subsequent leases are effectively treated as extending the earlier lease (*FA 2003, Sch 17A, para 5*). As each lease in the series after the first is granted (or substantially performed), any SDLT return made in respect of the earlier lease must be amended to show details for what is now deemed to be a longer lease, and any additional SDLT must be paid. Additional SDLT may arise in relation to rent (the NPV of the rent will have increased because the deemed lease is for a longer period) and/ or premium (if a further premium is paid, the premiums must be aggregated both to determine the rate of tax and to calculate the amount of tax).

Example 4.22 – successive linked leases

Harriet granted Ian a five-year lease of a warehouse commencing 1 September 2006 for a premium of £130,000 and a yearly rent of £50,000. The lease was executed on the start date without prior substantial performance. The lease agreement included an option for Ian to take a further five-year lease commencing on 1 September 2011 at the same rent, on payment of a further premium of £130,000. Ian exercises the option; the second lease is executed on 1 August 2011 (ie one month before commencement) and the additional premium is paid on 1 September 2011.

During September 2006, Ian submitted an SDLT return for the five-year lease, with premium £130,000 and yearly rent of £50,000. The total SDLT paid was £2,057, comprising £1,300 on the premium (charged at 1% because the rent is £1,000 or more, see **4.46**) and £757 on the rent. A further SDLT return is needed in respect of the second lease. The leases are linked, so there is deemed to be a ten-year lease at a flat rental of £50,000 per annum and a premium of £260,000, commencing 1 September 2006. The SDLT on such a lease is £10,458, comprising £7,800 on the premium (at 3%) and £2,658 on the rent. The SDLT paid on the original lease is deducted, leaving £8,401 payable as a result of the second lease. Although the second lease is not 'substantially performed' early, it is executed one month before commencement, so the further SDLT return and payment are due 30 days after execution, that is no later than 31 August 2011.

4.60 Successive leases are not necessarily linked. If, when the first lease was granted, there was no agreement (explicit or implied) that the next lease would be granted, and if the next lease was negotiated independently of the first, they are not likely to be linked. However, if the first lease contained an option for grant of a further lease, they probably are linked. HMRC tend to assume that successive leases are linked unless there is clear evidence to the contrary.

Other linked leases

4.61 Leases of different premises may be linked – for example, a tenant may take on leases of two shops in different towns from the same landlord, negotiated as a single deal. Additionally, the deemed lease arising from an abnormal increase in rent after the first five years of a lease (see **4.24**) is automatically linked with the original lease and with any previous such deemed leases (*FA 2003, Sch 17A, para 14(5)(b)*). However, this deemed lease runs in parallel with the original lease, so they cannot be 'successive'. The deemed lease arising from a variation to increase rent within the first five years of a lease is not automatically linked with the original lease – this is a matter to be determined in the light of the facts. For example, if the rent increase is a result of a statutory rent review, the leases are unlikely to be linked; if the increase relates to improvements of the premises contemplated when the lease was originally executed, the leases are likely to be linked.

4.62 Where leases are linked and the 'successive leases' rules do not apply (for example, leases of two properties agreed between the same parties as part of a single transaction), any premiums are aggregated to determine the correct rate of SDLT, which is then applied separately to each premium. The NPV of the rents under the leases are also aggregated to give a figure for total NPV (TNPV), and the tax on this is calculated in the normal way. The tax applicable to each lease is then calculated by applying the fraction NPV (for the individual lease)/TNPV to the overall tax on rent.

4.63 If the linked leases do not have the same effective date (or if some are and some are not wholly residential), and if, as a result, the zero rate threshold would be different for the separate leases, the tax on the TNPV must be calculated afresh for each lease before applying the NPV/TNPV fraction (*FA 2003, Sch 5, para 2*). This complexity means it is not possible to use the SDLT calculator on the HMRC website to make a direct calculation of the SDLT due on the leases. However, the calculator can still be used to calculate the NPVs for the individual leases, the remainder of the calculation then being performed manually.

Example 4.23 – leases linked but not successive

The facts are as in Example 4.8 above. Using the HMRC calculator, the NPV of the rents under the original 25-year lease is £164,814 and the SDLT paid was £148. The NPV of rents under the deemed notional 15-year lease arising from the abnormal rent increase is £253,382. The total NPV is therefore £418,196. The SDLT on a single lease with this NPV is (£418,196 – £150,000) × 1% = £2,681. There have been no changes in rates and thresholds which would affect this lease, so this can simply be allocated between the actual and notional leases as follows:

- Actual lease: £2,681 × £164,814/£418,196 = £1,056;
- Notional lease: £2,681 × £253,382/£518,196 = £1,624.

The original SDLT liability on the actual lease was £148, so the additional liability of £908 must be notified by way of an amended return, in the form of a letter to the Birmingham Stamp Office (see **6.15** and **Appendix A**).

Example 4.24 – linked leases calculation

The facts are as in Examples 4.5 and 4.10 above. The NPV of rent under the original lease is £207,915 and the SDLT paid was £579. The NPV of the deemed additional lease is £21,712, so the aggregate NPV is £229,627. The SDLT payable on a lease with this rental NPV is 1% of £(229,627 – 150,000), which is £796. Thresholds and rates are the same for both actual and deemed lease, so this calculation is appropriate for both leases. The revised SDLT attributable to the original lease is £796 × £207,915/£229,627, which is £720, and the SDLT attributable to the deemed additional lease is £796 × £21,712/£229,627, which is £75 (the £1 overall reduction arises from rounding and seems to be acceptable). As a stand-alone lease, the deemed lease arising from the rent increase would not have given rise to any SDLT charge but, because it is linked with the original lease, a charge arises.

Lease renewals

4.64 The interaction between the SDLT rules and commercial practice leads to complexity when a lease is renewed. As a result, the costs of compliance may be far greater than the amount of tax payable. Inevitably, the tax payable will depend on the rent (and premium, if any) payable under the new lease and the length of the lease. However, the tax may also depend on matters such as: when the *old* lease was executed; whether there has been a period of 'holding over' between expiry of the old lease and finalisation of the new; and how the parties agree to treat the holding-over period. A period of holding over occurs when the tenant remains in occupation after a lease has expired, usually while a new lease is negotiated.

Information required

4.65 This section lists the information which must be assembled in order to determine the SDLT consequences of a renewal. It then provides flow-charts, with illustrative examples covering most situations. The examples only apply where the new lease comes into effect after 18 July 2006; for new leases taking effect on or before that date, further advice may be required.

- Expiry date (E) of old lease and annual rent (R) at expiry.
- Whether old lease was executed, or is treated as having been executed for SDLT purposes, before 1 December 2003 (a 'stamp duty' lease) or after 30 November 2003 (an 'SDLT' lease). Note that a stamp duty lease may have become an SDLT lease if it was varied while SDLT was in force. If the old lease is a stamp duty lease, it is assumed that it was for a period of five years or more; if, exceptionally, a stamp duty lease with a life of less than five years is now renewed, further advice may be required.
- Stated start date (S) and end date (D) of new lease, and date (B) on which it was executed.
- Starting annual rent (Q) of new lease, together with usual information about rent review dates or other arrangements under which rent may change.
- Details about payments in respect of any 'holding over' period – for example, whether rent was paid at rate R, or at a greater rate and, if so, whether the greater payment was identified as rent for the period of holding over, or as a payment for entering into the new lease. Please see the relevant examples below for further information on this matter.

Old lease under stamp duty

4.66

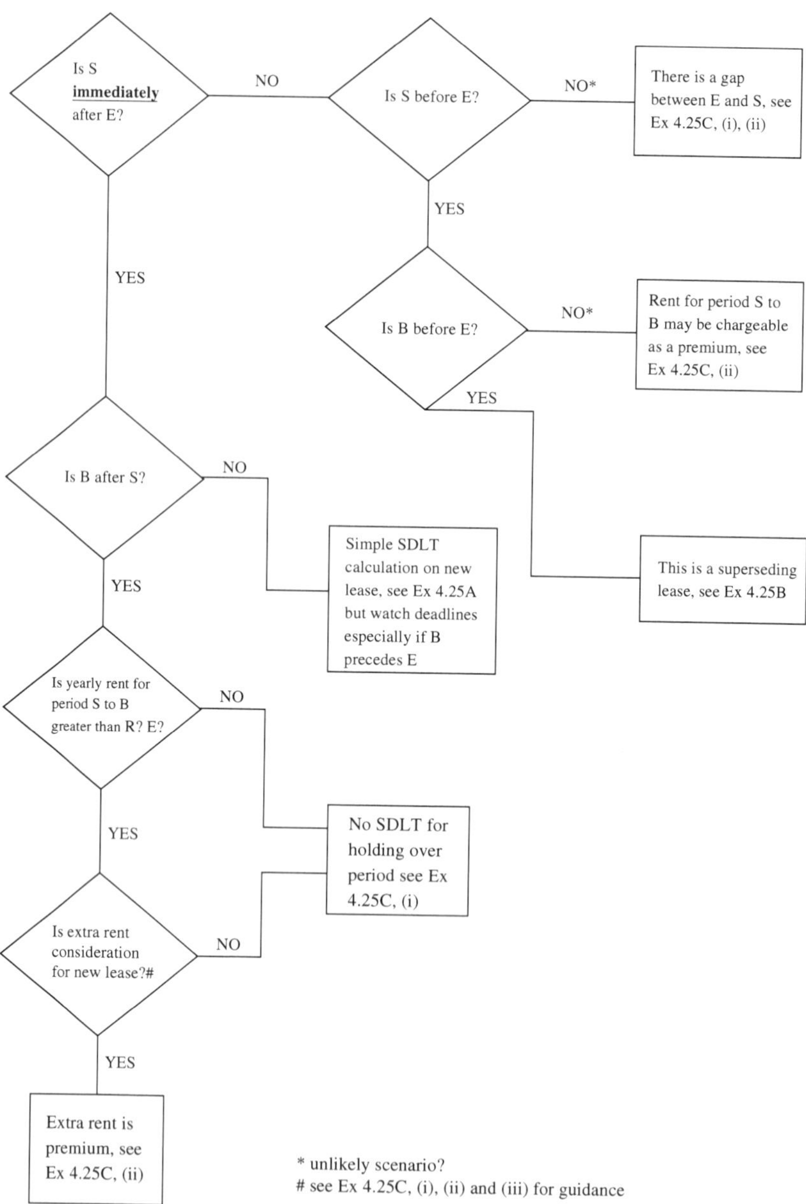

* unlikely scenario?
\# see Ex 4.25C, (i), (ii) and (iii) for guidance

Old lease under SDLT

4.67

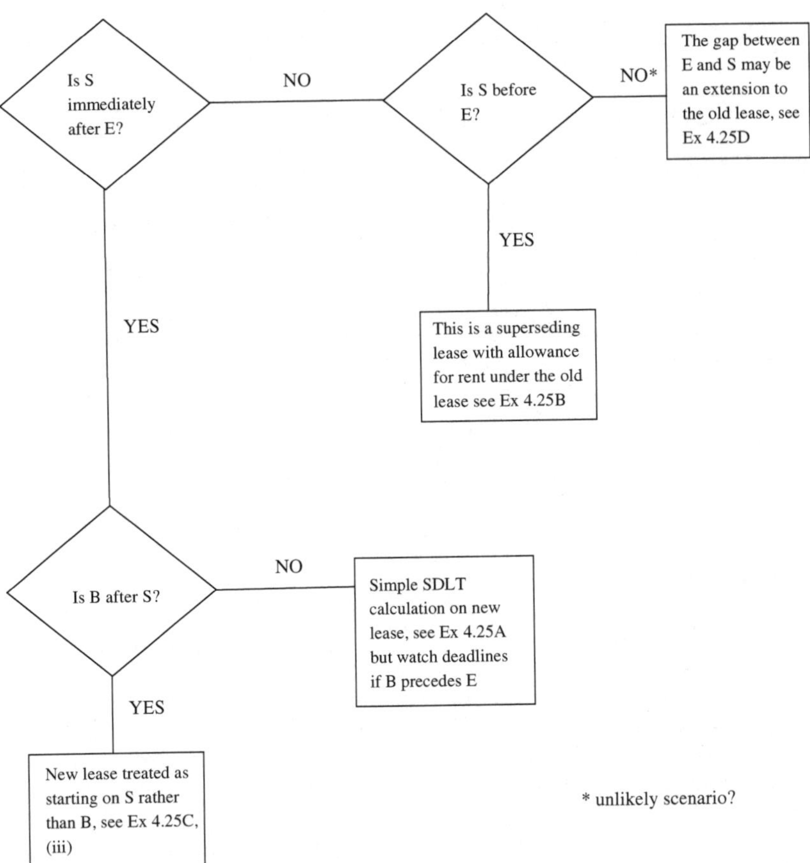

Lease renewal examples

4.68 The following examples are referred to in the flowcharts at **4.66** and **4.67**.

General fact pattern

ServiceCo occupies a commercial unit on lease from unrelated Propco. When the old lease was granted (more than five years ago), there was no agreement between the parties as to whether the lease would be renewed. The lease expires on 31 December 2010, at which time the annual rent is £100,000 including VAT. A new lease is negotiated, the commercial terms being for seven years from 1 January 2011 (except where noted below) at yearly rent of £120,000 including VAT. No separate premium is payable. There is a rent review due on 1 January 2016.

Example 4.25A

New lease is negotiated in advance and executed on 1 December 2010 to take effect on 1 January 2011. There are no complications, the HMRC calculator gives the NPV of the rent as £733,745, and the SDLT payable as £5,837. The rent review will not occur during the first five years of the lease and so can be ignored at present. When the review occurs, it will be necessary to check whether it leads to an abnormal increase in rent (see **4.25**). The calculation of SDLT is based on the lease commencing on 1 January 2011. However, because the lease was executed on 1 December 2010, the SDLT return and tax payment are due within 30 days of this date, ie before 31 December 2010, which is before the lease period commences.

Example 4.25B

As Example 4.25A, except lease is executed on 1 July 2010 and takes immediate effect, displacing the old lease. The new lease is again for seven years (that is, it expires in this case on 30 June 2017). The SDLT return and tax payment are due by 31 July 2010. If the old lease was a stamp duty lease, the basic calculation is the same as for Example 4.25A; no allowance is given in respect of the unexpired six months of old lease displaced by the new lease. If the old lease was an SDLT lease, an allowance is given in the SDLT calculation for the £50,000 rent which would have been paid under the old lease for the period from 1 July to 31 December 2010. See Example 4.10 for the method of calculation. The rent for the first year of the new lease is therefore taken to be £70,000 (that is, £120,000 less the £50,000 'allowance'). The HMRC calculator gives the NPV of the rent as £685,436 and the tax payable as £5,354.

Example 4.25C

New lease is finally executed on 1 July 2011, stated to be for seven years from 1 January 2011 at yearly rent of £120,000 but silent on matter of payment of rent for period before execution. ServiceCo has continued paying rent at yearly rate of £100,000, but pays an extra £10,000 immediately before lease is executed, to bring the yearly rate for the period of holding over (1 January to 31 June 2011) up to the new rent.

(i) Both parties are satisfied that the extra payment is in respect of occupation during the period of holding over and is not an inducement to the landlord to enter into the new lease. If the old lease was under stamp duty, continued occupation after expiry is treated as an extension of that lease which is not subject to SDLT on either the rent paid at the 'old' rate or the retrospective £10,000 rent increase. The same analysis would apply if the new lease was stated to commence on some date after 1 January 2011 – for example on 1 July 2011, the date of execution – such that there was acknowledged to be a gap between the end of the old lease and the start of the new. Note the position would have been different prior to the change of law on 19 July 2006. SDLT is payable in the normal way on the new lease which is deemed to commence on 1 July 2011 (and so be for a period of only 6 years 6 months if it expires on 31 December 2017).

(ii) The parties acknowledge that the extra £10,000 payment was made to persuade Propco to grant the new lease. If the old lease was under stamp duty, the continued payment of rent at the old rate during the period of holding over is treated as for an extension of the old lease, with no SDLT consequences. However, the additional £10,000 is treated as a premium for the new lease. SDLT is chargeable on this at 1% (the zero rate band is not available because the yearly rent is £1,000 or more; see **4.46**), in addition to SDLT on the rent for the period of the new lease from 1 July 2011. The same analysis would apply if the new lease was stated to commence on a date after 1 January 2011.

Often, on the renewal of a non-residential lease for a relatively short period and at modest rent, the NPV of the rent will fall below the £150,000 threshold. However, the 'premium' treatment of small sums in respect of the period of holding over will still give rise to the need to complete an SDLT return to report and pay very small amounts of tax (under £10 in some cases seen by the author).

(iii) If the old lease was under SDLT, the new lease is treated as beginning on the stated start date of 1 January 2011 and for a period of seven years. The £60,000 rent paid in respect of occupation in the six months to 30 June 2011 is taken into account as rent under the new lease, irrespective of whether the payment is acknowledged as being in respect of the new lease (*FA 2003, Sch 17A, para 9A*).

Example 4.25D

New lease is finally executed on 1 July 2011, stated to be for seven years from 1 July 2011, so there is a gap between expiry of the old lease and stated commencement date of the new. Yearly rent is £120,000 but lease is silent on matter of payment of rent for period before execution. ServiceCo has continued paying rent at yearly rate of £100,000, but pays an extra £10,000 immediately before lease is executed, to bring the yearly rate for the period of holding over (1 January to 31 June 2011) up to the new rent. If the old lease was under stamp duty, the treatment is covered under Examples 25C(i) and 25C(ii) above. If the old lease was under SDLT, the treatment of the period of holding over will depend on the precise legal status of this occupation by the tenant:

- If, in law, the old lease is treated as continuing (for example, under provisions of the landlord and tenant legislation), the continued occupation is treated initially as a one-year extension of the old lease. This is likely to lead to the need to recalculate the SDLT payable on that old lease and make an amended return (see **6.17**) and pay any additional SDLT due. Note that the deemed extension is for one year, even if the actual continued occupation (prior to the new lease taking effect) is for less than this. If the continued occupation continues for more than one year, the deemed extension period increases in one-year steps until it ends. However, the additional £10,000 will not be taken into account in calculating the additional SDLT, unless it amounts to an 'abnormal increase' in rent (on the numbers in the example, it does not).
- If the foregoing does not apply (perhaps because the lease disapplied the relevant landlord and tenant provisions), it may be that an implied new tenancy arises for the interim period and this will be separately subject to SDLT, but probably linked to the new lease, forming a pair of successive leases. Apart from possibly bringing deadlines forward, this should have the same net effect as the lease being stated as beginning on 1 January 2011, as in Example 25C(iii). In the present case, the landlord's acceptance of continued rent payment suggests this would be the case. However, it would save the need to even consider the matter if the new lease was expressed as beginning immediately after expiry of the old!
- Finally, it may be that the tenant's continued occupation is an act of trespass, or is under a tenancy at will. Such occupation has no SDLT consequences. However, it is likely to be difficult to demonstrate that this is the basis of occupation if a new lease is eventually executed.

WHEN DO SDLT OBLIGATIONS ARISE?

Grant of a lease

4.69 The concepts of 'substantial performance' and 'effective date' (see **2.9** and **2.38**) apply to transactions involving leases, but with some specific 'trigger points'. In the case of a new lease, there are typically several stages which may occur at different times. The first SDLT liability and obligation to submit a return will arise 30 days after the earlier of:

- the lease proper being executed, and
- the agreement for lease being substantially performed.

Substantial performance occurs on the earliest of:

- the first payment of rent being made,
- substantially the whole of any consideration other than rent (eg a premium) being paid,
- the tenant taking possession of substantially the whole of the premises, and
- in Scotland, missives of let being concluded which do not provide for subsequent execution of a definitive lease.

The tenant will be regarded as taking possession if he occupies the premises, including for the purpose of fitting out, or if he becomes entitled to enjoy other benefits of tenancy such as receipt of rent from a sub-tenant (see **2.9**). Where an agreement for lease is substantially performed before the lease is granted, this is deemed to be the grant of a notional lease on the terms provided for in the agreement.

4.70 When SDLT obligations have arisen on a notional lease as a result of substantial performance of the agreement, the subsequent grant of the real lease is also potentially subject to SDLT. At this point, the notional lease is deemed to be surrendered and overlap relief (see **4.35**) is given for SDLT paid on the notional lease. The practical effect is that, provided the lease is for the same rent and term (and premium, if any) as envisaged in the agreement for lease, no further SDLT is payable. In this case, by virtue of the combined effect of *FA 2003, s 77A(3)* and *Sch 17A, para 9*, no further notification to HMRC is required. However, difficulty can arise if the rent is uncertain, variable or payable other than in sterling.

4.71 First, if rent is payable in another currency and the exchange rate moves between substantial performance and completion, the sterling equivalent of the rent will differ at the two dates. If the sterling equivalent increases, extra SDLT will be payable. If the sterling equivalent decreases, no refund of SDLT will be due.

4.72 Second, for SDLT purposes, the term of the lease will normally be regarded as beginning no earlier than the date of grant. This may result in a rent review falling within the first five years of the term, making the rent 'uncertain' (see **4.37**). It may also be important in determining such matters as when further returns are required if rent is variable or uncertain (see **4.74**).

Deferral of SDLT

4.73 If (perhaps unusually) any amount of a premium is contingent or uncertain at the effective date and will not be payable until more than six months after the effective date, the lessee may apply to HMRC to defer payment of an appropriate amount of SDLT in the same way as for other land transactions (see **6.31**). However, it is not possible to apply to defer payment of SDLT arising in respect of rent, even if the amount of rent is uncertain at the effective date. This means that, if final settlement of the rent leads to a further SDLT liability, say at the end of the first five years of the lease, interest will be chargeable on that SDLT from the original due date (30 days after the effective date of the lease).

Uncertain or variable rent

4.74 The rent for the first five years of the lease may not be finally ascertained at the outset (for example, because the rent is based on results of a business or because there is a rent review within the first five years). It remains necessary to submit returns and pay SDLT on normal timescales. SDLT must be calculated on the basis of a 'reasonable estimate' of the rent. Details must then be notified and any additional SDLT paid within 30 days of the earlier of (a) the rent being finally ascertained and (b) the end of the fifth year. The rent for the first five years may not have been finally determined when the five-year deadline arrives (for example, it may depend on profits of a period for which accounts have not yet been finalised). In that case, it may be necessary at the five-year point to submit a further return on the basis of a revised reasonable estimate, and further amend this once the rent is finally determined. In either case for interest purposes, the effective date for the revision remains the original date of the lease, and interest will be charged on any SDLT paid more than 30 days from then.

Example 4.26 – timing of returns and tax payments

The facts are as in Example 4.17 above. Ken must submit an SDLT return and pay SDLT no later than 30 November 2011. At that time, he must make a reasonable estimate of what the rent will be, and it seems likely that his estimate will be £10,000 per quarter. The total rent payable over the first five years (and, therefore, the final SDLT liability) will not be known until some time after the end of the first five years. Because the actual rent is higher than the estimate, Ken must submit a further return by 29 November 2016 (that is, within 30 days of the end of the first five years), self-assessing the additional SDLT, which must be paid by the same date. If the correct figures are not known by this due date, Ken must make a reasonable estimate, then correct the return once the actual numbers are known. If any of this leads to additional SDLT being paid after 30 November 2011, interest will be charged on this additional tax from that date.

Informal occupation and holding over

4.75 It can be difficult to establish when SDLT obligations arise in cases of informal occupation. It is essential to establish the precise legal nature of the occupation. A periodic tenancy is initially regarded as a lease for one year. If the annual rent exceeds the relevant threshold, SDLT obligations arise 30 days after commencement. If the tenancy continues beyond one year, it is treated as a lease for two years, then three years and so on. At the commencement of each further year, it is necessary to consider whether the cumulative rent and/or period are sufficient to give rise to SDLT notification or payment obligations. If so, those obligations arise 30 days after the start of the year in question.

The position is similar where a lease does not have a stated end date. In some cases, the position may be similar where a tenant remains in occupation after the end of the lease. However, where the tenant is 'holding over' while a new lease is negotiated, the precise nature and timing of SDLT obligations in respect of the holding-over period depend on the provisions of the new lease (see **4.64** et seq).

Variation or surrender of a lease

4.76 There are no special rules relating to time for notifying and paying SDLT on the variation or surrender of a lease. The obligations arise 30 days after the earlier of:

- completion of the formalities giving effect to the variation (for example, the parties executing the relevant document), and
- 'substantial performance' of the variation.

Substantial performance has essentially the same meaning as set out in **4.69**, subject to the specific rule in the next paragraph.

Abnormal increase in rent

4.77 Where there is an abnormal increase in rent (see **4.25**), the notional new lease is deemed granted on the date on which the new rent first becomes payable (*FA 2003, Sch 17A, para 14(5)*). SDLT obligations arise 30 days after this date. Note this is not necessarily the same as the date from which the new rent applies.

RELIEFS

4.78 In general, reliefs and exemptions available for other UK land transactions also apply to transactions involving leases – see **Chapter 3** in respect of reliefs. Some of the reliefs are modified for lease transactions, particularly in relation to possible future clawback of the relief. There are a few additional reliefs which only apply to lease transactions.

Sale (or lease) and leaseback relief

4.79 Where a vendor sells or leases a major interest in a property to a purchaser and, in consideration (wholly or partly), the purchaser grants a lease (the 'leaseback') to the vendor out of that major interest, the leaseback may be exempt from SDLT (*FA 2003, s 57A*). The only other consideration permitted for the initial sale/lease (which must not be a sub-sale, see **3.8**) is cash and/or assumption, satisfaction or release of a debt; the vendor and purchaser must not be companies in a group relationship, such that they could qualify for group relief.

Overlap relief

4.80 This is mentioned at **4.34**, and applies if a lease is granted which supersedes a previous lease of substantially the same premises, which itself was subject to the SDLT regime. In calculating SDLT on the new lease, the rent for the 'overlap period' (that is, the period which would have been covered by the old lease but is now covered by the new) is reduced by the rent which would have been paid under the old lease if that had been left to run its course (*FA 2003, Sch 17A, para 9*). The relief may also apply where the new lease is granted to someone who acted as guarantor under the original lease, or in certain circumstances where the new lease is granted to someone who was a sub-tenant of the original lessee.

This relief is in addition to the general principle set out in *FA 2003, Sch 17A, para 16* that, where a lease is surrendered in consideration of the grant of another, neither the surrender nor the grant counts as consideration for the other.

Exercise of collective rights by tenants of flats

4.81 Tenants holding long leases of flats may have the right to gain control of the freehold. This may be achieved, for example, by the tenants jointly forming a company or other entity to buy the freehold. Although the amount paid by any individual tenant may not be large enough to give rise to any SDLT liability, the total amount payable by the company may be very large, possibly attracting SDLT at the top 4% rate. This is clearly unfair in comparison with a leaseholder of an equivalent house, who may be able to buy the freehold as an individual without triggering an SDLT charge. *FA 2003, s 74* provides a relief, under which the rate of SDLT to be applied is determined by dividing the total consideration payable by the company or other entity by the number of flats involved. In its original form, the relief only applied to a specific type of company expected to be established under the *Leasehold Reform, Housing and Urban Development Act 1993*. Unfortunately, the provisions of that Act allowing formation of such companies have never been brought into effect, so this relief was ineffective until amended by *FA 2009, s 80*. The form of entity buying the freehold is now not specified.

Chapter 5

SDLT and Partnerships

INTRODUCTION

5.1 The legislation specifically dealing with partnerships is in *FA 2003, Sch 15*. In this chapter, references to paragraph numbers without further identification are references to paragraphs of *Schedule 15*. *Part 1 (paras 1–4)* and *Part 2 (paras 5–8)* set out general provisions, including confirmation of the treatment of an ordinary acquisition of a chargeable interest from an unconnected vendor. *Part 3 (paras 9–40)* was inserted by *FA 2004* and contains the detailed rules applying SDLT to almost all other transactions of partnerships which own, acquire or dispose of chargeable interests. The heading, suggesting that the *Part 3* provisions only apply in 'special' circumstances, is misleading!

5.2 The UK tax system has always had difficulty working out how to deal with partnerships – in particular, whether to treat them as separate entities distinct from their members or as mere aggregations of separately taxed members – and SDLT continues that uncertainty. When SDLT was introduced, many partnership transactions were initially left entirely within the stamp duty rules, while the Government tried to work out how best to deal with them under SDLT. Since the enactment of *FA 2004*, SDLT has generally applied to transactions by partnerships or partners, but with modification of and additions to the general rules. Substantial changes were made to the rules by *FA 2006, FA 2007* and *FA 2008*. The last of these amended the *FA 2007* changes with retrospective effect when it was realised that the earlier provisions caused major problems for some very large, widely held property investment vehicles.

5.3 This difficulty and uncertainty is reflected in the fact that HMRC's Stamp Duty Land Tax Manual does not, at the time of writing, include definitive guidance on the treatment of many partnership transactions. Guidance was issued in draft, in conjunction with the enactment of *FA 2004*, but this has not been finalised nor even amended to reflect subsequent changes in the legislation, so it is of limited use. It may be found at www.hmrc.gov.uk/so/pftmanual.htm. The June 2010 issue of HMRC's Stamp Tax Bulletin (www.hmrc.gov.uk/so/bulletin-jun-2010.htm) shows guidance in relation to partnerships as still 'in preparation'; it is hoped that definitive guidance will be issued soon.

5.4 Three types of UK-based partnership are recognised:

- a (general) partnership within the Partnership Act 1890;
- a limited partnership (LP) registered under the Limited Partnerships Act 1907; and
- a limited liability partnership (LLP) formed under the Limited Liability Partnerships Act 2000 or the Northern Ireland equivalent.

The SDLT rules seek to treat all three types of entity in the same way; they also apply the same treatment to any 'firm or entity of a similar character' formed under the laws of another country. Difficulties arise because the three types of entity listed above and many equivalent overseas entities have quite different legal and commercial characteristics. As a result, the SDLT treatment of a particular transaction may be logical in one case (say, involving a general partnership) but less so in another (say, involving an LLP). These differences have been a factor in the use of partnerships to mitigate SDLT costs, and many of the special rules which now apply were originally intended to combat perceived avoidance. Particular issues arise from the fact that LLPs (together with Scottish LPs and many overseas equivalents) are bodies corporate for the purposes of general law and many other tax purposes, but are treated as 'transparent' as regards ownership of land for SDLT purposes (see, for example, **3.18**).

GENERAL PRINCIPLES AND ORDINARY TRANSACTIONS

General principles

5.5 Property held by or on behalf of a partnership is treated as held by or on behalf of the partners (and not the partnership); a land transaction entered into for the purposes of a partnership is treated as entered into by or on behalf of the partners (and not the partnership); this is so even if the partnership is regarded as a body corporate or other legal entity for other purposes, such as ability to enter into contracts and to own property (*para* 2). However, the partners at the effective date of the transaction have joint and several liability for payment of any tax (*paras 6, 7*). They also have responsibility, in some circumstances together with any partners who join after the effective date, for payment of any penalty, for example for failure to make a return or notify liability. Although this means all partners have responsibility for compliance, they may nominate 'representative partners' to act on behalf of the partnership. Any such nomination must be notified to HMRC (*para 8*).

5.6 If there is a change in the membership of a partnership, it is nonetheless treated as the same continuing partnership, provided at least one member before the change remains a member afterwards (*para 3*). Thus, despite the assertions in the previous paragraph, there are ways in which a partnership is treated as a separate entity.

Partnership share

5.7 In order to calculate the chargeable consideration for many partnership transactions, or even in some cases to determine whether a chargeable transaction has occurred, it is necessary to know the shares which the different partners have in the partnership. For most SDLT purposes, a partner's share in a partnership is defined as the proportion in which he is entitled to share in the income profits of the partnership at the effective date of the transaction (*para 34(2)*). When property is transferred out of a partnership, a more complicated definition applies, although in many cases it produces the same result (see **5.23**). Entitlement to capital, or to capital profits, does not enter into the calculation. The definition causes practical difficulties – partnerships often decide the precise sharing of profits after the year end, once total profits and the contribution of each partner to them are known. In such cases, it may be necessary to complete an SDLT return and pay tax based on estimated shares, then amend the return once profit shares are finally settled. Since profit shares do not normally vary from day to day, the reference to the 'effective date' is usually taken to mean the accounting period containing the effective date.

Ordinary transactions

5.8 If a partnership (or a partner on behalf of a partnership) enters into a land transaction with a person who is completely at arm's length, that transaction is treated in the same way as an equivalent transaction not involving a partnership. The only modification is that the partners have joint and several responsibility for any compliance matters. A person is completely at arm's length if he is neither a partner (whether current, joining or departing) nor connected with a partner. Connected for these purposes is as defined by *Corporation Tax Act 2010 (CTA 2010), s 1122*, although the automatic connection of partners with each other is omitted. It follows that, for such an arm's-length transaction, SDLT is generally chargeable by reference to the value of the actual consideration, and it is only necessary to consider the market value of the property itself where that would be required for a non-partnership transaction (eg for exchanges of property interests).

SPECIAL PROVISIONS

5.9 The application of the SDLT rules to arm's-length transactions is relatively straightforward. Complications arise when there is a connection between the partnership and the other party, ie where the other party is a partner (current, departing or joining) or is connected with a partner. It is necessary to consider separately the implications of the partnership acquiring or disposing of property, including modification of an existing interest where that would be treated as an acquisition or disposal under general SDLT rules. It is also necessary to consider the implications of changes in the membership or relative interests of the members in a partnership which owns property; in certain cases, such changes are deemed to give rise to a corresponding transfer of property interests between partners.

5.10 In general, when partnership transactions are subject to the 'special provisions', SDLT is charged by reference to the market value of the property interest in question and the proportion of the property which is deemed to be transferred. In the original version of the legislation, any actual consideration given was also taken into account. The rules were amended in 2006 to remove this link. Actual consideration (other than any change in partnership share) is now irrelevant in these cases. However, there are anti-avoidance rules; in some circumstances, amounts which are commercially equivalent to consideration may trigger these (see **5.17**).

5.11 The legislation sets out formulae which must be applied to the market value of the property in question to determine the deemed consideration for the transaction. The formulae appear complex, but are generally seeking to achieve a relatively simple overall effect, which is to ensure that tax is charged on the economic transfer of value which takes place.

Example 5.1 – simple partnership case

Eric and Ernest are in a general partnership, sharing equally. They agree to admit Eddie as an equal partner (so each partner has a one-third share in profits, losses and assets) in return for Eddie agreeing, inter alia, to contribute freehold premises to the partnership. The property is transferred to Eric and Eddie jointly to hold on trust for the partnership (this is a normal arrangement, because a general partnership is not a body capable of holding the title to land). In the absence of any other complicating factors, SDLT is chargeable by reference to two-thirds of the market value of the property. This is the proportion which has economically changed hands by transfer to the other partners; Eddie still has a one-third interest in the property through his membership of the partnership, so no SDLT is charged on that proportion.

5.12 Inevitably, real transactions do include complicating factors, and HMRC are keen to minimise perceived avoidance. Therefore, the basic formulae are supplemented by definitions and rules for special cases which must be taken into account. It would not be safe to assume that the simple apportionment set out above gives the correct SDLT charge, without checking the specific facts of the case against the detailed rules.

Acquisition by a partnership

5.13 Under *para 10*, when a chargeable interest is acquired by a partnership from a partner, or from a person who becomes a partner as a result, or from a person who is connected with either, SDLT is charged on deemed consideration equal to:

$$MV \times (100 - SLP)\%$$

where MV is the market value of the chargeable interest at the effective date of the transfer, and SLP is the 'sum of the lower proportions'. A five-step calculation is required to determine SLP, set out in the legislation (*para 12*) as follows:

(1) Identify the 'relevant owner(s)'. These are persons who have an interest in the property immediately before it is transferred and are partners or connected with partners immediately after the property is transferred.

(2) For each relevant owner, identify the 'corresponding partner(s)'. These are persons who are partners immediately after the transfer and who are relevant owners or are individuals connected with relevant owners. For these purposes, a company may be regarded as an individual connected with a relevant owner *only* if it holds property as trustee and is connected by virtue of *CTA 2010, s 1122(6)* (trustee connected with settlor etc).

(3) For each relevant owner, take the proportion of the property to which he is entitled immediately before the transfer and apportion it between any one or more of his corresponding partners. Where a relevant owner has more than one corresponding partner, the apportionment may be performed in whatever manner gives the best result.

(4) Find the 'lower proportion' for each person who is a corresponding partner in relation to one or more relevant owners. The lower proportion is the lower of:

   (a) the proportion apportioned to him under (3) above, and

   (b) his partnership share immediately after the transfer.

(5) Add together the lower proportions for each partner who is a corresponding partner. This is the SLP.

Example 5.2 – calculating the sum of the lower proportions

Alfred, Betty and Carl are in partnership, sharing 40%, 40% and 20% respectively. Betty and Carl are sister and brother; apart from the partnership, Alfred is not related to or connected with Betty or Carl. The partners agree to buy a building from Danielle, who is Betty and Carl's sister, for £500,000. The calculation steps are as follows:

(1) The only relevant owner is Danielle, because she owns 100% of the property before the transfer.

(2) Betty and Carl are corresponding partners because they are individuals connected with the only relevant owner, their sister Danielle.

(3) Danielle was entitled to 100% of the property before the transfer. We choose to apportion this 50% to each corresponding partner, Betty and Carl.

(4) For Betty, her partnership share immediately after the transaction is 40%, and the proportion apportioned to her under (3) is 50%, so her lower proportion is 40%; for Carl, his partnership share immediately after the transaction is 20%, and the proportion apportioned to him under (3) above is 50%, so his lower proportion is 20%.

(5) The sum of the lower proportions is 40% (Betty) plus 20% (Carl), which is 60%.

The consideration for SDLT purposes is therefore MV × (100 – 60)%, or 40% of the market value, ie £200,000. In this relatively simple case, it can be seen that this represents the proportion of the property effectively transferred to Alfred, the partner who is not connected with the original owner of the property.

5.14 In most cases before the transfer, the property will be owned by one person, so there will be only one relevant owner. If two or more persons own a property as beneficial joint tenants ('owners', rather than 'tenants', in Scotland), they are treated as owning as tenants in common, in equal shares.

Connected companies

5.15 The restriction to individuals in step (2) was introduced by *FA 2007, s 72*, and is designed to prevent the use of a partnership arrangement to transfer property to a connected company without suffering SDLT on the full market value of the property. Other anti-avoidance rules are dealt with at **5.17** and **5.27**.

Example 5.3 – partnership including connected company

Derek sets up a company, Fiddler Ltd, in which he is the sole shareholder. Derek and Fiddler Ltd form a limited partnership in which Derek is the limited partner with a 1% share and Fiddler Ltd is the general partner with a 99% share. Derek transfers a valuable property to the partnership. The steps to calculate the proportion of market value on which SDLT is charged are as follows:

(1) Derek is the only relevant owner with 100%.

(2) Derek is also the only corresponding partner. Fiddler Ltd cannot be a corresponding partner, as it is not an individual.

(3) Therefore, Derek's 100% ownership before the transfer must be apportioned 100% to Derek as corresponding partner after the transfer.

(4) Derek's partnership share immediately after the transfer is only 1%, so his lower proportion is 1%; Fiddler Ltd is not a corresponding partner, so it does not figure in the calculation.

(5) The SLP is therefore 1%, and SDLT is chargeable on the 99% of the market value effectively transferred to Fiddler Ltd.

Lease at rent and other transactions

5.16 The same principle applies where the acquisition takes the form of the grant of a lease at rent to the partnership from a partner or person connected with a partner. In that case, the calculation set out above is applied to each year's rent. The resulting apportioned rent figures are then used to calculate the SDLT on the net present value (NPV) of the rent in the normal way (see **4.50**). The same principle also applies where there is a variation of a lease or other chargeable interest which, on normal principles, is regarded as an acquisition by the partnership from a partner or person connected with a partner.

Example 5.4 – lease at rent, partnership shares vary

Twin sisters Gloria and Grace carry on a market research business in partnership with Harry, with whom they are not otherwise connected.

Partnership profit-sharing ratios are adjusted at the end of each year in accordance with the partnership deed, using a formula which takes account of matters such as business won, hours worked etc. Gloria grants a 20-year lease to the partnership (strictly, to the partners jointly to hold on behalf of the partnership) at a time when the profit sharing ratios are 25% to Gloria, 40% to Grace and 35% to Harry. The lease is for a rent of £25,000 per annum (thought to be market rent) and no premium, with a market rent review at the end of every fifth year. The partnership has the option to surrender the lease at each rent review date. The calculation steps are as follows:

(1) Gloria is the only relevant owner, owning 100% of the property before the grant of the lease.

(2) Gloria and Grace are corresponding partners, as they are the relevant owner or an individual connected with the relevant owner.

(3) Gloria's 100% ownership of the property before the grant of the lease is apportioned between Gloria and Grace – we choose to apportion 50% to each.

(4) Gloria's partnership share immediately after the grant of the lease is 25%, and Grace's is 40%. In each case, this is less than the apportioned ownership under (3), so in each case the partnership share is the lower proportion.

(5) Therefore the SLP is 25% + 40% = 65%, and the NPV of the remaining 35% of the rent, ie £8,750 per annum, is subject to SDLT. In this particular case, the NPV is less than £150,000, so no SDLT will be payable, but it will be necessary to submit an SDLT return (see **6.2**).

Two years later, the partners agree that the estimate of the market rent was wrong and it should have been £35,000 per annum. They therefore agree to vary the lease to increase the rent to this sum with effect from the start of the third year. At that time, the profit-sharing ratios are Gloria 30%, Grace 30% and Harry 40%. The variation to increase the rent is treated as the grant of a further lease for the remaining 18 years at a rent equal to the increase, which is £10,000 per annum – see **4.22** in this regard. Carrying out the SLP calculation shows that the NPV of 40% of this rent, or £4,000 per annum, is subject to SDLT. On its own, this would be too little to give rise to an SDLT cost. However, in this case, the deemed further lease is probably linked with the original lease (see **4.58** et seq). As a result, SDLT will be payable on both the original lease and the deemed further lease as a result of this rent increase. See Example 4.24 for an illustration of the calculation required.

Withdrawal of money after acquisition of property

5.17 The transfer of property from a partner or person connected with a partner to a partnership marks the start of a three-year period within which certain other events can lead to a further SDLT charge (*para 17A*). If, during that period, the partner concerned withdraws from the partnership money or money's worth which does not represent income profit, but:

- is capital withdrawn from the partners' capital account, or
- arises from the partner reducing his interest or ceasing to be a partner,

the withdrawal is treated as a chargeable land transaction. Where the original transfer was from a person connected with a partner, withdrawal of value by either the partner or any person connected with the partner is treated as a chargeable transaction. However, presumably, the connected person would have also to be a partner to be able legitimately to withdraw capital etc.

If the partner (or, where the original transfer was from a person connected with a partner, the partner or a person connected with the partner) has made a loan to the partnership, the repayment of any of the loan or a withdrawal of any amount by that person which does not represent income profit of the partnership is also treated as a chargeable land transaction.

In either case, the chargeable consideration is the smaller of:

- the amount withdrawn from or repaid by the partnership, and
- the market value of the land at the date of the original land transfer, reduced by any amount which has already been charged to SDLT.

If the withdrawal of money or money's worth is also subject to SDLT as a transfer of an interest in a PIP (see **5.30**), the SDLT charged under the 'withdrawal of money' provision is reduced by the amount of any charge under the 'transfer of interest in PIP' provision (*para 17A(8)*). If a '*paragraph 12A* election' (see **5.38**) has been made in respect of the property transfer, no SDLT arises on a subsequent withdrawal of value.

Example 5.5 – repayment of loan after transfer

Using the facts as in Example 5.2, the partnership does not have enough ready cash to pay the whole price of the building purchased from Danielle, so it is agreed that £350,000 will be left outstanding as a loan from Danielle to the partnership, with interest being charged at 2% above the Bank of England base rate, payable monthly in arrears. The loan arrangement has no effect on the SDLT charge on the initial transfer of the property to the partnership. One year later, after a purge on debtors, the partnership has enough cash and pays off the loan. The loan repayment is taken to be a land transaction, and SDLT is chargeable on the partnership. However, SDLT was paid on £200,000 when the property, with a value of £500,000, was transferred to the partnership. The chargeable consideration for the deemed land transaction cannot exceed the part of that market value which has not yet been taxed. So, SDLT is chargeable on £300,000, and not on the full £350,000 loan repayment. Note that this limitation is assessed by considering the market value of the property when it was transferred, and not the value at the time of the loan repayment or other withdrawal of value.

Had the partnership borrowed from a bank at the outset and paid Danielle in full, the SDLT charge on the original land transfer would still have been based on £200,000, but the subsequent repayment of the bank debt would not have given rise to an SDLT charge. It is difficult to see any policy reason for this discrimination, which therefore looks rather like a poorly directed anti-avoidance provision.

Transfer to a PIP may also involve transfer of partnership interest

5.18 The charge on the partnership when a new or existing partner (or someone connected with him) transfers a chargeable interest to the partnership does not depend on the amount or form of consideration given by the partnership. As suggested in Example 5.1, the consideration could take the form of admitting a new partner or increasing a partner's share. This acquisition of, or increase in, partnership share will be regarded as a transfer of an interest in a partnership. If the partnership is a property investment partnership (PIP), this transfer will be separately subject to SDLT (see **5.30**), chargeable on the new partner or the partner whose share has increased. This is in addition to the charge on the partnership arising from the acquisition of the property. The transaction is an exchange. This fact should not affect the calculation of SDLT because, both in transactions between a partnership and its partners (or persons connected with them) and in an exchange, SDLT is calculated by reference to the market value of the chargeable interests acquired (albeit indirectly, where partnership interest is acquired) rather than the consideration given. As noted below (see **5.34** and **5.36**), the newly transferred property is not taken into account in determining the SDLT charge on transfer of the partnership interest, so there is no double charge.

Example 5.6 – admission of partner, transfer of property

X Ltd and Y Ltd are limited partners in Spendit LP, a limited partnership which owns shopping centres and is clearly a PIP. The general partner is a Jersey-registered company with a negligible partnership share. X has a 40% partnership share, and Y has 60%. The shopping centres are worth £100 million. It is agreed that Z Ltd will be admitted as a limited partner with a partnership share of 30%, so that X's share drops to 28% and Y's to 42%. By way of payment, Y will transfer a further shopping centre to Spendit LP, with a value of £45 million. Apart from membership of Spendit LP, there are no other connections between X, Y and Z.

- **Transfer of property to Spendit**: The calculation set out at **5.13** shows that Spendit is liable for SDLT on 70% of the £45 million value of the property brought to the partnership by Z Ltd.
- **Transfer of partnership share to Z Ltd**: Z Ltd is deemed to have acquired an interest in the 'relevant partnership property' owned by Spendit before Z Ltd joined. The consideration is the market value of the property multiplied by the partnership interest acquired, ie 30%. Whether the shopping centres already owned by Spendit are relevant partnership property will depend on their history, and the question of whether the transfer to Z Ltd is 'Type A' or 'Type B' (see **5.33** and **5.35**).

Disposal by a partnership

5.19 Disposal of a chargeable interest should not directly give rise to any SDLT obligations for the partnership; it is for the purchaser to deal with any SDLT. If disposal is to an unrelated third party, the purchaser will be liable for SDLT in the normal way, based on consideration given. However, if disposal is to a partner or person connected with a partner, special rules come into play (*para 18*). These are similar to those outlined in the previous paragraph; their purpose is to ensure the purchaser pays SDLT only on the proportion of the property which he and/or connected individual partners did not already own indirectly through membership of the partnership. As in the previous paragraphs, SDLT is charged on deemed consideration equal to:

$$MV \times (100 - SLP)\%$$

where MV is the market value of the chargeable interest at the effective date of the transfer, and SLP is the 'sum of the lower proportions'. Again, a five-step calculation is required to determine SLP, set out in the legislation (*para 20*) as follows:

(1) Identify the 'relevant owner(s)'. These are persons who have an interest in the property immediately after it is transferred and are partners or connected with partners immediately before the property is transferred.

(2) For each relevant owner, identify the 'corresponding partner(s)'. These are persons who are partners immediately before the transfer and who are relevant owners or are individuals connected with relevant owners. For these purposes, a company may be regarded as an individual connected with a relevant owner *only* if it holds property as trustee and is connected by virtue of *CTA 2010, s 1122(6)* (trustee connected with settlor etc).

(3) For each relevant owner, take the proportion of the property to which he is entitled immediately after the transfer and apportion it between any one or more of his corresponding partners. Where a relevant owner has more than one corresponding partner, the apportionment may be performed in whatever manner gives the best result.

(4) Find the 'lower proportion' for each person who is a corresponding partner in relation to one or more relevant owners. The lower proportion is the lower of:

    (a) the proportion apportioned to him under (3) above, and

    (b) his partnership share immediately before the transfer.

(5) Add together the lower proportions for each partner who is a corresponding partner. This is the SLP.

Example 5.7 – transfer of property to partner

Alfred, Betty and Carl are (still) in partnership, sharing 40%, 40% and 20% respectively. Betty and Carl are siblings, Alfred is not related to them. Betty decides to withdraw from the partnership and it is agreed she will take one of the properties in satisfaction of her entitlement to partnership capital. The calculation of Betty's SDLT liability is as follows:

(1) The only relevant owner is Betty, because she owns 100% of the property after the transfer.

(2) Betty and Carl are corresponding partners because they are, or are connected with, the only relevant owner, Betty.

(3) Betty is entitled to 100% of the property after the transfer. We choose to apportion this 50% to each corresponding partner, Betty and Carl.

(4) For Betty, her partnership share immediately before the transaction is 40%, and the proportion apportioned to her under (3) is 50%, so her lower proportion is 40%; for Carl, his partnership share immediately

before the transaction is 20%, and the proportion apportioned to him under (3) above is 50%, so his lower proportion is 20%.

(5) The sum of the lower proportions is 40% (Betty) plus 20% (Carl), which is 60%.

The consideration for SDLT purposes is therefore MV × (100 – 60)%, or 40% of the market value. In this simple case, it can be seen that this represents the proportion of the property effectively transferred from the partner who is not connected with the final owner of the property. Again, the same principles apply in relation to rent if the 'transfer' is the grant of a lease at rent.

5.20 In most cases after the transfer, the property will be owned by one person, so there will be only one relevant owner. If the transfer is to two or more persons as beneficial joint tenants ('owners', rather than 'tenants', in Scotland), they are treated as owning as tenants in common, in equal shares.

Transfers between partnerships

5.21 The possibility is recognised that a property may be transferred from one partnership to another and that there may be connections or commonality between the partners. In that case, it is necessary to perform calculations of the chargeable consideration twice: once as set out at **5.13** (transfer to a partnership from connected owner); and once as explained at **5.19** (transfer from a partnership). The chargeable consideration is then to be taken as the higher of the two amounts thus calculated (*para 23*).

5.22 The restriction to individuals in step (2) is again (see **5.15**) designed to prevent the use of a partnership arrangement to transfer property to a connected company without suffering SDLT on the full market value of the property. Transfer to a company which was a partner before the transfer leads to SDLT being chargeable on the proportion of the market value of the property which the company did not already economically own by virtue of its partnership share. Transfer to a company which is not a partner, but is merely connected with a partner, leads to SDLT being chargeable on the full market value of the property. This, however, is subject to the possible application of reliefs to the transfer (see **5.39**).

Partnership share – special rules

5.23 As noted above (see **5.7**), for most SDLT purposes, partnership share is defined as the proportion in which the partner is entitled to share in income profits. A more complex analysis and calculation are required to determine the partnership share of any relevant partner, when this is required for step (4) in the SLP calculation on transfer of a chargeable interest out of a partnership (*para 21*). The complexity arises from an attempt to negate early SDLT mitigation which used partnership structures. In a straightforward case, if stamp duty or SDLT (based on market value or arm's-length consideration) has been paid on all properties acquired after 19 October 2003 and, where necessary, on transfers of partnership interests, the share of any partner should simply be the proportion in which he is entitled to share in income profits. However, to be certain of having the right numbers, it is necessary to work through the following steps:

(1) Check whether the chargeable interest which is the subject of the transfer (or from which any lease is granted, if the transaction is the grant of a lease):

  (a) was transferred to the partnership before 20 October 2003, or

  (b) was transferred to the partnership on or after that date, and either the instrument of transfer has been duly stamped or SDLT has been duly paid on the transfer.

  If neither (a) nor (b) applies, the partnership share of the partner is treated as zero.

(2) Assuming the partnership share is not zero under step (1), find the 'relevant date':

  (a) If (1)(a) applies and the partner was a partner on 19 October 2003, that is the relevant date.

  (b) If (1)(a) applies and the partner became a partner after that date, the date he became a partner is the relevant date.

  (c) If (1)(b) applies and the partner was a partner when the property was transferred to the partnership, the relevant date is the date of that transfer.

  (d) If (1)(b) applies and the partner became a partner after the property was transferred to the partnership, the relevant date is the date he became a partner.

(3) Find the partner's actual partnership share on the relevant date.

(4) Add to the share determined under (3) any increases in the partner's share, where:

  (a) if the increase resulted from a transfer which occurred on or before 22 July 2004, the instrument of transfer has been duly stamped with *ad valorem* stamp duty, and

  (b) if the increase resulted from a transfer which occurred after that date, any SDLT payable in respect of the transfer has been duly paid.

(5) Deduct from the result of (4) any decreases in the partner's partnership share during the period from the day after the relevant date to the day before the date on which the transfer of property out of the partnership occurs.

It can, therefore, be seen that a great deal of historic information may be needed to determine what should be a simple matter of a partner's partnership share.

Transfer from a corporate partnership

5.24 The rules are modified if a property is transferred from a partnership whose members are entirely bodies corporate and the SLP is 75% or more (*para 24*). In this case, no reduction is given for the SLP, and the consideration is deemed to be equal to the market value of the property (and, if the transfer is the grant of a lease at rent, the full NPV of the rent is subject to SDLT). This situation can only occur when the transferee is a partner with a 75% or higher partnership share. In this situation, the only way to reduce the SDLT charge is to claim group relief on the transfer. Group relief is modified for partnership transactions to allow for this (*para 27*; see **5.40**).

Transfer of an interest in a partnership

5.25 Whether a true transfer of an interest in a partnership is possible depends on the law governing the partnership, and the terms of the partnership deed or other agreements governing such matters. In some cases, it may be possible to achieve an effect equivalent to a transfer, only by one partner withdrawing capital or in some other way relinquishing some or all of his entitlement as partner, while another person becomes a partner, introduces new capital or increases his entitlement in some other way. For most transactions, the legislation makes these distinctions irrelevant, defining a transfer of an interest in a partnership as any occasion on which a person acquires or increases a partnership share (*para 36*). This is regarded as a transfer of partnership interest to the person acquiring or increasing partnership share and from the other partners. This is a very wide definition, covering not only situations where a person makes payments to other partners to acquire or increase his partnership share, but also where a person introduces capital on admission to the partnership, such that the actual value of the other partners' interests remains unchanged. The definition of transfer of a partnership interest was introduced from 19 July 2007; prior to that, a definition applied which did refer to changes in the actual value of each partner's interest. HMRC's draft guidance on partnership transactions still reflects the old definition, and should no longer be relied on.

5.26 When the special rules for partnership transactions were first introduced, *any* transfer of a share in any partnership which owned UK property was treated as a transfer of an equivalent share in the UK property. It was eventually accepted that this placed an unnecessary administrative burden on ordinary trading partnerships which happened to own their premises – profit-sharing ratios within large professional partnerships may change several times each year, and each could give rise to complex SDLT calculations as well as the need to value the property held. Therefore, *FA 2006* restricted the scope of the charge on transfers of partnership interests, so that it now only applies to transfers of interests in 'property investment partnerships' (PIPs). As a result, a transfer of an interest in a partnership which is not a PIP will not give rise to SDLT obligations, unless caught by anti-avoidance provisions (see the next paragraph).

Transfer pursuant to earlier arrangements

5.27 If:

- a chargeable interest is transferred to a partnership from a partner or person connected with a partner,
- that person or partner then transfers any or all of his partnership interest under arrangements which were in existence at the time of the land transfer, and
- the partnership transfer would not otherwise be a chargeable transaction,

the partnership transfer is a chargeable land transfer (*para 17*). The partners are treated as the purchaser under this deemed transaction, and the chargeable consideration is the market value of the land at the date of the land transfer multiplied by the proportionate share in the partnership transferred under the arrangements. However, this treatment does not apply if an election is made in respect of the land transfer under *para 12A* (see **5.38**). As in other cases (see **3.19**), arrangements are defined as including any scheme, agreement or understanding, whether or not legally enforceable.

5.28 The practical implication is that, if a partner transfers a chargeable interest to the partnership and shortly after transfers his partnership interest, HMRC are likely to question whether the transactions are part of a single arrangement. The deemed land transaction arising as a result of such a transfer of an interest in a partnership is notifiable (by completion of an SDLT return) only if the deemed consideration is sufficient for tax to be payable. For example, if the initial property transfer to the partnership did not involve grant of a lease at rent and if there are no linked transactions, the subsequent transfer of partnership interest will not be notifiable unless the deemed consideration exceeds the zero rate limit of £125,000 or £150,000 for residential or non-residential/mixed property respectively.

Property investment partnerships

5.29 A property investment partnership (PIP) is defined as a partnership whose sole or main activity is investing or dealing in chargeable interests, whether or not the activity includes the carrying out of construction activities on the land (*para 14(8)*). So, a partnership which invests in property in order to receive rent, or buys and sells property in order to make a profit (whether as a trade or an investment activity), or buys, develops and sells in order to make a profit, is a PIP if this is its sole or main activity.

If a partnership carries on more than one activity, some of which do not consist of investing or dealing in chargeable interests, it will be necessary to determine which is the main activity. In many cases, this may be obvious, but it may be difficult in borderline cases, where the partnership perhaps devotes similar effort to two activities, only one of which is caught, and derives similar levels of profit from them. In such a case, it may be necessary to carry out detailed analysis of time spent on the different activities, capital employed in each and profits derived from each, in order to form a defensible view. Unfortunately, there is no room for compromise or apportionment – the partnership must be classified as wholly a PIP or not a PIP. If a partnership is a PIP, all property held must be considered as potential 'relevant partnership property' (as defined below); there is no exemption for any property which may be held for the purposes of a minority 'non-PIP' purpose.

Transfer of an interest in a PIP

5.30 A transfer of an interest in a PIP is treated as a chargeable transaction if the 'relevant partnership property' (see next paragraph) includes a chargeable interest. The consideration for the chargeable transaction is a proportion of the market value of the relevant partnership property; the proportion is the proportion by which the transferee's partnership share increases. Where the transfer of an interest in a PIP is one side of an exchange, the interest in the PIP is deemed to be a major interest in land if any of the relevant partnership property is a major interest – this then confirms the need to calculate SDLT by reference to the market values of the relevant partnership property (see **2.29**).

Example 5.8 – retirement of partner, linked transactions

DEF Partnership is a PIP with three partners D, E and F, each with a one-third partnership share. F decides to withdraw; as a result, the shares of D and E each increase to 50%. The relevant partnership property has a value of £1.2 million. Each of D and E is treated as the purchaser under a chargeable transaction with consideration of one sixth of £1.2 million, or £200,000 (one sixth being the proportion by which their respective partnership shares increase). In the author's view, the two acquisitions are linked (see **2.36**) because they form a series or composite transaction between the same vendor (F) and purchasers D and E, who are connected within the terms of *CTA 2010, s 1122*. Note that, for the purposes of determining whether transactions are linked, the automatic connection of partners applies. The draft HMRC guidance on partnerships appears to suggest that the transfers are not linked (see SDLTM35400, Example (1), available at www.hmrc.gov.uk/so/pftmanual.htm#14), and this is a matter which should not have been affected by changes in the law since the draft guidance was issued. However, this was only ever draft guidance, so it cannot be relied on!

Relevant partnership property

5.31 There are two definitions of relevant partnership property, depending on whether the transfer is classified as Type A or Type B (see **5.33–5.35**). This distinction, with its related rules, is the main concept introduced by the *FA 2008* changes to *FA 2003, Sch 15*. The intention of the legislation is to ensure SDLT is paid where a partnership structure is used to transfer economic ownership of property between partners for consideration. However, it seeks to avoid difficulties for partnership structures used in widely held property investment schemes or where transfers occur for no consideration (for example, normal periodic adjustments of profit-sharing ratios). However, it is necessary to work through the definitions in any particular case. It would not be safe to decide that no SDLT charge arises purely on the basis of the general intention of the legislation. It is important to note that the distinction between Type A and Type B transfers is relevant only for deciding whether the partnership holds relevant partnership property and, if yes, its value. Both types of transfer are potentially subject to SDLT. However, in many Type B transfers, there will be no relevant partnership property and so no SDLT liability.

Market rent leases

5.32 Leases which satisfy certain very stringent conditions are referred to as 'market rent leases' and are always excluded from relevant partnership property. Therefore, if a partnership only holds leases of this kind, no transfer (whether Type A or Type B) will be a chargeable transaction. In practice, such partnerships are likely to be rare. To qualify as a market rent lease, a lease must have been granted for a market rent only (ie no premium and no arrangements for any future premium). Furthermore, either it must be for a term not exceeding five years or, if for a longer term, it must provide for market rent reviews at no longer than five-yearly intervals. Note that the rent review must provide for adjustment to a market rent, which means it must be possible for the rent to fall if market rents have declined. Most rent review clauses provide for upward-only reviews, and such a lease cannot qualify as a market rent lease, even though the inability of the rent to fall may have no practical effect. An anti-avoidance condition requires that there should not have been any amendment to the lease since it was granted which itself leads to the rent being less than a market rent immediately after the transfer of the partnership interest.

Example 5.9 – market rent leases, anti-avoidance rule

Partner X has a 99% share in the XY partnership which is a PIP. X grants a 200-year lease to the partnership at a market rent, with five-yearly market rent reviews. The partnership pays SDLT on the 1% of the NPV of rent, representing the 1% effectively transferred to Partner Y. X then agrees to reduce the rent to a peppercorn. This is a transfer to the partnership (see **4.28**), and the partnership pays SDLT on the 1% of the market value of the transfer (in practice, the value of the transfer is probably close to the market value of the freehold property). The partnership now owns virtually the whole economic value of the freehold property. X then transfers 98% of his partnership share to Y, for consideration. When it was granted, the lease was a market rent lease. But for the prohibition on subsequent amendments, it might still count as a market rent when the partnership share is transferred. The anti-avoidance condition ensures that the lease is not excluded from relevant partnership property. The value of the lease is, therefore, taken into account in determining any SDLT payable on the transfer of the partnership interest.

Type A transfers

5.33 Two situations give rise to a Type A transfer (*para 14(3A), (3B)*). The first occurs when the whole or part of a partner's interest as partner is transferred to another person (whether or not an existing partner) in return for consideration in money or money's worth. For the legislation to make sense, this must mean consideration given to the partner whose interest reduces (or to someone else at that partner's behest). The mere contribution of capital to the partnership by the person who gains partnership share does not amount to the giving of consideration for these purposes. The second occurs when a new partner joins and an existing partner withdraws money or money's worth from the partnership, thereby reducing or extinguishing his partnership share. However, this is not a Type A transfer if the withdrawal of money or money's worth comes from resources available to the partnership prior to the transfer.

Example 5.10 – a Type A transfer

The PQR partnership is a PIP with three partners, P, Q and R, sharing profits equally. The partnership holds assets worth £1 million and cash on deposit of £200,000. P decides to retire. At the same time, the other partners decide to admit S as a new partner with a 20% share. S introduces capital of £240,000 for this share. The partnership uses £200,000 of this cash and the £200,000 previously on deposit to pay out P's capital. This is a Type A transfer.

5.34 If the transfer of an interest in a partnership is Type A, all chargeable interests held by the partnership are regarded as relevant partnership property, apart from market rent leases (see **5.32**) and any property transferred to the partnership in connection with the transfer of partnership interest (*para 5*).

Example 5.11 – Type A transfer, relevant partnership property

The assets held by the PQR partnership (see Example 5.10) consist of: various plots of freehold building land purchased from third parties at various times and currently valued at £600,000; a long leasehold office transferred from P in 2006 and valued at £200,000; a warehouse leased from a third party; and sundry loose furniture and stock-in-trade valued at £150,000. The warehouse lease is at rent, subject to five-yearly market rent reviews and qualifying as a market rent lease (see **5.32**). However, local rents have increased dramatically since the last rent review 18 months ago. Because this lease has the benefit of three and a half years at the current rent, now substantially below current market levels, it is considered to have a value of £50,000.

The freehold building land and long leasehold offices, total value £800,000, are relevant partnership property for a Type A transfer. However, the warehouse lease is not relevant partnership property and may be ignored. The total partnership share transferred is 33.3%, being the share relinquished by the retiring partner: 20% of this goes to the new partner S for deemed consideration of £160,000 (20% of £800,000); and 6.7% goes to each of the continuing partners Q and R for deemed consideration of £53,336 each.

These are three separate transfers, so the question arises as to whether they are 'linked' (see **2.36**). If they are not linked, S will pay SDLT of £2,000, being 1% of £200,000; Q and R will pay no SDLT, because the consideration paid by each is below the threshold, but each will have to notify the transaction. If they are linked, the aggregate consideration will be £306,672, so each partner will pay SDLT at 3% on the consideration he is deemed to give. It is difficult to see how the transfers to Q and R can be anything other than linked, but aggregation of consideration for these transfers does not in itself give rise to a charge. It may be possible to argue that the transfer to S is not linked with the other transfers because, when the transfers were agreed, S was not a partner and so was not connected with Q and R. To strengthen the position, P, Q and R would be well advised to agree the surrender of 13.3% of P's capital *before* it is agreed to admit S on surrender of P's remaining 20%.

Type B transfers

5.35 Any transfer of an interest in a PIP which is not a Type A transfer is a Type B transfer (*para 14(3C)*). This includes:

- a transfer which is the result of an adjustment of profit-sharing ratios between the partners, with no partner paying any other for the transfer and no new partner being introduced; or
- a transfer which is the result of a partner (X) reducing his share or exiting the partnership, where no payments are made by any other partner and either no new partner is admitted, or, if a new partner is admitted, any amount withdrawn from the partnership by X is paid out of resources which were available to the partnership before the transfer. It is considered that 'resources' here include previously arranged loan facilities.

Example 5.12 – a Type B transfer

The XYZ partnership is a PIP with three partners, Z, Y and Z, sharing profits equally. The partnership holds assets worth £1 million and cash on deposit of £200,000. X decides to retire. It is agreed that X will take £400,000 cash in settlement of his partnership capital and accumulated profits. The partnership borrows £200,000 from its bank to fund this cash payment. Since no new partner has been admitted and no existing partner has paid anything for his increased partnership share, this is not a Type A transfer, so it must be a Type B transfer. Care is needed here. If Y or Z gives any additional security to the bank in relation to the borrowing, this could be interpreted as giving consideration for the additional partnership share acquired on withdrawal of X, making it a Type A transfer. Treatment as Type B will be more secure if the borrowing from the bank is arranged before X decides to retire.

Relevant partnership property for Type B transfers

5.36 In addition to market rent leases, the following property is excluded from relevant partnership property in a Type B transfer (*para 14(5A)*):

- any chargeable interest transferred to the partnership in connection with the transfer of partnership interest. For example, if an incoming partner pays his contribution to capital by transferring a property to the partnership, that property is not relevant partnership property. It is reasonable to exclude this from any SDLT calculation on the transfer of partnership share, since there will be a separate SDLT calculation/charge in respect of this property transfer (see **5.13**);
- any chargeable interest transferred to the partnership on or before 22 July 2004. This is the date from which this kind of partnership transaction was brought within the SDLT regime;
- any chargeable interest not economically attributable to the partnership interest transferred. For example, it may be that other partners have sole rights to profits and proceeds of a property, so that the partner receiving the partnership share gains no interest in that particular property – although this is an arrangement more commonly seen in relation to the premises of professional and trading partnerships than the assets of PIPs;
- any chargeable interest in respect of which an election has been made under *para 12A* (see **5.38**); and
- any other chargeable interest which was not acquired from a partner (existing or newly admitted) or from someone connected with such a partner.

The net result of these exclusions is that relevant partnership property for a Type B transfer consists only of property transferred to the partnership from a partner or connected person, after 22 July 2004, in respect of which no election has been made under *para 12A*, which is not a market rent lease, and which is not held solely for the benefit of partners other than the recipient of the transfer.

Notifying liability

5.37 A land transaction consisting of the transfer of an interest in a PIP is notifiable just like any other land transaction by completion of an SDLT return, but *only* if the deemed consideration, together with that for any linked transactions, is high enough to give rise to an SDLT liability (*para 30*). This contrasts with many other land transactions, where notification is needed even when no SDLT liability arises.

Paragraph 12A election

5.38 Normally, when a property is transferred to a partnership from one or more partners, or persons connected with partners, SDLT is not charged on the full market value, as explained at **5.13**. However, it is possible for a PIP to make an election under *para 12A* to disapply that rule and have SDLT charged on the full market value of the property. The property is thereafter effectively treated as if it had been acquired from an unconnected third party. The election must be made in the SDLT return for the transaction and, once made, is irrevocable.

If the election is made, it will normally increase the amount of SDLT payable immediately, since there will be no reduction in deemed consideration for the part of the property effectively remaining in the ownership of the transferor or his corresponding partner(s). This is not likely to be an attractive option in many cases, but may be worthwhile where the extra SDLT is not very large and it is anticipated that there will in future be Type B transfers of partnership interests. The election will then exclude the property from the calculation of SDLT on such transfers (see **5.36**).

Reliefs

5.39 For the avoidance of doubt, *FA 2003, Sch 3, para 1* (exemption for transfer for no chargeable consideration) is specifically disapplied to transactions involving partnerships. Apart from that, other reliefs and exemption generally do apply (*para 25*).

5.40 A transfer of property to or from a partnership may qualify for relief in just the same way as a transfer to or from another entity. The wording of the group relief provisions is modified to ensure that:

(1) relief is granted by reference to the partnership share of the partner(s) which are in the same group as the transferor/transferee company (*para 27A*), and

(2) in the case of a transfer to a partnership, relief is clawed back if those partners cease to be in the same group as the transferor while the partnership still holds the property or an interest derived from it (*para 27*).

5.41 A transfer of an interest in a partnership may qualify for relief if a direct transfer of relevant chargeable interests held by the partnership would have qualified. The wording of disadvantaged areas and charities relief are modified to ensure that:

(1) disadvantaged areas relief only applies if the proportion of the consideration for the overall transaction relating to residential property in a qualifying area does not exceed the limit of £150,000 (*para 26*), and

(2) charities relief applies only if all of the chargeable interests held by the partnership are held for charitable purposes – that is, there is no partial

relief if the partnership holds some properties for charitable purposes and some not (*para 28*).

SUNDRY PROVISIONS

5.42 Stamp duty continues to apply to a document which transfers an interest in a partnership, if that partnership holds stock or marketable securities; see **8.55** (*paras 31–33*).

The acquisition of a partnership interest is only subject to SDLT as set out above (*para 29*). If an interest in a partnership is acquired in some other way, it is not subject to SDLT.

Example 5.13 – non-chargeable acquisition of partnership interest

Cubit LLP is a business advisory partnership with 53 partners, employing 371 staff working out of 11 offices. Cubit has various interests in its office buildings, and a portfolio of business premises which it lets out, but rental income forms only 20 to 30% of its income, the balance coming from advisory and consulting activities. It is therefore considered that Cubit is not a PIP. The partners decide to admit three new partners, two from the existing workforce and one by direct appointment from outside. Each partner contributes £20,000 partnership capital (funded, in the case of the existing staff, by a corresponding loan from the partnership, to be repaid out of profit share) and has an initial profit share of 0.25%.

On the general definition, this amounts to three transfers of partnership interest to the new partners. However, as Cubit is not a PIP, and the transfers are not in connection with the transfer of chargeable interests in UK land, nor are they 'pursuant to earlier arrangements' involving transfers of chargeable interests, the transfers of partnership interests are not within the charge to SDLT.

Partnership property – guidance

5.43 HMRC's original draft guidance on SDLT and partnerships declared:

> 'Partnership property is any interest or right held by or on behalf of a partnership, or the members of a partnership, for the purposes of partnership business. This means that property held by one of the partners and used for the purposes of the partnership business is partnership property.'

This outrageous view effectively suggested that, if a partner allowed the partnership to store goods in his garage on an informal basis for no payment, the garage became partnership property. The guidance was amended by SDLT Technical News Issue 5 (August 2007) to agree with the more reasonable position stated for other taxes in Business Income Manual BIM72058. At the time of writing, Technical News has been withdrawn from the HMRC website and it is difficult to find any reference to the current guidance.

Retrospective taxation?

5.44 The *FA 2007* changes contained the usual transitional provisions to ensure that they did not apply retrospectively to transactions already started at the time the changes were announced (2pm on 6 December 2006). The *FA 2008* changes then removed those transitional provisions. As a result, it appears that the rules, as amended by *FA 2008*, apply to all transactions, even those commenced before any of the changes were announced. If currently dealing with the completion of transactions which commenced so long ago, careful analysis will be required to establish whether the current rules lead to greater taxation than would have been the case under the pre-2007 rules and, if so, whether this is retrospective taxation which may be susceptible to challenge.

Chapter 6

SDLT Administration and Compliance

INTRODUCTION

6.1 This chapter deals with questions of what must be notified to HMRC, on whom the responsibility for notification and payment of SDLT falls, and the processes involved. It details deadlines, costs of missing them, and occasions on which payment of SDLT may validly be postponed. It explains how to claim repayment if a payment of SDLT proves excessive. Finally, it reviews the powers which HMRC have to enquire into and amend returns, assess unpaid or underpaid SDLT and seek penalties. The relevant legislation is in *FA 2003, ss 76–99* and *Schs 10–14*, and the *SDLT (Administration) Regulations 2003, SI 2003/2837*. The *SDLT (Electronic Communications) Regulations 2005, SI 2005/844*, govern the electronic submission of SDLT returns. Precise references are given in appropriate paragraphs below.

SDLT is within the regime for disclosure of tax avoidance schemes (DOTAS), but with its own rules for determining what must be disclosed. Responsibilities in relation to DOTAS are dealt with in **Chapter 7**.

NOTIFICATION

What is notifiable, and by whom?

6.2 In general, (real) land transactions (see **2.7** for definition) are notifiable unless exempt. There is a list of exemptions, which also render the transaction non-notifiable, at **3.7**. If none of the exemptions apply, the transaction is notifiable even if no SDLT is payable. It is especially important to note that a transaction is not excused from being notified merely because a relief is available to reduce or remove the SDLT liability – reliefs must be claimed in a return.

Deemed land transactions also give rise to the obligation to notify. In many cases, a real transaction is deemed to be a land transaction (or to be the acquisition of a chargeable interest, which is automatically a land transaction; see **2.7**). Examples include the substantial performance of a contract before completion (see **2.10**), or variation of a lease to reduce the rent or term (see **4.28** and **4.29**). In other cases, actions or events are deemed to amount to transactions which are specifically stated to give rise to an obligation to submit an SDLT return. An example is on final determination of uncertain consideration or rent, if that leads to further SDLT becoming payable (see **2.20**).

Two cases involving anti-avoidance provisions are specifically stated to be notifiable. These are the 'notional land transaction' under *FA 2003, s 75A* (see **7.5** et seq), and the deemed transaction on substantial performance of a contract providing for conveyance to a third party (see **3.9**). In both of these cases, most of the exemptions do not apply; so, for example, a deemed transaction under one of these sections is notifiable even if the consideration is below the normal £40,000 notification threshold. However, the exemptions from notification relating to secondary transactions in 'alternative finance' arrangements (see **3.33**) and transfers of partnership interests (see **5.37**) *do* apply. It is not clear why some exemptions should apply while others do not, and this may simply be the result of poor structuring of the legislation. Making these notional transactions notifiable places responsibility for interpretation and application of the general anti-avoidance rules firmly on the taxpayer.

Exempt transactions

6.3 If a transaction is exempt, there is no obligation to notify it to HMRC (*FA 2003, s 77A*). However, the taxpayer does still have the obligation to maintain records relating to the transaction for at least six years (see **6.62**). When SDLT was introduced, it was possible for the taxpayer to 'self certify' that the transaction was exempt. The self certificate could then be used as evidence that SDLT obligations had been completed, allowing the land transaction to be registered. Self certificates were abolished by *FA 2008*; when registering an exempt transaction, it is now necessary simply to inform the Land Registry that the transaction is exempt.

6.4 Sometimes, taxpayers choose to complete returns for transactions which appear to be exempt. This is commonly done to guard against future allegations of failure to notify, where exemption is dependent on a treatment of the facts which could be susceptible to challenge. This is considered in more detail at **6.48**.

Responsibility for notifying

6.5 Responsibility for notification and payment of any tax falls on the purchaser (*FA 2003, s 76*; SDLTM50100). The identity of this person is usually self-evident, being the person who gains beneficial ownership of the land interest. However, there are several provisions identifying the purchaser in particular circumstances:

- When property is transferred to a partnership, or where value is withdrawn from a partnership after such a property transfer (see **5.13** and **5.17**), all of the partners are purchasers and have joint and several responsibility for notification. They may nominate one or more responsible partners, but this does not remove the responsibilities of individual partners if the nominated partners fail in their duties (*FA 2003, Sch 15, paras 6–8*).
- When a lease is varied to shorten the term, the landlord is the purchaser. If it is varied to reduce the rent, the tenant is the purchaser (*FA 2003, Sch 17A, para 15A*).
- Where trustees of a settlement other than a bare trust acquire beneficial ownership of a property, they are purchasers (*FA 2003, Sch 16, para 4*). The obligation to make a return may be discharged by any one or more of the trustees, but subsequent obligations, for example in relation to enquiries by HMRC, then fall on the trustees who signed the return. Where trustees (or nominees) acquire a property under a bare trust, the person on behalf of whom the acquisition is made is normally treated as the purchaser (*Sch 16, para 3(1)*). However, if the acquisition by bare trustees takes the form of the grant of a lease to them, they are treated as purchasers of the whole beneficial interest in the lease (*Sch 16, para 3(2)*; see **2.18**). In origin, this is an anti-avoidance provision.
- Where the Official Solicitor is acting for a person under a disability (for example, mental incapacity), the Official Solicitor may notify on behalf of that person (*FA 2003, Sch 10, para 1B*). However, the person for whom the Official Solicitor acts remains the purchaser and therefore is liable for tax, interest and penalties where these arise.

How to notify

6.6 Notification is by submission of a land transaction return (LTR) to HMRC. The LTR is due within 30 days from the effective date of the transaction (see **2.8**). The legislation provides for the 30-day period to be shortened by regulation; in the early days of consultation on modernising stamp duty, a senior member of the Stamp Office suggested that the eventual target period might be five days. For many commercial transactions, this would be an impossibly tight deadline, and fortunately such shortening of the deadline does not seem imminent.

Paper forms

6.7 An LTR must be in a form and containing information prescribed by regulations, or in such other form as has been 'approved by the Board', ie HMRC (*FA 2003, Sch 10, para 1*). The principal regulations are the *SDLT (Administration) Regulations 2003, SI 2003/2837*. These include a facsimile of the general LTR (form SDLT1) and supplementary forms required in some cases (forms SDLT2, SDLT3 and SDLT4). These are reproduced at **Appendix B**. The regulations permit use of a different form if approved by HMRC. If paper forms are to be submitted, it is not acceptable to use copies. Each SDLT1 has a unique reference number (the unique transaction reference number or UTRN), and an original form must be used for each return. Previously, it was acceptable to use photocopies of blank supplementary forms, but HMRC's latest instructions insist on originals of these too. Insistence on a single original paper form causes difficulties in some cases, especially when the required signatories are scattered over several locations or perhaps located overseas; electronic submission may be easier in such cases. Supplies of forms may be obtained from HMRC; see **Appendix A**. Forms must be completed in black ink (*reg 9(1)*) to aid machine reading. Further guidance on the completion of the forms is set out at **6.19** et seq.

6.8 Routine paper returns should be sent to the processing centre at Netherton; see address in **Appendix A**. Apart from the return, any supplementary forms, a cheque in payment of the SDLT (if paying by cheque) and a plan (if one is provided), no correspondence or other documents should be included. This requirement is mentioned in the guidance notes (SDLT6) at the very end of Part 1 (General Guidance). For guidance where it is considered necessary to submit other information or documents to HMRC, see **6.48**. HMRC request that the papers be submitted without folding, in an A4 or larger envelope, as folding may cause problems with machine reading. They also encourage payment by bank transfer, other direct instruction to the bank or other electronic means (including debit cards) where possible, to minimise the risk of payment going astray. Links to appropriate destination bank account details are at www.hmrc.gov.uk/payinghmrc/stamp-land.htm, which should be consulted whenever payments are made in case account details change. For users of the ARTL system (see **6.13**), payment is automatically collected from the nominated bank account.

Electronic returns

6.9 The *SDLT (Electronic Communications) Regulations 2005, SI 2005/844*, permit delivery of LTRs electronically and, on this basis, HMRC offer the facility to submit LTRs via the internet once the person making the submission has registered for the purpose. The forms can be completed and submitted using basic software provided free of charge by HMRC, or by using commercial software which has more features. The forms are fundamentally the same as the paper versions, and the guidance set out below (at para **6.19** et seq) applies equally to the electronic forms. Links to appropriate paragraphs of HMRC's own guidance on completion, equivalent to the booklet SDLT6 for paper returns (see **6.20**), should be available as each section of the return is completed. The online forms are 'intelligent', in that they decide which sections to present for completion in accordance with sections already completed; they should, therefore, make it clear when completion of supplementary forms is required. Part-completed forms can be stored for later finalisation and submission. The software should also check for inconsistencies or omissions and prevent submission if these are found. It will not, however, check for technical errors, so the fact that submission is allowed does not guarantee that the return is correct! The electronic forms are just as restrictive and limited as their paper counterparts, so the same difficulties arise in ensuring adequate disclosure (see **6.19** and **6.48**).

6.10 Paper returns have to be signed by the purchaser(s) (*FA 2003, Sch 10, para 1(1)(c)*), but clearly this is not possible for electronic forms. Instead, before an agent is permitted to submit the final return, he must confirm that the purchaser has approved the draft return and that appropriate evidence of this is held. The only fact which is allowed to be missing from the draft approved by the purchaser is the effective date. This allows the forms to be drafted before completion of the transaction, approved by the purchaser, and then finalised and submitted immediately on the effective date (*Sch 10, para 1A*).

6.11 When a return is submitted online, the HMRC certificate (form SDLT5) is issued automatically and immediately. This contrasts with submission of paper returns, when there may be a delay of several days or even weeks before the SDLT5 is received. The SDLT5 certificate must be submitted to the Land Registry to permit registration of the purchaser's interest or the change brought about by the transaction, so there is a clear advantage in receiving this immediately.

6.12 Before using the online submission facility, it is necessary to register with HMRC, following the process which begins with a link under 'Do it online' on the SDLT Index page of the HMRC website, at www.hmrc.gov.uk/sdlt/index.htm. The process includes waiting for postal delivery of a PIN before the service can be activated, so it is not a good idea to wait until a return is due before registering.

Scotland – the ARTL system

6.13 For many transactions involving registered land in Scotland, it is also possible for law firms (but not the general public) to deliver LTRs via the Registers of Scotland under the ARTL system for Automated Registration of

Title to Land (see SDLTM60150). Law firms must register with the Keeper of the Registers in order to use the system (many Scottish law firms have done so) and they will then receive appropriate training and instruction. Further details, including help with registering, are available at www.ros.gov.uk/artl. The system pre-populates the electronic SDLT return with some information about the property. The arrangement is intended as a trial for eventual extension to the rest of the UK. It is a long-held Government ambition to integrate collection and routine administration of SDLT with registration of land transactions, leaving HMRC to deal with policy and policing. To this end, the Edinburgh Stamp Office is now co-located with the Keeper of the Registers of Scotland. This may eventually lead to electronic submission of LTRs becoming compulsory but, for the time being, paper forms are still acceptable. Indeed, there are some transactions which cannot be processed through the ARTL system, and these must be dealt with by submission of paper or electronic returns in the normal way.

Computer-generated paper forms

6.14 When SDLT was introduced, as a first step towards automation, it was possible to complete return forms on screen (using software provided by HMRC or independent suppliers) before printing out, signing and submitting the printed copy. Because these computer-generated forms did not bear a unique number (UTRN, see **6.7**), HMRC provided separate numbered payslips for payment of SDLT. The number from the relevant payslip was added to the computer-generated return form and functioned as its UTRN. Software was then developed to summarise information in the forms in a barcode printed on the forms ('2D Bar-coded Forms') which could be machine read more easily. These methods of submitting returns have now been dropped; the choice is only between handwritten paper forms and full online submission.

Further and amended returns

6.15 A number of transactions and events, described at various points in this book, give rise to the requirement to submit a further LTR when one has already been submitted for the original transaction, or to amend the original LTR.

Example 6.1 – further return, variable rent

Dave enters into a seven-year lease of a pub; the lease is executed without prior substantial performance of any agreement. The rent is provisionally fixed at £30,000 per annum, but this is to be adjusted at the end of each year using a formula which takes account of turnover in the year just ended. An

LTR is submitted within 30 days of grant of the lease. At the end of the first five years, it is established that the rent has been above £30,000 in all years, so further SDLT is payable. A further return is due within 30 days of the end of the fifth year of the lease.

Example 6.2 – further return, clawback of relief

Dozy Ltd purchases a property from group company Dee Ltd and submits an LTR on which group relief from SDLT is claimed. Two years later, Dozy Ltd, while still owning the property, is sold to a third party. Dozy Ltd must make a further return reporting the withdrawal of group relief within 30 days of whichever step leads to its old parent group ceasing to have beneficial ownership of its shares.

Example 6.3 – further return, final determination of consideration

Beaky Ltd buys a property from connected company Mick Ltd and makes an LTR, paying SDLT based on an estimated market value. Six months later, it is discovered that the market value was under-estimated. Beaky Ltd must amend the original return to show the correct value, within 30 days of discovering the error. Nine months after the original transaction, it is realised that Beaky and Mick are group companies. Beaky may, if it so wishes, further amend the return to claim group relief and seek repayment of the SDLT paid. However, amendment is not compulsory because it would lead to a decrease in the SDLT charge.

6.16 It is important to establish whether the required action is:

(1) submission of a new return for a new transaction, which may or may not be linked with the original transaction;

(2) submission of a further return for the original transaction, perhaps now modified in the light of subsequent events or facts; or

(3) amendment of the return originally submitted in respect of the original transaction.

In some cases, (1) will be necessary as well as either (2) or (3). As noted below, there is no practical difference between (2) and (3). Even where amendment is not *required*, a purchaser may voluntarily amend a return within 12 months of the filing deadline for the original return (for example, in order to claim a relief which was omitted from the original return, or to correct a calculation error which led to payment of the wrong amount of SDLT). If an error is discovered which led to an underpayment of SDLT, it is an offence to fail to amend the return which may give rise to a penalty (see **6.53**). A new return for a new transaction is generally made by completion of a new SDLT1 (whether paper or online), together with supplementary forms if necessary. If the new transaction is linked with a previous transaction, there is space on the return to note this fact. This linking may also lead to the need to amend the return, or to submit a further return, for the original transaction.

Example 6.4 – further return, later linked transaction

The facts are as in Example 2.11. Tanya submits an LTR (using form SDLT1) in respect of the first house purchase, before 8 February 2011. This shows tax chargeable £1,600, being £160,000 at 1%. When the second purchase completes, Tanya submits an LTR (another form SDLT1) in respect of the second purchase, showing tax chargeable £6,000, being £200,000 at 3%. She also makes a further return in respect of the original purchase, showing the tax now increased to £4,800. With this return, Tanya pays the additional tax of £3,200 now due on the first purchase. The new return for the second purchase, the further return for the first purchase and the payments of £6,000 and £3,200 respectively are all due by 14 July 2011. As noted below, the further return in respect of the first purchase is made by letter, not completion of form SDLT1.

How to submit further and amended returns

6.17 In principle, submission of a further return for the original transaction and amendment of the original return are different processes; the legislation specifies which is required in each situation. In practice, HMRC guidance states that each requirement is to be satisfied by submission of a letter to the Birmingham Stamp Office (see **Appendix A**) (www.hmrc.gov.uk/sdlt/return/amend.htm). The letter must quote the UTRN which appeared on the original return and set out details of the changes and/or further information, including any further payment required. The letter should refer to the appropriate numbered boxes on the original return, so it is important that a copy of that return be retained. Where the legislation specifies that a further return must be submitted but, in practice, HMRC require that a letter be sent, they are presumably relying on the fact that the regulations permit use of a form other than SDLT1 'in a form that has been approved by the Board' (see **6.7**). In the case of minor corrections not affecting the substance of the transaction, HMRC may be willing to accept amendment by telephone, but in the author's view it is always safer to write.

6.18 HMRC may also unilaterally correct minor errors and omissions, in which case notice must be given to the person(s) who submitted the return (*FA 2003, Sch 10, para 7*; SDLTM60100). The person(s) to whom notice is given may reject the amendment:

- by re-amending the return within the permitted 12 months, or
- if notice is received from HMRC later than nine months after the filing date, by giving notice that the amendment is rejected within three months of the date of issue of HMRC's notice.

This facility to correct obvious errors was well used in the early days of SDLT, but it is now much more likely that a return with errors which prevent processing will be rejected and will require re-submission after correction by the taxpayer. A major point in favour of online submission is that many errors are highlighted and must be corrected before the return can be submitted.

Practical completion of return forms

6.19 The return forms are input documents for an automated system, and the paper versions are designed to be machine read, which is why the regulations specify completion in black ink (*SI 2003/2837, reg 9*). The forms contain a series of numbered boxes and are very limited and limiting in terms of information which may be included. Some boxes are for matters such as names, addresses, dates and monetary amounts; beyond this, they are completed by inserting 'X' to show that a particular statement applies, or by inserting a letter or number to indicate which statement or item applies from a list.

6.20 Guidance on completion, including lists of the relevant codes, is contained in booklet SDLT6 'How to complete your Land Transaction Return'. Paper copies of the latest version of this may be ordered from the HMRC publications office, online at www.hmrc.gov.uk/contactus/staustellform.htm or by post from the HMRC publications department (see **Appendix A**). The booklet is also available as a downloadable PDF file at www.hmrc.gov.uk/so/sdlt6.pdf, or as an online html document starting at www.hmrc.gov.uk/sdlt6/index.htm. Even if the paper or PDF version of SDLT6 is used, it is generally safest to check the online version for recent changes; at the time of writing, the latest paper version is dated September 2009 and it contains some references to items on the HMRC website which are no longer current.

6.21 The LTR has two functions:

(1) to set out the information to establish the amount and timing of liability to SDLT; and

(2) to provide the Government with statistical information (which was previously collected under the stamp duty regime from the 'Particulars Delivered' or PD form submitted with many transfer documents) (*FA 2003, Sch 10, para 1(4)*).

In relation to (2), the information on the LTR is significantly more detailed – some would say intrusive – than that on the PD form. In particular, in relation to the purchase of properties leased to multiple tenants, the purchaser is required to collate a lot of detail which may not be readily available. The author is aware of cases where the need to gather this information has delayed submission of returns beyond the due date. It is, therefore, important to be aware of the requirements and to begin gathering information as early as possible to minimise this risk.

6.22 In general, the manner of completion of the boxes is self-evident or adequately explained by the instructions in the SDLT6 document, although careful close reading of the instructions is essential. This section of the book does not aim to replicate SDLT6, and therefore provides comment only where something useful can be added. There is one important caveat: HMRC's instructions for completion of some of the forms have changed significantly over the last few years. The reader must take care to follow the latest instructions.

Form SDLT1

6.23

Box	**Heading**	**Comment**
2	Description of transaction	Care is needed because the meaning of terms used in the guidance notes differ slightly from normal legal meanings – a transfer of a leasehold interest is A (other, involving lease), not F (conveyance or transfer).
3	Interest transferred or created	Code LG is labelled 'long leasehold', but in fact length of lease is irrelevant. Any lease at a ground rent with vacant possession is LG.
5	Restrictions etc	This requires judgement as to what is unusual; the entry in this box has no effect on whether the form will be processed, but omission of facts which could influence how HMRC views the transaction may make it more difficult to resist a discovery assessment later (see **6.47**).

Box	Heading	Comment
9	Reliefs	'PFI relief' (see **3.11**) must be claimed as code 28. The relief may reduce consideration to zero, but a return showing zero consideration will be rejected. If this applies, the normal approach seems to be to insert consideration of £1 and write a 'further information' letter to HMRC (see **6.48**) explaining that this has been done. A new code (32) was introduced from June 2010 for first-time buyer's relief (see **3.35** for details).
10	Consideration	It is a common error to put an entry here when a lease is granted at a premium. If a lease is granted, this box must be left blank – the premium is reported later in box 22 (where a zero is required if there is no premium).
13	Linked Transactions	The 'total consideration' box should show the aggregate capital consideration paid for linked transfers of freeholds and existing leases, plus any premiums paid on grant of new leases or amendment of existing leases where these are also linked. This should include amounts in respect of the transaction(s) reported on this SDLT1. However, it should not include any amount in respect of the NPV of rent on any leases. There is no place on the return to show the aggregate NPV of rents under linked leases. The aggregate NPV must be taken into account in calculating the entry in box 25 (Tax due in respect of NPV) – see **4.58** et seq and Example 4.23 for an illustration of the significance of this.
26	Number of properties	See **6.27** for use of schedules where six or more properties are involved.
28	Address	In paper returns, if the address does not fit in the space available, start writing it here and simply put on form SDLT3 the part which does not fit – do not write the whole address on the supplementary form, or you may receive an SDLT5 certificate with a jumbled address for the land, which the Land Registry may reject.
30, 31	Title number and NLPG UPRN	If this information is not readily available, these boxes can be left blank. This will have no effect on whether the form is processed successfully.
59	Agent authority	Accidentally leaving this blank is a major cause of agents failing to receive SDLT5 certificates or other communications from HMRC.

Form SDLT4

6.24

Part 2	About leases	Where a property is transferred while subject to more than one lease to tenants, the first lease is reported in questions 16 to 21 of form SDLT1. HMRC *originally* required details of all other leases to tenants to be reported on form SDLT4, or (where multiple leases were involved) as a schedule to SDLT4. This requirement caused confusion, because form SDLT4 is designed (and mainly used) for reporting details of leases which are themselves the subject of the transaction. HMRC have now clarified the matter: if the property transferred is subject to more than one lease to tenants, details of all except the first lease are to be reported on a schedule to form *SDLT1*, not on form SDLT4. A pro-forma schedule is available at www.hmrc.gov.uk/so/sdlt-sublease-guide.htm, but equivalent schedules created for the purpose are acceptable.

Guidance notes, SDLT6 – section after main guidance on how to complete forms

6.25

6.7	Deferment cases	These notes do not make it clear that they only apply where the taxpayer has already obtained HMRC agreement to deferment – see **6.34** for details of what is required to obtain that agreement.

SPECIAL CASES

Linked transactions

6.26 Generally, separate transactions require separate returns, and it is generally acceptable to report acquisition of separate properties on separate forms SDLT1, even if they are acquired under a single transaction or arrangement. Where two or more linked transactions (see **2.36**) have the same effective date, *FA 2003, s 108(2)* provides that the purchaser(s) may opt to make a single land transaction return as if all of the transactions formed a single notifiable transaction. If there are two or more purchasers, they must make the return jointly, which implies they have joint and several liability for payment of the SDLT and any interest and penalties which may arise from late submission/payment or errors. The statute indicates that the 'single return' approach is available for any such linked transactions. However, HMRC impose restrictions because a single LTR form can only cope with two or more transactions if they are sufficiently similar (see section of SDLT6 dealing with section 13 of SDLT1 form). Therefore, it is only permitted to report two or more transactions on a single return if:

- the vendor(s) and purchaser(s) for each are identical;
- the transactions all fall within the same category (that is, one of the following: transfer of freehold; grant of lease; other transaction involving lease; other transaction); and
- either no relief is being claimed, or the same relief is claimed in respect of all transactions.

Multiple properties

6.27 Where linked acquisitions are reported on one form SDLT1, details of one of the properties must be included on form SDLT1, with the others on separate forms SDLT3 (and forms SDLT4 where the transaction includes the grant of leases). If six or more properties are acquired under a single transaction, it is possible to submit the SDLT3 and any SDLT4 information on schedules rather than on separate forms (SDLTM60125). HMRC will provide guidance on acceptable formats for such schedules. The guidance notes suggest calling the SDLT helpline in the first instance but, in the author's experience, direct contact with Birmingham Stamp Office Complex Transactions Unit is best (see **Appendix A** for contact details). It is usually possible to construct a suitable spreadsheet; HMRC require an electronic copy, even if a paper copy is sent with a paper return, to allow them to copy and paste information into their systems. Most of the information entered on these schedules is for the purposes of Government statistics rather than determining tax liability and, where information is not readily available, HMRC will often accept schedules with gaps – it is worth asking!

When to notify

6.28 In general, the deadline for submission of a land transaction return is 30 days from the effective date of the transaction (*FA 2003, s 76(1)*). If an amended or further return is required as a result of an event occurring after the effective date, the return is due within 30 days of that event. In the case of a lease with uncertain or variable rent (see **4.37**), the latest date for submission of an amended return is 30 days after the end of the fifth year of the term of the lease. Where the rent depends on the annual results of a business, this may be before the rent for the fifth year has been finally determined. In that case, the return should be submitted using a reasonable estimate of the rent, and then amended as necessary once the rent is finally determined. As noted at **6.17**, if a return is submitted in respect of the original transaction, further and amended returns are to be submitted by way of a letter to Birmingham Stamp Office, not by completion of further forms.

Penalties for late submission

6.29 If a return is submitted up to three months late, a penalty of £100 is chargeable, irrespective of whether SDLT is chargeable or whether the SDLT is paid on time. If the return is more than three months late, the penalty increases to £200. In addition, if a return is filed 12 months or more late, a tax-geared penalty may be charged. This penalty may be up to 100% of the tax chargeable on the relevant transaction (*FA 2003, Sch 10, paras 3–4*; SDLTM86120).

PAYMENT OF SDLT

Payment methods

6.30 Originally, payment of SDLT was linked to the submission of the return, so that the return was not regarded as duly submitted unless and until any SDLT had been paid. This link was broken by *FA 2007*, so that submission of the return and payment of the SDLT are now regarded as separate actions. The breaking of the link makes it very important to ensure that HMRC can identify sums received and attribute them to the correct return. To this end, the 11-digit UTRN of the related return must be quoted when SDLT is paid. SDLT may be paid by sterling cheque drawn on a UK bank, payable to 'HM Revenue & Customs Only', followed by the UTRN. If a single cheque is used to pay SDLT on several returns, the UTRNs should be listed on the back of the cheque, with the amount of SDLT against each. The cheque may be sent by post to the processing centre at Netherton (see **Appendix A**), or paid in at a bank or Post Office using the payslip(s) from the paper return(s). Alternatively (and, in the eyes of HMRC, preferably), payment may be made by any of the usual electronic or bank transfer methods. Relevant bank account details for these purposes are at www.hmrc.gov.uk/payinghmrc/stamp-land.htm.

Due date and deferment

6.31 SDLT is generally due 30 days from the effective date of the transaction – usually the earlier of substantial performance of the agreement and legal completion of a transfer or execution of a lease (see **2.8**). There is no automatic right to defer payment where there are delays in paying consideration, occupying the property or determining the amount of consideration. If, for any reason, the amount of consideration has not been finally determined when payment of SDLT falls due, payment must be based on a reasonable estimate. Further SDLT may then be due once the consideration is finally determined, and this must generally be paid within 30 days of that final determination. However, interest will be chargeable on this additional SDLT from the original due date of the main payment, unless deferment has been granted in respect of the additional tax.

6.32 If, at the effective date of a transaction:

- the SDLT cannot be finally determined because any amount of consideration is uncertain or contingent, and
- any part of that consideration falls or may fall to be paid more than six months after the effective date,

the taxpayer may apply to defer payment of SDLT on the consideration which falls to be paid later (*FA 2003, s 90*; *SI 2003/2837, Pt 4*). However, it is not possible to defer payment on any element of the consideration which is certain at the effective date or later date of application, has already been paid by then, or is known to become payable within six months of the effective date. Deferment is only possible if uncertainty about the consideration arises from future events. Deferment is not possible in respect of any SDLT which arises on rent under a lease, but deferment may be possible in respect of SDLT on a lease premium.

6.33 If deferment is granted, the notification of that fact will set out details of when further payments of SDLT must be made. If the specified payments are made by the specified dates, interest will not be charged. If payments are late, interest will be charged only from the dates on which they should have been made. The fact that deferment can be interest-free is the principal reason for going to the trouble of making an application.

Example 6.5 – deferment

On 1 January 2011, Elvis agrees to buy a freehold block of flats from Cliff for £10 million payable now and up to a further £5 million payable on 1 January 2012. The amount payable on 1 January 2012 will be determined in accordance with a formula where the only variable is the net rents received in the year to 30 June 2011. The agreement is completed without prior substantial performance on 31 March 2011. Cliff must pay SDLT on the £1 million consideration no later than 30 April 2011. He may apply to defer payment on the additional consideration because (a) that consideration falls to be paid more than six months after the effective date of the purchase, and (b) the amount cannot be determined at the effective date (or later date of application) since it depends on rent receipts for a period ending after that date. However, if the contingent amount had depended on the net rents for the year to 31 March 2011, deferment would not have been possible. Although, at the effective date, that amount might not have been finally worked out, it would in principle be possible to know the amount at that date, so the amount is not 'uncertain' as defined by *FA 2003, s 51*.

Applying for deferment

6.34 An application for deferment must be made no later than the due date for the original return, ie 30 days after the effective date (*FA 2003, s 90*). It is understood that this deadline is rigidly enforced, and HMRC encourage early submission of applications, even before the transaction is finalised if possible. Application is made by letter to the Birmingham Stamp Office (see **Appendix A**), marked 'SDLT Deferment Application' (SDLTM50900). The letter must set out:

- the identity of the purchaser;
- the location of the land involved;
- the nature of the contingency/uncertain payment;
- the amount of consideration for which deferment is sought (or a best estimate where it is uncertain);
- as full details of the times of expected payments as it is possible to give;
- a reasoned opinion as to when this part of the consideration will cease to be contingent or can be ascertained;
- a calculation of the SDLT payable on the total of the actual and the contingent/uncertain consideration (based on best estimates); and
- a calculation of the SDLT in respect of which the application to defer payment refers.

HMRC are entitled to ask for further information, and are likely to do so if the transaction is unusual or if avoidance is suspected. If deferment is denied, it is possible to appeal (see **6.58** et seq), but in practice this will be worthwhile only where very large sums are at stake.

Interest on SDLT

6.35 As with other taxes, interest is charged on SDLT which is paid late (*FA 2003, s 87*), at the rates set by regulation under *FA 1989, s 178*. In general, the rate is the same as for income tax and NIC (see www.hmrc.gov.uk/rates/

interest-late.htm#itnic for details). In most cases, tax is late if it is paid after the due date, which is 30 days after the 'relevant date'. The relevant date in various situations is as follows:

(1) for an ordinary acquisition of a chargeable interest, whether by transfer or grant of a lease, the effective date;

(2) where certain events occurring after execution or earlier substantial performance of a lease are treated as the grant of a new lease (eg abnormal increase in rent (see **4.25**), or transfer after a relief was claimed on grant (see **4.15**)), the date of the event which is treated as the grant of a new lease;

(3) where a relief is withdrawn as a result of a later event (eg group relief withdrawn because the purchaser leaves the group within three years), the date of the event giving rise to the withdrawal;

(4) where the tax arises on an earlier transaction as a result of a later linked transaction (eg because aggregation of consideration throws the original transaction into a higher rate band), the effective date of the later linked transaction;

(5) where tax arises on a 'growing' lease (see **4.11**), the day on which the lease becomes treated as being for a longer fixed term; and

(6) where deferment has been granted as set out at **6.34**, the date on which the deferred SDLT payment is due.

However, when further tax arises after the normal due date and none of items (2) to (6) applies, interest is chargeable from the original due date, ie 30 days after the effective date of the original transaction.

When SDLT is repaid, interest is payable (*FA 2003, s 89*), again at the same rates as generally apply to direct taxes as set under *FA 1989, s 178*. Such interest is not income for tax purposes. The interest is payable for the period from receipt of the tax by HMRC to the date of repayment.

Example 6.6 – relevant date and interest charge

On 1 May 2011, David enters into a five-year lease of a property at a provisional rent of £200,000 per year, but the amount is to be finally determined by reference to performance of the business carried out in the property during the five years. On 29 June 2011, David pays SDLT on the basis of the £200,000 annual rent. On 15 May 2016, just after the end of the lease, the annual rent is finally determined to be £225,000. The SDLT liability is recomputed, and the additional SDLT is due 30 days after the date on which the rent is finally determined. However, interest is charged on this further SDLT from 30 June 2011, being 30 days after the effective date of the lease.

Collection and Enforcement

6.36 SDLT is due and payable, whether under a self-assessment (that is, as a result of submission of a return), or under a determination or assessment by HMRC, unless deferment has been granted as outlined above or postponement has been agreed/granted (see below). HMRC are empowered to enforce payment of outstanding SDLT by distraint ('diligence' in Scotland) or by civil proceedings in magistrates' courts (for amounts not exceeding £2,000), county courts, the High Court or Scottish equivalents (*FA 2003, Sch 12*).

HMRC ENQUIRIES

6.37 The process for HMRC to enquire into an SDLT return is similar to that which applies to other direct tax returns (*FA 2003, Sch 10, Pt 3*). It begins by HMRC giving notice of enquiry to the purchaser before the end of the enquiry period; it ends when HMRC gives a 'closure notice'. This may be given because HMRC are satisfied that their enquiry is complete or because the Tax Tribunal gives a direction to that effect on application by the purchaser. The enquiry period is potentially relatively short, being nine months from:

- the filing date (which is itself 30 days after the effective date; see **2.8**) if the return was filed on time,
- the actual date of filing if the return was late, or
- the date of amendment if the return is amended by the purchaser.

6.38 However, if the notice of enquiry is given as a result of an amendment to the return, and the normal enquiry period for the original return has ended (or an enquiry into the original return has already been completed), the enquiry is limited to matters to which the amendment relates or are affected by the amendment. Outside these time limits, HMRC may only pursue potential underpayment of tax by making a 'discovery assessment' (see **6.46**).

Example 6.7 – time limits for enquiry into return

On 1 March 2011 (effective date and date of completion), Hattie Ltd buys a business from Eric Ltd. Payment takes the form of Hattie accepting responsibility for debts of the business amounting to £2 million plus an issue of shares in Hattie Ltd to Eric Ltd with a market value of £1 million. The business includes a property provisionally valued at £1.5 million. On 20 March 2011, Hattie Ltd submits an LTR on the basis of this valuation, claiming relief under *FA 2003, Sch 7, para 8* (acquisition relief; see **3.21**). Hattie Ltd pays SDLT at 0.5% accordingly. On 1 February 2012, Hattie Ltd gives notice to amend the return, decreasing the value attributed to the property to £1.2 million. On 15 February 2012, HMRC give notice of enquiry into the return. The normal enquiry period for the original return ended on 31 December 2011 (nine months after the filing date), so the enquiry may only deal with matters affected by the amendment. In this case, it is considered that the enquiry may relate to the valuation of the property but not to the availability of acquisition relief.

6.39 As part of an enquiry, HMRC may demand to see documents and information, giving at least 30 days' notice (*FA 2003, Sch 10, para 14*). The purchaser may appeal against such a demand (see **6.59**). If no appeal is lodged, or after any appeal is settled, initial and daily penalties may be imposed for failure to produce the outstanding documents and information. In addition to a general right to demand documents and information from the purchaser, HMRC are given powers to seek information and documents from third parties, including tax accountants and other advisers. Exercise of these powers is subject to consent or review by the Tax Tribunal or, in some cases, a judge or sheriff. Situations in which these powers may be invoked are beyond the scope of this book. The relevant parties will normally require specialist advice in these cases.

6.40 While an enquiry is in progress, HMRC may amend the return if they conclude that additional tax is due and amendment is necessary to prevent a loss of the tax (*FA 2003, Sch 10, para 17*). Written notice of the amendment must be given to the purchaser. This power is normally only used where a prima facie underpayment has been established, but the taxpayer refuses to make an appropriate payment on account, suggesting there may be a risk of eventual default. The purchaser may appeal to the Tax Tribunal against the amendment and may apply to have collection of any additional tax postponed. Postponement may be agreed by HMRC, or the question may be determined by the Tax Tribunal if the taxpayer and HMRC cannot reach agreement.

6.41 The purchaser may also amend the return, if the normal period allowed for amendment has not yet expired (*FA 2003, Sch 10, para 18*; see www.hmrc.gov.uk/sdlt/return/amend.htm). Voluntary amendment to correct any errors which have come to light may be taken into account in determining any penalty position (see **6.56**). HMRC may, however, reject the amendment if they do not agree with it.

6.42 HMRC and the purchaser may agree to refer matters to the Tax Tribunal during an enquiry (and, if they see fit, the First-tier Tribunal may pass the referral on to the Upper Tribunal). Subject to the normal rights of appeal through the courts, the decision of the Tribunal is binding on all parties.

6.43 Normally, enquiries are closed by HMRC giving notice of closure once they are satisfied no further amendments are required (*FA 2003, Sch 10, para 23*). The notice must make it clear whether any taxpayer amendments of the return are accepted. The purchaser may appeal to the Tax Tribunal against a closure notice (*Sch 10, para 35*). Alternatively, the purchaser may apply to the Tax Tribunal for a direction that the enquiry be closed (*Sch 10, para 24*). Details of procedure are on the Tribunals Service website (see **6.60**).

FAILURE TO DELIVER A RETURN

6.44 If a purchaser fails to deliver a return, or if HMRC believe that a return should have been delivered, HMRC may issue a notice requiring delivery of a return (*FA 2003, Sch 10, paras 5, 25–27*). At least 30 days' notice must be given and the transaction in question must be specified. If the person to whom the notice is given fails to comply, HMRC may apply to the Tax Tribunal for the imposition of a daily penalty. There does not appear to be any provision for appeal against such a notice, for example on the grounds that the purported transaction to which it relates has not taken place, or is not notifiable, or that the person to whom notice was given is not the purchaser. Any penalty is in addition to those which apply automatically for late submission (see **6.29**). Alternatively or additionally, if no return is forthcoming, HMRC may make a determination of the SDLT which they believe to be unpaid, and this is then treated as a self-assessment (that is, as if a return had been submitted) for the purposes of enforcement, including the charging of interest and penalties. A determination may not be made more than six years after the effective date of the transaction in question. If the taxpayer subsequently makes a self-assessment by delivering a return, provided this occurs not later than 12 months after notice of the determination is given or six years after the original due date for the return (whichever is later), the self-assessment displaces the determination. This, of course, then allows HMRC to launch an enquiry into the return. As an alternative, the taxpayer may appeal to the Tax Tribunal against the assessment, but only on the grounds that the transaction has not taken place or been substantially performed, or that it has but it is not notifiable. Logically, if such an appeal is successful, it should also displace any daily penalty awarded for failure to comply with HMRC's notice to deliver a return, but the legislation does not overtly say that this is so.

6.45 A further bizarre and potentially wholly unfair provision allows HMRC to treat a return (or any other document) as not having been delivered or made available if, whilst in their care, it has been destroyed or so damaged as to become illegible. The author is not aware of any case in which HMRC have in practice relied on this provision.

DISCOVERY ASSESSMENT

6.46 If a return has been made (or is deemed to have been made by virtue of a determination) and the enquiry period (see **6.37**) has not yet ended, any possible loss of tax will normally be investigated by launching an enquiry. Once an enquiry has commenced, if HMRC are concerned that recovery of additional tax is at risk, they may amend the return as described at **6.40**, thereby allowing action to be taken to collect the tax. Once the enquiry period has ended, or an enquiry has been completed, HMRC has no automatic right to reopen matters and seek further tax.

6.47 However, if no return has been made, or in certain circumstances where a return has been made but the time for launching an enquiry has passed, HMRC may assess any tax which they discover to have been underpaid (*FA 2003, Sch 10, Pt 5*). If a return has been made, a 'discovery' assessment may only be made to recover tax lost:

(1) as a result of fraud or negligence on the part of the purchaser or an agent or partner of the purchaser, or

(2) because, when the normal time for enquiry ended (or any previous enquiry was completed), HMRC could not, on the basis of information then available to them, have reasonably been expected to be aware of the loss of tax.

For the purposes of (2), information is available if it is contained in a land transaction return, has been furnished in the course of an enquiry, could reasonably be expected to be inferred from such information, or is notified to HMRC by the purchaser or a person acting on his behalf (*Sch 10, para 1(5)*).

6.48 In reliance on the last of these points, taxpayers and their agents often submit further information to HMRC at the time of submission of the LTR. HMRC guidance indicates that such further information should not be enclosed with paper returns, but rather should be sent to the Birmingham Stamp Office (see **Appendix A**), quoting the UTRN(s) of the return(s) to which it relates.

6.49 The decision as to what further information, if any, to submit requires careful thought. Submission of further information may increase the likelihood of the transaction being selected for enquiry. If the treatment originally adopted in the return is clearly correct, any such enquiry will normally be fruitless, but will incur administrative costs. Alternatively, if there is genuine doubt over the treatment of the transaction, it will be important to ensure that the information submitted is sufficiently comprehensive. If HMRC cannot see the full facts and circumstances to enable them to make their own judgement of the treatment adopted, they are likely to consider that a discovery assessment is justified, should further information come to their attention later.

6.50 The general time limit for HMRC to make a discovery assessment is six years from the effective date of the transaction. This period is extended to 21 years where fraud or negligence is involved and if the purchaser has died, shortened to three years from the date of death (or six years from the effective date of the transaction, if that is earlier). If the assessment is to recover an excessive repayment of SDLT, it may also be made at any time during an enquiry into the relevant return, or up to 12 months after the repayment is made, even if this is outside the normal time limit.

6.51 The purchaser may appeal against a discovery assessment and may apply to have payment of any additional tax postponed (*FA 2003, Sch 10, para 35*). As in other cases, postponement may be agreed by HMRC, or the matter may be determined by the Tax Tribunal.

MISTAKE IN RETURN ETC

6.52 If a mistake is discovered in a return within the period allowed for amendment (usually up to one year after the normal submission deadline), this should be dealt with by amending the return as set out at **6.41**. If this deadline is missed, it may be possible to make a claim for relief from excessive assessment arising from a mistake in a return. At the time of writing (September 2010) such a claim may be made up to six years from the effective date of the transaction, but it is proposed to reduce this period to four years for claims made on or after 1 April 2011 (*Finance (No 2) Bill 2010*, presumably destined to become *F(No 3)Act 2010, s 28*). There is no provision to extend either period where, for example, the return was made after the normal deadline (*FA 2003, Sch 10, para 34*). The proposed amendments from 1 April 2011 will place severe restrictions on the acceptable grounds for making a claim – for example, if there was a mistake in making or failing to make a claim or election, it will no longer be possible to correct this by way of a claim under these provisions. Making a claim under these provisions will also remove restrictions on HMRC's ability to make a discovery assessment. Therefore careful analysis will be required before deciding to pursue such a claim.

A claim for relief may also be made where a person believes he has been assessed more than once in respect of the same transaction. There does not appear to be any time limit on such a claim (*Sch 10, para 33*).

PENALTIES, FINES AND OTHER SANCTIONS

Penalties

6.53 As noted at **6.35**, it is the view of HMRC that interest charged when SDLT is paid after the date on which it ought to have been paid does no more than compensate the Government for loss of use of the money. As a separate matter, penalties are provided for various failures; these are generally in *FA 2003, Sch 10* and *Sch 11, para 6*. Some are fixed amounts and apply automatically; others are for variable amounts up to a ceiling. They apply as follows:

(1) Late submission of return – up to three months after the due date, £100; three months or more after the due date, £200.

(2) Late submission of return – 12 months or more after the due date, an amount up to the amount of tax chargeable on the transaction. This is in addition to the penalty chargeable under (1).

(3) Failure to submit return after HMRC have given a formal notice to deliver – up to £60 per day of continuing failure. This requires a direction from the Tax Tribunal and is in addition to any penalty under (1) and (2).

(4) Fraudulent or negligent delivery of incorrect return, or failure to correct return after error has come to light – up to the amount of understated tax. This penalty was brought into the general *FA 2007* regime for penalties for incorrect returns (*FA 2007, Sch 24*) by SI 2009/571.

(5) Failure to keep and preserve records as required – up to £3,000.

(6) Failure to produce documents or information after formal notice has been given – an initial amount of £50 and, for continued failure, a daily penalty of up to £30 (if imposed by HMRC) or £150 (if imposed by the court). However, these penalties cannot be imposed after the failure has been remedied, so they should be seen as encouragement to comply rather than punishment for not complying.

6.54 In principle, HMRC impose most penalties by making a formal determination (or, where indicated above, by seeking such a determination from the Tax Tribunal) and issuing notice of the determination to the taxpayer (*FA 2003, Sch 11*). The taxpayer may then appeal against the determination, initially to the Tax Tribunal, subsequently to the courts. In the case of fraud, penalty proceedings may be brought in the High Court (or the Court of Session in Scotland). The general time limit for determining a penalty or commencement of proceedings for a penalty is six years from the date on which the penalty was incurred. However, for tax-geared penalties, this is extended to three years after determination of the tax. A penalty for assisting in preparation of an incorrect return may be sought up to 20 years after the penalty was incurred.

6.55 In practice, most fixed and daily penalties are paid without formal determination. These penalties will be waived only in the most exceptional circumstances – for example, if the taxpayer is able to show that the return was completed and posted in good time, but lost in the post, or if the taxpayer's agent suffered a serious illness at just the wrong time. Details are given in leaflet SD7 available from the HMRC publications and stationery service (see **Appendix A**) or online at www.hmrc.gov.uk/leaflets/sd7.pdf.

6.56 Most tax-geared penalties are included in a negotiated settlement, where it is rare for the maximum amount to be imposed. The amount of any such penalty will depend on matters such as size and gravity of adjustment and taxpayer cooperation; some guidance is given in Tax Bulletin issue 71, which may be found on the HMRC website at www.hmrc.gov.uk/bulletins/tb71.htm.

Fines and other sanctions

6.57 Any person who conceals, destroys or falsifies a document, the production of which has been requested or required, or permits or causes such concealment etc, if convicted, is liable to a fine and/or up to two years' imprisonment. A person who fails to comply with a court order to produce documents or information may be held to be in contempt of the relevant court and may be fined and/or imprisoned accordingly. As with other taxes, criminal prosecution is possible for the most serious cases involving fraud, potentially leading to fines and/or imprisonment. Dealing with such matters is not within the scope of this book.

APPEALS

6.58 There are various references in this chapter to appealing against HMRC decisions, determinations and assessments. The normal rules for appeals on direct tax matters apply equally to SDLT (*FA 2003, Sch 10, Pt 7*). These are set out at www.hmrc.gov.uk/complaints-appeals/direct-tax-appeal.htm on the HMRC website. Initially, appeals are made to HMRC. This may be done either by using the form usually supplied with the notice of decision etc, or by letter. A letter of appeal must set out the details necessary to allow HMRC to identify the tax return or transaction and decision involved (usually the HMRC reference) and the grounds of the appeal.

6.59 In general, the appeal must be made within 30 days of the decision, assessment etc. If the taxpayer and HMRC are unable to reach agreement on the disputed matter, HMRC may offer an 'independent review' (that is, a review by one or more other HMRC officers). Within 30 days of such an offer, the taxpayer must decide whether to accept, or to refer the matter directly to the Tax Tribunal. If a review is accepted, it is still possible for the taxpayer to appeal to the Tax Tribunal if he does not accept the outcome of the review.

6.60 SDLT matters are dealt with by the First-Tier Tribunal (Tax) of the Tribunals Service. Guidance on making an appeal or reference to the Tax Tribunal, and the necessary forms, are available on the Tribunals Service website at www.tribunals.gov.uk/tax/FormsGuidance.htm, or may be obtained by writing to the Tribunal Service (see **Appendix A**).

RECORD KEEPING

6.61 Purchasers are required to keep and preserve whatever records may be required to enable the delivery of correct and complete returns (*FA 2003, Sch 10, Pt 2*). Such records include original contracts and transfer instruments, supporting maps, plans and other documents, and records of payments receipts and financial arrangements. The records must be kept for at least six years from the effective date of the transaction. They must also be kept until any enquiry into the return is completed, and until HMRC no longer have the right to enquire into the return, if these dates are later than the six-year time limit. It is acceptable to keep the information from the documents (for example, scanned copies) rather than the documents themselves. However, taxpayers may be concerned about the ability to demonstrate that such information is in accordance with the original document. So, in most cases, the original document is likely to be retained, albeit in a document storage facility, even if the information is also stored electronically.

6.62 The requirement to keep and preserve records applies where a return has to be made, but also where no return is required because the transaction is exempt (*FA 2003, Sch 11*) (see **6.3**). For most commercial transactions, the requirement to keep records for six years is reasonable and in line with other record-keeping requirements. In the case of routine home purchases, where the property may well be re-sold within the six years, the requirement is not so clearly justified. Many homeowners, unaware of the requirement, are likely to dispose of records in a shorter period.

Chapter 7

SDLT Anti-Avoidance Rules

INTRODUCTION

7.1 Prior to the introduction of SDLT in 2003, it was relatively easy to minimise stamp duty costs on many property transactions. It had proven difficult to introduce effective anti-avoidance rules for this document-based tax. These were major factors in the decision to replace stamp duty with SDLT, a transaction-based tax not reliant on the manner in which the transaction is documented. The initial SDLT rules were not perfectly drafted and, inevitably, transactions were structured to take advantage of this and minimise tax. Initially, HMRC tackled this by introducing targeted anti-avoidance rules intended to prevent exploitation of specific reliefs and treatments. Eventually, it was concluded that these were having only limited success and, on 6 December 2006, a general anti-avoidance rule for SDLT was introduced in the form of *FA 2003, s 75A*.

7.2 *Section 75A* was initially introduced by regulation; by the time it was confirmed by *FA 2007*, it had expanded to three sections, which now appear as *FA 2003, ss 75A–75C*. These sections demonstrate a hardening of attitudes to avoidance of SDLT, which is further illustrated by the June 2010 edition of 'Spotlight', HMRC's web publication about avoidance (see www.hmrc.gov.uk/avoidance/spotlights.htm), which makes it clear that HMRC intend to attack schemes which seek to exploit 'sub-sale relief'. Some of these schemes appear to have been structured in a way which seeks to fall outside the scope of *ss 75A–75C*, but the tenor of the Spotlight article suggests that HMRC will challenge whether this has been successful.

The final version of the provisions is in some ways more stringent than the original version, but is still stated to apply with effect from 6 December 2006. During the parliamentary debates on the *2007 Finance Bill* the Government was eventually persuaded that this could amount to retrospective taxation, so a clause was introduced (*FA 2007, s 71(3)*) to state that, for transactions entered into before Royal Assent, if the liability under the original version was less than that under the final version, the lesser liability would apply. This chapter deals with the final version of the rules. If, exceptionally, a transaction potentially within the scope of *s 75A* commenced prior to 19 July 2007 and is only now being dealt with, the transitional rules, which remain in *FA 2007*, should be checked.

7.3 SDLT is within the system for disclosure of tax avoidance schemes (DOTAS), but it has its own rules for determining what must be disclosed, and there are other differences from the system which applies to other taxes.

7.4 It is arguable that the introduction of *ss 75A–75C* has rendered some of the previous targeted anti-avoidance rules redundant, but they all remain in force too. This chapter looks first at the general anti-avoidance rule. It then provides a list of specific targeted rules – these are dealt with more fully in the relevant chapters examining the transactions or reliefs to which they apply. Finally, it explores the SDLT version of DOTAS.

GENERAL ANTI-AVOIDANCE RULE – FA 2003, SS 75A–75C

Introduction

7.5 The rules potentially apply to all transactions other than those consisting of simple single steps, unless specifically excepted. They operate by comparing the total SDLT actually paid on all steps with the SDLT which would be payable on a 'notional transaction'. If the SDLT actually paid is less, any real land transactions are disregarded and, in their place, the notional transaction becomes chargeable. Credit is given for any SDLT paid on real transactions, and further SDLT is payable to bring the total up to that on the notional transaction.

7.6 The test is completely objective – that is, there is no need to consider the motives of the parties. This means that a series of transactions which are not entered into with any intention of avoiding tax, but which happen to reduce the SDLT bill below that implied by the notional transaction, could still be caught. For this reason, it is not safe to ignore the rules merely because there is no avoidance motive; their application must be considered in all multi-step transactions.

7.7 HMRC have provided some guidance on the application of *ss 75A–75C*. This is in Technical News Issue 5 (August 2007) and may be found at www.hmrc.gov.uk/so/tech-newsletter5.pdf. The guidance gives examples of where the rules do or do not apply, but these are not always technically accurate. For example, it is stated that *s 75A* will apply to a contract for a husband to purchase a property from a third party, with a sub-sale to his wife (Technical News 5, para 14(4)), when in fact *s 75A* will not apply unless the total SDLT payable is less than would have been payable on the notional transaction. Most of the examples in the guidance involve the grant, variation or termination of leases. This confirms the nature of the avoidance against which the legislation is primarily directed.

When do the rules apply?

7.8 They apply where one person (V) disposes of a chargeable interest, and another person (P) acquires it or a chargeable interest deriving from it. It does not matter that there may be various steps between the disposal and the acquisition, nor does it matter if the chargeable interest goes through various transformations between the disposal and the acquisition. The legislation was introduced to deal with schemes which involved precisely that kind of step and transformation. If the asset disposed of or acquired is not a chargeable interest, the rules do not apply.

Example 7.1 – no transfer of a chargeable interest

X Ltd owns 100% of the shares of Y Ltd. Y Ltd owns a valuable property. X Ltd makes a loan to Y Ltd, allowing Y Ltd to pay a cash dividend to X Ltd, thus reducing the value of Y Ltd to £1. X Ltd then sells the shares of Y Ltd to unrelated party Z Ltd. Assuming there are no other steps, *s 75A* does not apply to the transaction, because there has been no disposal or acquisition of a chargeable interest. Shares in a company are not 'chargeable interests', even if the company's only asset is property. However, this may change in future – from time to time, the Government has threatened to introduce land-rich company rules, which may deem shares in such a company to be chargeable interests.

7.9 The rules only apply if there are 'a number of transactions' (which may include non-land transactions) involved in the disposal and acquisition. To make sense of this provision, 'a number' must be taken to mean more than one. However, 'transaction' includes an agreement, offer or undertaking not to take a specified action, and any kind of arrangement, even if it would not normally be described as a transaction. In other words, apparently unilateral acts and failures to act may be regarded as transactions. It does not matter when the transactions occur – they merely have to occur 'in connection with' the disposal and acquisition. The transactions are referred to as 'scheme transactions'.

7.10 The legislation lists examples of 'scheme transactions' as follows, but makes it clear this is not an exhaustive list:

- acquisition of a lease derived from a freehold formerly owned by the vendor;

- sub-sale to a third party;
- grant of a lease to a third party subject to a right to terminate;
- exercise of a right to terminate a lease or take some other action;
- agreement not to exercise a right to terminate a lease or take some other action; and
- variation of a right to terminate a lease or take some other action.

It is clear from this list that transactions involving the grant and termination of leases were foremost in HMRC's collective mind when the rules were written. Although not exhaustive, this list is important when considering 'incidental transactions' (see **7.12**).

Example 7.2 (part 1) – scheme caught by ***s 75A***

Agnes owns a freehold residential property worth £2 million. She grants a lease to Bill to hold as nominee for herself. Bill is a friend but not otherwise connected with Agnes. The terms of the lease are as follows:

- yearly rent, one peppercorn, no premium; and
- term one month, but with an option (exercisable before the end of the month) to extend to 100 years in return for payment of £1.

There is no SDLT on the grant of the lease because it is treated as granted beneficially to the nominee (see **2.18**), and there is no reason to substitute the actual consideration with market value or any other figure. However, on the assumption that the option is likely to be exercised, the value of the freehold interest is now minimal. Agnes sells the freehold to Claire for £1. Again, there is no SDLT on this sale as there is no reason to substitute anything else for the actual consideration.

Agnes then undertakes to refrain from exercising the option to extend the lease if Claire pays her £2 million. There could possibly be an argument that this is a land transaction subject to SDLT, but in real, slightly more complicated arrangements based on this general structure, it was considered that this was not a land transaction. The overall result then is that Claire has spent £2 million to acquire a property but paid no SDLT.

There are a number of transactions, comprising the grant of the lease, sale of the freehold and undertaking not to exercise the option, so this series of transactions is potentially caught by *s 75A*.

The notional transaction

7.11 The rules only apply if the total SDLT paid on all transactions in the scheme is less than the amount which would be payable on a 'notional land transaction'. This notional transaction is defined as a transaction effecting the transfer from V to P, for consideration equal to the largest amount (aggregated if more than one):

- given by or on behalf of any one person, or
- received by or on behalf of V,

for the scheme transactions. Reference to a notional land transaction sometimes causes confusion, because the legislation does not specify the nature of the transaction. However, this is unimportant. All that matters in this regard is that there is deemed to be a chargeable transaction for a specified amount of consideration, which determines the minimum SDLT charge.

Incidental transactions and reliefs

7.12 In measuring the consideration for this notional land transaction, certain amounts must be left out of account. The amounts are:

- the consideration for any transaction which is merely incidental to the transfer of the chargeable interest (see **7.16**); and
- any consideration paid in respect of a transaction covered by the following reliefs in *FA 2003*:
  - *s 60* (compulsory purchase facilitating development);
  - *s 61* (compliance with planning obligations);
  - *ss 63, 64* (demutualisation of insurance company or building society);
  - *s 65* (incorporation of limited liability partnership);
  - *s 66* (transfers involving public bodies);
  - *s 67* (transfer in consequence of reorganisation of parliamentary constituencies);
  - *s 69* (acquisition by bodies established for national purposes);
  - *s 71* (acquisition by registered social landlord);
  - *s 74* (collective enfranchisement by leaseholders);
  - *s 75* (crofting community right to buy);
  - *Sch 6A* (relief for acquisition by housing intermediaries etc); and
  - *Sch 8* (charities relief).

These various reliefs are considered in more detail in **Chapter 3**. Without these exclusions, many of the reliefs would become relatively useless in real-life transactions which often involve multiple steps for entirely innocent reasons. Perhaps of more importance are the reliefs which are not listed above, the most important of which are the group, reconstruction and acquisition reliefs set out in *FA 2003, Sch 7*. HMRC are concerned that these reliefs may be exploited in ways which were not intended, and are not keen to facilitate this (although this does beg the question of who is to judge the intention of reasonably plain legislation).

Example 7.2 (part 2) – SDLT payable under *s 75A*

The total SDLT paid on the basis of the scheme transactions is nil. The consideration for the notional transaction is £2 million (plus £1), being the aggregate amount given by Claire. Therefore, *s 75A* applies and the SDLT payable is £2 million at 4% (or 5% after 5 April 2011). This scheme is precisely the kind of arrangement that *s 75A* appears to be designed to block.

Effective date

7.13 The effective date of the notional transaction is the last date of completion of a scheme transaction or, if earlier, the last date of substantial performance of a scheme transaction. In the example above, this is likely to be the date on which Claire pays Agnes £2 million. If the transaction was a simple sale for £2 million, the effective date would typically be the date on which the consideration was paid, so this appears reasonable.

Exclusions from s 75A

7.14 The potential scope of *s 75A* is very wide. In particular, it could inhibit a legitimate arrangement of transactions in order to come within the terms of a relief or favourable treatment. To guard against this, there are two specific exclusions in *s 75A* itself, and some general restrictions on application set out in *ss 75B* and *75C*.

7.15 *Section 75A* does not apply if the only reason for the reduced SDLT is that *FA 2003, ss 71A–73* (alternative property finance reliefs; see **3.31**) or *Sch 9* (right to buy etc reliefs; see **3.37**) apply. It is important to remember that the exclusion only applies if these reliefs are the *only* reason for the SDLT saving. A combination of steps which qualify for one of the reliefs with other steps risks losing the protection of the exclusion and bringing the whole transaction within the scope of *s 75A*.

Section 75B – incidental transactions

7.16 Consideration for a real transaction in a series may be ignored in calculating the consideration for the notional transaction, if the real transaction is 'merely incidental' to the transfer of the chargeable interest from V to P. There is no comprehensive definition of 'merely incidental'. The legislation gives three examples of transactions which may be incidental, as follows, but the list does not claim to be exhaustive:

- a transaction undertaken for the purpose of constructing a building on the land;
- a transaction for the sale of anything other than land; and
- a loan or other provision of finance to enable someone to pay for part of the process by which the land transfer takes place.

Since the legislation only says these transactions 'may' be incidental, the list is of very limited use. It is further limited by the statement that transactions in the list at **7.10** are not incidental. A transaction cannot be regarded as incidental if it forms part of the process by which the transfer of the chargeable interest is effected, or if the transfer is conditional on completion of the transaction.

Example 7.3 – incidental transactions

The facts are as in Example 7.2 above, but Claire also pays Agnes £25,000 for the furniture and other chattels in the house. This is a payment for something other than land. Subject to confirmation that this represents a 'just and reasonable' allocation of the overall amounts paid, this will be regarded as an incidental transaction, and the amount paid will not be taken into account in determining the consideration for the notional land transaction.

Section 75C – other exclusions and conditions

7.17 A transfer of shares or securities is ignored for the purposes of *s 75A* if (but only if) it would otherwise be the first of a series of scheme transactions. This allows a degree of corporate reorganisation in order to permit a claim to relief on a subsequent land transaction.

7.18 If a real transfer equivalent to the notional transaction would have been eligible for a relief, the relief applies to the notional transaction.

7.19 If the notional transaction is a transfer to an associated company, *FA 2003, s 53* applies to deem the consideration to be at least equal to market value (see **2.27**).

7.20 If there are two notional transactions which, together, amount to an exchange, *FA 2003, Sch 4, para 5* applies to deem the consideration for each notional transaction to be equal to the market value of the interest deemed transferred under that notional transaction.

Example 7.4 – exclusion of first step, transfer of shares

Henry owns all of the shares in two companies (Anne Ltd and Jane Ltd). Anne Ltd owns the freehold of a property which is let to Jane Ltd at a rent which is below the market rate. The lease held by Jane Ltd therefore has a capital value. Henry wants to put the value of the property into a single company, partly to extract cash and, later, to raise finance. Henry transfers the shares of Jane Ltd to Anne Ltd for payment in cash. He then arranges for Anne Ltd to transfer the freehold property to Jane Ltd as a contribution to capital (claiming group relief from SDLT), at which point the lease held by Jane Ltd collapses into the freehold by operation of law.

This is a series of transactions forming part of a single scheme. There is a transfer of property from Anne Ltd to Jane Ltd. This is for no consideration, but as a transfer to a connected company it is deemed to be for market value consideration. The notional transaction is the transfer from Anne Ltd to Jane Ltd, which is deemed to be for market value consideration by virtue of the application of *s 53* as noted above. The SDLT paid (nil) is less than would be payable on this notional consideration, so *s 75A* potentially applies. However:

(1) As the first step in the series, the transfer of shares of Jane Ltd to Anne Ltd is ignored. There is, therefore, only one step in the transaction (the transfer of the property to Jane Ltd), so *s 75A* does not apply.

(2) If there were other steps such that this was not enough to disapply *s 75A*, the notional transfer (being a transfer from Anne Ltd to Jane Ltd) should qualify for group relief just as the real transfer does. So, even if *s 75A* does apply, the SDLT charge should be removed by group relief.

7.21 It should be noted that the application of a relief to the notional transaction is subject to the normal conditions and restrictions which would apply in relation to that relief for a real transaction. So, in the example above, if Anne Ltd were to dispose of the shares of Jane Ltd within three years of the transfer of the property, the notional group relief would be clawed back, and it would be necessary to reconsider the application of *s 75A* to the original transaction.

7.22 Other provisions which are applied to the notional transaction as they would apply to a real transaction are as follows:

- an interest in a property-investment partnership (see **5.29**) is treated as a chargeable interest; and
- if any of the scheme transactions is entered into in connection with a transfer of an undertaking (such that *FA 2003, Sch 7, paras 7–8* apply), the notional transaction is also treated as entered into in connection with the same transfer.

7.23 Where V or P is a partnership, the normal partnership rules were originally applied in relation to a notional transaction which comprises a transfer of land to or from the partnership, from or to a partner or someone connected with a partner (see **5.13** and **5.19**). However, it was concluded that this might allow avoidance. *FA 2010, s 56* therefore amended *s 75C(8)* and inserted *s 75C(8A)* to ensure that the rules in *FA 2003, Sch 15, Pt 3* do not apply to any notional transaction which consists of a transfer to or from a partnership. As a result, any such notional transaction will be subject to SDLT as if it was a transfer between two ordinary persons. This may produce an unfair result where an actual transfer to a partnership involves more than one step, thus bringing *s 75A* into play.

Example 7.5 – unjust result from application of *s 75A*

RST is a partnership of three otherwise unconnected individuals R, S and T, who share partnership profits equally. The partnership requires further premises. R's wife owns a suitable building which is currently vacant and in need of refurbishment. R's wife leases the building to R for 10 years for no premium and a peppercorn rent. In turn, R sub-lets the building to the partnership for 10 years at a market rent, but with the first year rent-free to reflect the cost of refurbishment which the partnership will incur.

If the transactions are regarded separately, no SDLT arises on the lease from R's wife to R, and SDLT will be chargeable on the partnership in respect of only 67% of the NPV of rents on the lease to the partnership: 33% of the NPV represents the interest effectively retained by R through his membership of the partnership (see **5.11** et seq for an explanation of this).

If the transactions are regarded as a series within *s 75A*, the notional transaction will be the grant of a lease at rent from R or R's wife (it does not matter which, for these purposes) to the partnership. The normal partnership rules will not apply, and the full NPV of rents under the lease to the partnership will be subject to SDLT. The SDLT cost will, therefore, be increased by the application of *s 75A*, even though there was no avoidance in the original series of transactions.

7.24 *Section 75C(5)* and *(10)* makes it clear that any apportionment of amounts for the purpose of measuring consideration on the notional transaction must be on a just and reasonable basis, and that any SDLT paid in respect of an actual transaction which is ignored under *s 75A* is to be treated as paid in respect of the notional transaction. This, therefore, should avoid any element of double charge. However, it is possible that *s 75A* could apply to more than one group of steps in a complex series of transactions. This could lead to more than one charge under *s 75A*, even where a 'simple' transfer of the property from the original vendor to the ultimate purchaser would only have led to a single charge.

SPECIFIC ANTI-AVOIDANCE RULES

Introduction

7.25 Many of the conditions surrounding reliefs or treatments could be regarded as anti-avoidance rules. Their purpose is to ensure that the relief or treatment is only available in the circumstances envisaged by the Government. Nonetheless, there are some specific rules which may be recognised as having been included to counter particular arrangements and may be properly regarded as anti-avoidance provisions. These specific rules are described at various points in this book, when dealing with the transactions or circumstances in which they may apply. For convenience, they are also listed below, with references. Some seek to attack specific structures which are considered to give rise to a tax advantage; others only apply if there is an avoidance motive. The rules apply whether or not the transaction is caught by *FA 2003 ss 75A–75C*; indeed, by denying a relief or treatment, the specific rules may ensure that the transaction is not within the terms of the general anti-avoidance rule.

Subject	**Description**	**Statute (*FA 2003*) or other reference**	**Reference in this book**
Sub-sale relief	Alternative contracts	*ss 44A, 45A*	**3.9**
Sale and leaseback relief	Not combined with other reliefs	*s 57A(3)(c), (d)*	**3.34**

Subject	Description	Statute (*FA 2003*) or other reference	Reference in this book
Group, reconstruction and acquisition reliefs	Motive test	*Sch 7, paras 2(4A), 7(5), 8(5B)*	**3.22**
	Arrangements	*Sch 7, paras 2, 8(4)*	**3.19**
	Clawback on leaving group	*Sch 7, paras 3, 4A*	**3.24**
	Clawback on change of control	*Sch 7, paras 9, 11*	**3.27**
	No combination with sub-sale relief	*s 45(5A)*	**3.10**
Alternative finance reliefs	Not combined with group or sub-sale relief	*s 73A* *s 45(3)*	**3.33** **3.10**
	Arrangements to change control of financial institution	*s 73AB*	**3.32**
Charities relief	Change of use from charitable	*Sch 8, para 2*	**3.43**
Partnerships	Arrangements to transfer	*Sch 15, para 17*	**5.27**
	Withdrawal of value after land transfer	*Sch 15, para 17A*	**5.17**
Trusts	Grant of lease to bare trustee	*Sch 16, para 3(4)*	**2.18**
Leases	Assignment of lease after relief claimed on grant	*Sch 17A, para 11*	**4.15**
	Loan or deposit in conjunction with grant	*Sch 17A, para 18A*	**4.44**
Building contracts	Separation of building and land contracts	*Prudential Assurance v CIR* [1992] STC 863	Example 2.6

SDLT AND DISCLOSURE OF TAX AVOIDANCE SCHEMES (DOTAS)

Introduction

7.26 *FA 2004, Pt 7* introduced obligations for the notification of schemes for the avoidance of direct tax (potentially including SDLT). The legislation sets out the nature of the obligations in general terms and states on whom they fall. The detailed application to most taxes was then laid out in the *Tax Avoidance Schemes (Information) Regulations 2004, SI 2004/1864*. SDLT was not initially in the list of taxes covered, but was added by the *Tax Avoidance Schemes (Information) (Amendment) Regulations 2005, SI 2005/1869*, with effect from 1 August 2005. The nature of SDLT schemes brought within the rules was set out in the *SDLT Avoidance Schemes (Prescribed Descriptions of Arrangements) Regulations 2005, SI 2005/1868*. As explained below, the rules for identifying notifiable SDLT schemes set out in these regulations are very different from the rules for other taxes.

7.27 It is important not to be misled by the title – the regime is not restricted to complex avoidance schemes, but may apply to the simplest modification to a transaction to reduce the tax cost. The parties to a transaction and anyone advising them may be required to make disclosure to HMRC in a very short timeframe. There are penalties for failure to comply. For many advisers, the original penalties were insignificant, but the stigma of being identified as non-compliant was regarded as worse than any financial penalty. *FA 2010, Sch 17* increased the maximum potential penalty to £1 million, which is likely to be significant to all advisers. Many firms of advisers have instituted systems and procedures to ensure rapid identification of obligations. However, such systems are worthless unless the individuals providing advice are vigilant and recognise occasions when the rules apply.

Application to SDLT

7.28 SDLT was brought within the DOTAS regime from 1 August 2005. From that date, the rules apply to prescribed arrangements where the property in question is not purely residential and has a value of £5 million or more. Residential property with a value of at least £1 million was then brought within the rules from 1 April 2010 by *SI 2010/407*. Note that mixed residential/non-residential property is within the rules if the total value is £5 million or more and/or if the residential element is £1 million or more.

Scheme reference numbers (SRNs)

7.29 As with other taxes, HMRC provide a scheme reference number (SRN) for each scheme disclosed (*FA 2004, s 311*). Prior to 1 April 2010, promoters of SDLT schemes were not obliged to notify users of the SRN, and users had no obligation to notify HMRC of the number of any scheme used. This was because HMRC's primary concern was to understand the nature of SDLT avoidance arrangements rather than to challenge specific schemes. However, it must be assumed that HMRC now feel sufficiently educated to challenge SDLT schemes. From 1 April 2010, as is the case with other taxes, the SDLT SRN must be provided to users and reported by them to HMRC, along with other information (*FA 2004, ss 312–313*). HMRC have provided a new form for this purpose at www.hmrc.gov.uk/aiu/form-aag4sdlt.pdf.

HMRC guidance

7.30 HMRC have provided general guidance on the application of the DOTAS rules. This may be found online at www.hmrc.gov.uk/avoidance/dotas-sdlt250210.pdf, or paper copies may be obtained from HMRC's publications department (see **Appendix A**). Some sections of this guidance do not apply to SDLT, and other sections apply only to SDLT.

Notifiable arrangements and proposals

7.31 A notifiable arrangement is any arrangement which:

(1) falls within the description set out in the regulations (*SI 2005/1868*); and

(2) might be expected to enable any person to obtain a tax advantage as a main benefit from the arrangement (*FA 2004, s 306(1)*).

This is a two-pronged test. The mere obtaining of a tax advantage does not make the arrangement notifiable – it must also fall within the description set out in the regulations. Equally, an arrangement which happens to fall within the description set out in the regulations, but which does not have a tax advantage as a main benefit, is not notifiable. However, in the light of the severe penalties for failure to notify under these rules, most advisers 'play safe' and make a disclosure in all uncertain cases.

7.32 A notifiable proposal is a proposal for arrangements which would be notifiable if entered into (*FA 2004, s 306(2)*).

No hallmarks

7.33 In relation to income, corporation and capital gains tax, notifiable arrangements are those which have certain characteristics, referred to as 'hallmarks'. For those taxes, an arrangement is not notifiable unless it has one or more of the hallmarks. The 'hallmarks' have no application in relation to SDLT. Rather, the rules operate the other way round. *All* arrangements relating to residential property worth £1 million or more, and/or non-residential or mixed property worth £5 million or more, are notifiable, unless they fall within certain exclusions set out in *SI 2005/1868*.

7.34 The exclusions are expressed in the form of six steps which the arrangement might involve, and two rules setting out which combinations of steps are acceptable. The order of the steps is no important. The steps are set out in the regulations as follows:

> '**Step A: Acquisition of a chargeable interest by special purpose vehicle**
>
> The acquisition of a chargeable interest in land by a company created for that purpose ("a special purpose vehicle").
>
> **Step B: Claims to relief**
>
> Making–
>
> (a) a single claim to relief under any of the following provisions of the Finance Act 2003–
>
> (i) section 57A (sale and leaseback arrangements);
>
> (ii) section 60 (compulsory purchase facilitating development);
>
> (iii) section 61 (compliance with planning obligation);
>
> (iv) section 64 (demutualisation of building society);
>
> (v) section 64A (initial transfer of assets to trustees of unit trust scheme) *(note: this relief was abolished by FA 2006 for transactions after 21 March 2006)*;
>
> (vi) section 65 (incorporation of limited liability partnership);
>
> (vii) section 66 (transfers involving public bodies);
>
> (viii) section 67 (transfer in consequence of reorganisation of parliamentary constituencies);
>
> (ix) section 69 (acquisition by bodies established for national purposes);
>
> (x) section 71 (certain acquisitions by registered social landlords);
>
> (xi) section 74 (collective enfranchisement by leaseholders);
>
> (xii) section 75 (crofting community right to buy);
>
> (xiii) Schedule 6 (disadvantaged areas relief);
>
> (xiv) Schedule 6A (relief for certain acquisitions of residential property);
>
> (xv) Schedule 7 (group relief and reconstruction acquisition reliefs);
>
> (xvi) Schedule 8 (charities relief); or
>
> (xvii) Schedule 9 (right to buy, shared ownership leases etc.);
>
> (b) one or more claims to relief under any one of the following provisions of the Finance Act 2003–

(i) section 71A (alternative property finance: land sold to financial institution and leased to individual);

(ii) section 72 (alternative property finance in Scotland: land sold to financial institution and leased to individual);

(iii) section 72A (alternative property finance in Scotland: land sold to financial institution and individual in common); or

(iv) section 73 (alternative property finance: land sold to financial institution and resold to individual).

Step C: Sale of shares in special purpose vehicle

The sale of shares in a special purpose vehicle, which holds a chargeable interest in land, to a person with whom neither the special purpose vehicle, nor the vendor, is connected.

Step D: Not exercising election to waive exemption from VAT

No election is made to waive exemption from value added tax contained in paragraph 2 of Schedule 10 to the Value Added Tax Act 1994 (treatment of buildings and land for value added tax purposes).

Step E: Transfer of a business as a going concern

Arranging the transfer of a business, connected with the land which is the subject of the arrangements, in such a way that it is treated for the purposes of value added tax as the transfer of a going concern.

Step F: Undertaking a joint venture

The creation of a partnership (within the meaning of paragraph 1 of Schedule 15 to the Finance Act 2003) to which the property subject to a land transaction is to be transferred.'

7.35 The two rules setting out which combinations are acceptable are as follows:

'**Rule 1**

Arrangements involving Steps B, D, E and F are excluded arrangements unless rule 2 applies.

Rule 2

Arrangements are not excluded arrangements if they–

(a) include all, or at least two of, steps A, C and D; or

(b) involve more than one instance of step A, C or D.'

7.36 It is important to bear in mind that these rules merely make certain transactions exempt. Any multi-step transaction involving any steps other than steps A to F listed above, where the unlisted step(s) are essential to obtain the SDLT advantage, *cannot* be exempt from disclosure, no matter what combination of listed steps it involves.

Example 7.6 – step not in list, notification required

Notax LLP, a firm of tax advisers, develops a scheme for SDLT-free acquisition of leasehold commercial buildings. The scheme involves the client setting up an SPV (not a listed step), the SPV entering into a joint venture with the vendor (Step F), the SPV acquiring an interest in the property (Step A), and a claim to group relief (Step B). Under the rules set out above in **7.35**, this includes only one instance of a step listed in rule 2, so the scheme should be exempt from notification. However, the scheme also involves a step which is not listed but is essential to obtaining the tax advantage – setting up an SPV – so the scheme is not exempt from notification. In practice, it seems that few real schemes will be exempt from notification under these rules.

Arrangements which are 'substantially the same'

7.37 Separate, different schemes must be disclosed separately. However, once a scheme has been disclosed, no further disclosure is needed if the same scheme is implemented again, whether for the same or different clients. Equally, if subsequent implementation involves only minor differences such that the two schemes are substantially the same, no further disclosure is required (*FA 2004, s 308(5)*). HMRC have provided some guidance as to when schemes may or may not be regarded as substantially the same, as follows:

> 'In our view a scheme is no longer substantially the same if the effect of any change would be to make any previous disclosure misleading in relation to the second (or subsequent) client.
>
> In general provided the tax analysis is substantially the same we will regard schemes as "substantially the same" where the only change is a different client including a different company in the same group.
>
> We will not regard schemes as substantially the same where there are changes to deal with changes in the law or accounting treatment, changes in the tax attributes e.g. schemes creating income losses instead of capital losses or other legal and commercial issues.' (DOTAS guidance, February 2010, p 68)

7.38 From 1 April 2010, arrangements are excluded from the need to disclose if they are the same, or substantially the same, as arrangements first made available for implementation before that date. Where such arrangements related to non-residential property, they should have been disclosed under the rules then in force; however, this concession means that, in relation to residential property, only novel or significantly changed schemes need be disclosed.

Example 7.7 – arrangements which are 'substantially the same'

Tax advisory firm Fiscality has developed an arrangement which allows a company to grant a lease to a fellow subsidiary at low SDLT cost, so there is no need to claim group relief and therefore no clawback if the lessee leaves the group. The arrangement requires the establishment of an orphan company registered overseas to hold an interest in the land as nominee. The arrangement was disclosed under the DOTAS rules before 1 April 2010, and was used by two separate clients of Fiscality. In December 2010, Fiscality concludes that using a nominee company established in a different overseas jurisdiction would make it easier to administer the arrangement without affecting the tax analysis. In the author's view, if the only change is to use a company established in a different jurisdiction purely for convenience, the new arrangement will be 'substantially the same' as the old arrangement and no new disclosure obligation will arise.

Shortly afterwards, Fiscality concludes that the tax analysis will be strengthened if the order of execution of two steps in the arrangement is reversed. This change will be sufficient to prevent the new arrangement from being 'substantially the same' as the old, and a new disclosure obligation will arise when the new version is 'made available for use' or, if earlier, when Fiscality first become aware of a transaction forming part of arrangements implementing the new version of the scheme (see **7.54**).

Promoters and introducers

7.39 *FA 2010, Sch 17* amends the provisions relating to identity and obligations of 'promoters', and introduces a new concept of 'introducers'. The amendments take effect from a date to be fixed by regulations. At the time of writing (September 2010), the regulations have not been issued. On the basis of past experience, issue of the regulations should be announced in the news section of the HMRC website at www.hmrc.gov.uk/so/news.htm. The following paragraphs are written on the assumption that the *FA 2010* amendments have been activated, but the sections affected by the amendments are in *italics* and indicated thus: #.

7.40 From the beginning, the primary obligations have fallen on 'promoters'. A promoter is a person who, in the course of a tax advisory, banking or securities house business and in relation to a notifiable arrangement or proposal:

(1) is to any extent responsible for the design of the proposed arrangements, or

(2) *# makes a 'firm approach' to another person with a view to making the proposal available for implementation by that person or anyone else, or*

(3) makes the proposal available for implementation by any person.

7.41 *# The second point was inserted by FA 2010, Sch 17 to ensure the responsibility net is spread as widely as possible. A firm approach is made if, at a time when the arrangements have been 'substantially designed', information about them, including an explanation of the tax advantages, is communicated to anyone with a view to entering into transactions forming part of the proposal. Arrangements are substantially designed if, at that time, the nature of the transactions is sufficiently developed for it to be reasonable to believe that someone would enter into them (or into transactions not substantially different from them) in order to obtain the expected tax advantage.*

7.42 Prior to *FA 2010*, the expression 'substantially designed' did not appear in the legislation, but HMRC relied on a similar concept to determine whether a scheme had been 'made available'. In the view of HMRC, a 'marketed scheme' (see **7.56**) is made available if it is communicated to a potential user in sufficient detail at a time when it 'has been developed to such a stage that the promoter has a high degree of confidence in the tax analysis applying to it' (Guidance, para 10.3.1). The rules are expressed in wide, all-inclusive terms, so that reporting obligations may arise at a very early stage.

7.43 The question of whether an arrangement is substantially designed or developed to such a stage etc is particularly unclear. In any case in which HMRC may allege that a promoter has failed to make timely disclosure, they may be expected to wish to see copies of emails, notes of telephone conversations and other similar evidence, to show the process by which the scheme was developed.

Example 7.8 – timing of obligations

Notax LLP is developing an arrangement which, they believe, will allow purchase of houses at much reduced SDLT cost. On 1 February 2011, Mark, a partner in Notax, attends a conference with leading tax counsel at which counsel advises that their technical analysis is generally sound. Counsel highlights areas needing some further attention, such as the country of incorporation of a new company required to execute the arrangement. On 2 February 2011, Judith, another partner in Notax who has not been involved in developing the proposal, calls business contact Kim at the local branch of estate agent Houseller plc to tell him about the wonderful tax wheeze her firm has just developed, and to encourage Kim to talk to suitable house purchasers about it with a view to introducing her firm to them. There is an agreement in place between Notax and Houseller under which commissions are paid for successful introductions. Kim is not a tax person, so Judith does not give him any technical details, but she does outline the general steps required and explains that, if successful, the arrangement would reduce the SDLT cost of house purchase to less than one tenth of what it would otherwise be.

It is almost certain that Judith has fallen within paragraph (2) above and has triggered Notax LLP's disclosure obligations on 2 February 2011. It does not matter that Judith has given no technical details, or that she personally was not involved in developing the arrangement because, in the eyes of HMRC, Notax LLP as an entity is carrying on a tax advisory business and is the promoter.

7.44 *# A person is an introducer if he makes a marketing contact with another person in relation to a notifiable proposal. A marketing contact is made if the first person communicates information about the proposal to the second person, including an explanation of the expected tax advantage, with a view to anyone entering into the proposed arrangements. An introducer, provided he is not also a promoter, has no direct disclosure responsibilities, but may be required by HMRC to pass on to them such information as he has about the scheme.*

Example 7.9 – an 'introducer'

 # In Example 7.8, Kim immediately calls customer Irena who is negotiating to buy a UK house for about £2 million. He passes on the outline information received from Judith, and asks Irena to think about talking to Notax LLP. Kim is not working for or as a tax adviser or a bank or securities house, so neither he nor Houseller can be a promoter. However, since Houseller stands to earn commission from the introduction, this is undoubtedly a 'marketing contact'. Therefore, Houseller is an introducer.

Example 7.10 – no obligations

Following on from the previous example, Irena (who works for an advertising agency) mentions the Notax scheme to a colleague who is also about to buy an expensive house, passing on the contact details for Notax. Neither Irena nor her employer is carrying on a business as a tax adviser or a bank or securities house. Therefore, Irena cannot be acting as a promoter. # *This is a casual discussion with a colleague – Irena does not stand to make any financial gain from passing the information on to her colleague. Therefore, this is unlikely to be a marketing contact, and neither Irena nor her employer should be regarded as acting as an introducer.*

Who is not a promoter?

7.45 A person who is only involved in the design of a scheme, and is not in any way involved in implementation or organising or managing implementation, is not a promoter if:

- his input is benign – that is, the advice he gives does not contribute to the tax-saving aspect of the scheme (for example, advice as to whether a particular shareholding arrangement permitted a claim to group relief would be benign, but advice as to how to change the arrangement in order to qualify for group relief would not be benign), or
- he is not acting as a tax adviser – for example, an unrelated lawyer consulted only on the company law implications of a proposal would not be acting as a tax adviser, or
- he could not reasonably be expected to have sufficient information to know whether there is a disclosable scheme, or to be able to make that disclosure – for example, a newly appointed tax adviser might ask the outgoing tax adviser for an opinion on the implications of a proposed action (in the light of previous transactions) and the new adviser might use that advice in devising a notifiable proposal. However, if the outgoing adviser is not given any details of the proposal, he probably could not reasonably be expected to have sufficient information to know whether there is a disclosable proposal or to make disclosure.

7.46 A person who acts purely as an intermediary or introducer, without being involved in design, implementation or management of implementation, is not a promoter (but HMRC may demand information from such a person when the changes in *FA 2010, Sch 17* are activated; see **7.44**).

Co-promoters

7.47 If two or more persons are promoters in relation to the same (or substantially the same) proposal or arrangement, it is possible for only one disclosure to be made, and for this to be made by one of them. Provided:

(1) the other promoter holds or is provided with the information disclosed to HMRC,

(2) the disclosing promoter provides HMRC with a note of the name and address of the other promoter, and

(3) (if the co-promoter becomes a co-promoter after initial disclosure has been made) the disclosing promoter provides the other promoter with a note of the SRN,

the co-promoter is exempt from making disclosure. Where the proposal or arrangement made by the co-promoter is not identical with that disclosed, it is for the co-promoter to decide whether it is sufficiently similar for the exemption to apply. Co-promoters are not exempt from other obligations, such as providing their client with SRNs.

Overseas promoters

7.48 In principle, the DOTAS rules apply to a promoter resident outside the UK. However, in practice it may be difficult for HMRC to enforce compliance, especially where the promoter is not carrying on business through a UK permanent establishment. If no promoter is resident in the UK, and the overseas promoter does not comply with DOTAS obligations, the obligations fall instead on any person (the 'client') who enters into any transaction forming part of the arrangements. Note that the obligations fall on 'any person who enters into any transaction …', which therefore includes the vendor, even though any tax advantage will normally accrue to the purchaser. A vendor who does not know about any arrangements which the vendor may be implementing cannot be faulted for failing to disclose them. However, it is common for a vendor to know at least something of the purchaser's arrangements, so this is a matter over which vendors must take care.

These disclosure obligations are removed from the client(s) if a promoter complies with them.

Arrangements with no promoter

7.49 If a person enters into a transaction forming part of notifiable arrangements in relation to which there is no promoter (for example, a scheme which the taxpayer has developed himself), that person has responsibility for making an appropriate disclosure. This includes the situation where a scheme is devised by one company in a group and used by another in the same group. The group company devising the scheme is not regarded as a promoter but the company using the scheme must make disclosure.

Promoters with the benefit of legal privilege

7.50 In some circumstances, promoters who are lawyers may be able to resist providing some of the information required under DOTAS, on the grounds that the information is subject to legal privilege. If this happens, any user of the scheme is required to make the same disclosure as would be required if there was no promoter (see previous paragraph). However, as noted at **7.60**, the time limit for making disclosure is five days and not the 30 days which applies for 'in-house' schemes.

Duties of promoters

7.51 Promoters (or persons entering into a transaction if there is no promoter, or if there is no promoter in the UK and no overseas promoter complies with DOTAS):

- must provide HMRC with certain prescribed information (see **7.61** et seq), and
- must do this within the prescribed period after the relevant date (see **7.60**).

Promoters must make the disclosure by completing and submitting form AAG1, which may be downloaded for manual completion or completed and submitted online, as noted at **7.53**. In response to this, HMRC will normally provide a scheme reference number (SRN). The promoter must notify the SRN to any person to whom he is providing services in relation to the scheme, or any scheme which is substantially the same (see **7.37**). This notification must be made on form AAG6 (SDLT), available from the HMRC publications and forms address (see **Appendix A**) or downloadable from www.hmrc.gov.uk/aiu/aag6_sdlt.pdf. Note that this form is SDLT specific, and differs from the equivalent form used for other taxes. The number must be passed on within 30 days of the later of:

- the promoter first becoming aware of any transaction which forms part of the arrangements, and
- HMRC notifying the promoter of the SRN.

7.52 As noted above, the requirement to notify the SRN for SDLT schemes to the client was new from 1 April 2010.

Duties of scheme users

7.53 Also from 1 April 2010, obligations were imposed on users of SDLT schemes and others to whom an SRN is notified. Anyone who is notified of an SRN is now required to report their use of the scheme to HMRC, quoting the SRN. Some SDLT schemes operate by taking the transaction out of the charge so that, if the scheme works, there is no obligation to submit an SDLT return; in any case, the SDLT return has no space to report an SRN. To ensure relevant details are captured, HMRC have provided a new SDLT-specific version of form AAG4 (form AAG4 (SDLT)) for scheme users to report details. This may be ordered from HMRC's publications department or downloaded from www.hmrc.gov.uk/aiu/form-aag4sdlt.pdf. Alternatively, the form may be completed and submitted online via a link at www.hmrc.gov.uk/aiu/forms-tax-schemes.htm. Use of this form is now compulsory in all cases.

7.54 Anyone to whom an SRN is provided is also required to notify it to anyone else they reasonably expect to be a party to, and to gain a tax advantage from, implementation of the scheme, using form AAG6 (SDLT), as noted at **7.51**. This must be done within 30 days of the later of:

- first becoming aware of any transaction which forms part of the arrangements, and
- receiving notification of the SRN.

Time for disclosure – promoters

7.55 The rules relating to timing of disclosure by promoters are the same as for other taxes. A scheme promoter is required to make disclosure within five days (excluding weekends and bank holidays) of the 'relevant date'. The relevant date is the earlier of the date on which the notifiable proposal is 'made available for use', and the date on which the promoter first becomes aware of any transaction forming part of arrangements implementing the proposal.

7.56 The legislation does not state when a proposal is regarded as 'made available for use'. The HMRC guidance draws a distinction between bespoke and marketed schemes. A marketed scheme – that is, one which is developed for possible use by a range or category of users – is made available when it:

- has been developed to such a stage that the promoter has a high degree of confidence in the tax analysis applying to it; and
- is communicated to the first potential user in sufficient detail that he could be expected to:
  - understand the expected tax advantages; and
  - decide whether or not to enter into it.

HMRC accept that, where a firm of advisers has an internal approval process, a proposal will not normally be regarded as made available before that approval has been given.

7.57 In contrast with this, a bespoke scheme – that is, one which is designed for a specific client's situation – is not generally regarded as being 'made available'. For such a scheme, the relevant date will therefore be the date on which the promoter first becomes aware of any transaction forming part of the arrangements. There is a danger here where more than one individual in a firm of advisers has contact with the client; if the first individual to learn that a transaction has been implemented does not understand the significance of this, the five-day deadline may easily be missed.

7.58 Occasionally, an adviser may outline a partially developed planning idea to a client, in such general terms that no proposal can yet be regarded as made available for use. The client may then do further development work and proceed to implement its own version of the arrangement without further reference to the adviser. It might be thought that, in this situation, the adviser has not made a notifiable proposal and has no disclosure obligations. However, even here the legislation seeks to impose obligations on the adviser. Having provided the basic idea, the adviser is likely to be regarded as 'to any extent responsible for the design of the proposed arrangements' and therefore a promoter. If no disclosure of the proposal has previously been made, the adviser is required to make disclosure within five days of first becoming aware of any transaction forming part of the notifiable arrangements. It is very difficult to be sure of capturing such information – good communications with clients and robust internal systems are essential!

Time for disclosure and other notification – scheme users

7.59 As noted at **7.29**, the general requirement for users to notify use of SDLT schemes was introduced in April 2010. The rules governing timing of this notification are *not* the same as for other taxes. The differences mirror the tight timetable for submission of SDLT returns. The deadlines are as set out below. Guidance on the nature and content of the various forms is provided below.

Forms for disclosure and notification

7.60

Form	**Responsible person**	**Reason**	**Deadline for receipt by HMRC or other party**
AAG1	Promoter	Disclosing scheme	5 days from making available or becoming aware of first transaction in scheme
Submission of AAG2	User	Disclosing scheme from overseas promoter, no other disclosure made	5 days from entering into first transaction in scheme
Submission of AAG3	User	Disclosing scheme from lawyer claiming legal professional privilege	5 days from entering into first transaction in scheme

Form	Responsible person	Reason	Deadline for receipt by HMRC or other party
Submission of AAG3	User	Disclosing internally developed scheme, no external promoter	30 days from entering into first transaction in scheme
AAG4 (SDLT)	User	Notifying use of scheme with UK promoter (or overseas promoter who complies with disclosure requirement)	30 days from later of receipt of SRN and effective date of first transaction in scheme
Giving form AAG6 (SDLT) to others involved	Promoter and user	Informing other users of SRN	30 days from later of receiving SRN and becoming aware of first transaction in scheme

Content of disclosure

7.61 The forms noted above prescribe the information to be provided. The forms are reproduced at **Appendix B**. Paper copies may be ordered from the HMRC publications department (see **Appendix A**). Alternatively, PDF versions (for manual completion and posting) may be downloaded, or the forms may be completed and submitted online, via links at www.hmrc.gov.uk/aiu/forms-tax-schemes.htm. Most of the forms are the same as those used for disclosure of other direct tax schemes, but there are SDLT-specific versions of forms AAG4 and AAG6. Most of the entries required on the forms are self-explanatory, and help on completion is available, if needed, in the HMRC guide mentioned at **7.30**.

7.62 The only sections of the forms which commonly cause difficulty are those in forms AAG1 to AAG3 relating to the description and explanation of the scheme. HMRC guidance (Guidance on DOTAS, para 11.3.4) on this subject is as follows:

> 'Sufficient information is required to be provided such that an Officer of the Board of HMRC is able to understand how the expected tax advantage is intended to arise. The explanation should be in straightforward terms and should identify the steps involved and the relevant UK tax law. Common technical or legal terms and concepts need not be explained in depth.
>
> If the scheme is complex then copies of any prospectus or scheme diagrams will help us understand what is proposed but even where you send such documents you must still use form AAG 1. Where such documents are supplied there is no objection to these documents excluding information that would identify a client.'

7.63 Each form has a separate section for identification of relevant statutory provisions, but in the author's view it is also likely to be necessary to refer to appropriate sections of legislation in the body of any description and explanation.

New requirement to notify HMRC of users

7.64 *# Under FA 2004, s 313ZA, inserted by FA 2010, Sch 17, a promoter who provides services to a client in connection with the arrangements will be required to give information about the client to HMRC. This requirement will be activated by regulations which have not yet been issued at the date of writing (September 2010). The regulations will specify the information which the promoter must provide. The deadline will be the same as the deadline for notifying the client of the scheme reference number (SRN).*

Example 7.11 – details to be disclosed

The following is an example of the level of detail which may be appropriate in describing/ explaining a scheme. There is no suggestion that what follows is a description of a scheme which is currently or has previously been valid or effective!

Title of arrangement: Partner retirement plan

Explanation:

(1) This arrangement permits a partner to withdraw from a property-investment partnership and a new partner to join the partnership at reduced SDLT cost.

(2) Statutory references are to Finance Act 2003.

(3) ABC is a property-investment partnership as defined in Schedule 15 para 14(8), established in [overseas territory]. The partners are A, B and C who are all individuals and otherwise unconnected and who share equally in the profits and capital of the partnership. Although the majority of ABC's assets are chargeable interests (none of which was acquired from a partner or person connected with a partner), substantial other assets are held including property assets situated overseas.

(4) A wishes to retire and will withdraw value equal to his 33% share in the partnership capital; it is proposed to admit D, another individual who is not connected with A, B or C. D will contribute cash to secure a 33% share in the capital of the partnership.

(5) The partnership deed will be amended to specify that individual partners' shares entitle them to share in the economic value of specific assets. As a result, A's share will entitle him to share in the economic value of the overseas assets and a one-third share in just one chargeable asset; the shares of the other partners will entitle them to share in the economic value of the remaining chargeable assets plus a smaller share in the values of the non-chargeable assets. The values will be such that the overall partnership share of each partner will be unchanged. Appropriate legal advice has been obtained confirming that such subdivision is effective under the law of [overseas territory]. Copies of the current deed and draft amendment are available for inspection if required.

(6) The partnership will use a combination of cash already held and cash borrowed from a bank under an existing overdraft facility to pay A the value of his partnership share.

(7) D will contribute cash on admission to the partnership and will become entitled to the interests in assets relinquished by A.

Analysis:

(8) The division of assets into categories and subdivision of partnership interests will not affect any partner's partnership share as defined by Schedule 15 paragraph 34(2); therefore it will have no SDLT consequences.

(9) The withdrawal of A and admission of D will be a Category A Transfer of partnership interest as defined in Schedule 15 paragraph 14(3B). However the only relevant partnership property as defined in Schedule 15 paragraph 14(5) is the one UK property in which A has an economic interest. SDLT will be chargeable accordingly by reference to 33% of the market value of that property alone, in accordance with Schedule 15 paragraph 14(6) & (7).

Statutory provisions:

Finance Act 2003 Schedule 15 paragraphs 14(3B), (5)(c), (6), (7) and 34(2).

Information powers

7.65 If HMRC suspect that a scheme has not been disclosed, they are entitled to require anyone they suspect of being a promoter to formally state whether they consider a scheme to be disclosable and, if not, why not. The notice from HMRC will give a time by which a reply must be given – potentially, as short as ten days later – and penalties may be imposed for non-compliance. Beyond that, there are powers to require information to be given, but these generally require an order of the Tax Tribunal. These situations are beyond the scope of this book.

Penalties

7.66 The Tax Tribunal may impose penalties for failure to disclose a notifiable proposal or arrangement or for late disclosure, and for failure to comply with orders requiring disclosure or provision of information. The amount of the penalty may be up to £5,000, plus further amounts of up to £600 (or, in some cases, £5,000) for each day during which the failure continues. Any person in danger of suffering such penalties will doubtless require specialist advice beyond the scope of this book.

Chapter 8

Stamp Duty – General Rules

INTRODUCTION

8.1 The last comprehensive consolidation of stamp duty legislation was in the *Stamp Act 1891 (SA 1891)* and the *Stamp Duty Management Act 1891*. Unsurprisingly, the law has changed massively since then. The main changes have been to remove particular assets or transactions from the charge, so that *SA 1891, Sch 1*, which originally defined the scope of the tax, is now largely irrelevant. However, the principles set out in the body of *SA 1891* still apply, some sections of that Act having been amended by 21st-century *Finance Acts*.

Subsequent stamp duty legislation is scattered across more than a century of *Finance Acts*. Specific exemptions often appear in other legislation (for example, an exemption for transfers in the privatisation of rail services; see *Railways Act 1993, s 112* and *Sch 9*). For this reason, when dealing with Government-sponsored transactions, it is usually worth checking enabling legislation for exemptions. However, for most transactions the key legislation is found in *FA 1986, ss 66–85*, *FA 1999, Sch 13* and *FA 2003, ss 125* and *195*.

8.2 Since 1 December 2003, stamp duty has been chargeable only on transactions in stock and marketable securities, and Transfers of interests in partnerships with stock or marketable securities amongst their assets. (In this book, the expression 'Transfer' is capitalised to make it clear that this is a reference to the potentially stampable document.) The restriction to stock and marketable securities is in *FA 2003, s 125*; however, the charge on Transfers of partnership interests is then reinstated by *FA 2003, Sch 15, paras 31–33*. The latter provision was something of a 'last minute' amendment, when it was realised that it might otherwise be possible to escape stamp duty on Transfers of securities by first contributing them to a partnership, then transferring the interests in the partnership. It is doubtful whether the charge on partnership interests has any significant practical effect. The application to partnerships is considered at **8.55**; the imposition of stamp duty on certain *issues* of securities is dealt with at **8.53**. The following paragraphs deal primarily with the application of stamp duty to Transfers of stock and marketable securities.

8.3 Although, in principle, stamp duty is chargeable on Transfers of a wide range of shares and securities, in practice the transfer of most debts is exempted by either the 'loan capital exemption' or the 'non-marketable debenture' exemption (see **8.16–8.17**). Transfers of units in unit trusts are outside the scope of stamp duty, but are instead subject to a special SDRT regime (see **10.30**).

8.4 There is no direct compulsion to pay stamp duty on Transfers – enforcement is indirect, arising from the fact that a stampable document cannot be used to register title or as evidence in a civil court unless duly stamped (*SA 1891, ss 14, 17*). It is sometimes asserted that a document which ought to be stamped but has not been stamped is not legally valid. This is not true. The problem is simply that the document cannot be used as evidence. So, in many cases, if sufficient evidence of the terms of a contract can be adduced without reference to any (stampable) document, it should be possible to enlist the help of the courts in enforcing the contract, even if no stamp duty has been paid. This principle was widely relied on when stamp duty applied to transfers of assets such as goodwill, when contracts were entered into on the basis of oral agreements and conduct (see **11.30**).

In most cases, the legislation does not specify who should pay stamp duty (the exception is an agreement for sale of an equitable interest); but, in practice, the purchaser/ transferee will normally pay or arrange stamping in order to cancel any SDRT charge (see **10.11**) and to be able to register ownership of the asset.

SCOPE – DOCUMENTS

Stamp duty on Transfers

8.5 A 'Transfer' is a document (the legislation used to refer to 'conveyance or transfer', but it seems to be thought that 'conveyance' should be reserved for land transactions, so references to that word were largely removed from the stamp duty legislation by *FA 2003*). The concept of a Transfer is bound up with the separation in English law between legal and beneficial ownership. Under English law, parties may agree to buy and sell an asset; they may take actions, such as payment of consideration and perhaps physically handing over the asset, to give effect to the agreement. However, for certain assets such as land and shares, this is not sufficient to complete the process. At this point, the purchaser may have some form of beneficial ownership of the asset, but he does not have legal title. He only gains legal title when all steps to perfect the transfer of title, as required by law, have been completed – and, in the case of UK shares held in certificated form, this includes execution of an appropriate Transfer document. (A different process applies to shares held in dematerialised form, such as quoted shares held in CREST – see **10.20** for further details.)

8.6 In the UK, the most common form of share Transfer is a stock transfer form. However, other documents may also function as Transfers. In particular, a document under which the registered owner of legal title acknowledges that he holds as trustee or nominee for someone else – a 'declaration of trust' – can function as a Transfer (see **8.13** and Example 9.3).

Restricted to Transfers on sale

8.7 Stamp duty is currently payable only if the Transfer is 'on sale' (*FA 1999, Sch 13, para 1*) – that is, there is valuable consideration which counts for stamp duty purposes. A Transfer for no consideration (eg a gift) used to be subject to a fixed £5 stamp duty charge, which could sometimes be escaped by completing a certificate on the form. But, in a welcome piece of administrative simplification, *FA 2008, Sch 32* abolished the fixed £5 charge for Transfers completed on or after 13 March 2008. From that date, such a Transfer is simply not liable. There is no requirement to complete any certificate and the Transfer is deemed to be 'duly stamped' as soon as it is executed.

Small transaction exemption

8.8 At the same time, the main charging provision in *FA 1999, Sch 13, para 1* was amended by *FA 2008, s 98*, to remove the stamp duty charge where consideration does not exceed £1,000. If an appropriate certificate is added to the Transfer, the document does not require stamping or submission to the Stamp Office – a significant reduction in administrative hassle. However, if there are other linked transactions, it is only possible to certify if the *total* consideration for all relevant assets transferred in the same transaction or set of linked transactions does not exceed £1,000.

8.9 In arriving at the total consideration, it is only necessary to take account of types of consideration which 'count' for stamp duty purposes (see **8.24**). It is also possible to leave out of account any consideration attributed on a just and reasonable basis to 'goods, wares or merchandise' (such as stock in trade of a retail business), intellectual property or goodwill, provided the Transfer itself does not also act to transfer those assets. It would be unusual for a share Transfer to also transfer other assets, but this is a point where care may be needed in drafting documents (STM4.16 et seq).

However, amounts allocated to some other assets, especially debts and other financial assets, cannot be left out of account, even though no stamp duty will be chargeable in respect of them. Therefore, where there are such assets, a stock transfer form or other document transferring shares with a value below £1,000 may not qualify for certification, simply because the value of other relevant assets transferred under the same agreement take the total over £1,000.

8.10 Current prints of commercially produced stock transfer forms are usually pre-printed with a suitable certificate, merely requiring a 'X' in the appropriate box before signature. It is HMRC's view that:

(1) the certificate should be an integral part of the Transfer, not on a separate piece of paper (STM4.9) (it is not clear what should be done if there is simply no space on the transfer document to insert a certificate), and

(2) if the certificate is added after execution of the Transfer, it should be signed on behalf of all parties to the Transfer (STM4.14). Signature on behalf of the vendor is considered the more important and, in practice, such documents are not always signed by the purchaser.

8.11 Where a pre-printed certificate is not present, the following wording would be appropriate:

> 'The transaction effected by this instrument does not form part of a larger transaction or series of transactions in respect of which the amount or value, or aggregate amount or value, of the consideration exceeds £1,000.'

Example 8.1 – consideration below £1,000

Ian transfers to Joan the assets of his business trading under the name Tidy Gardens and comprising 100 shares in Tidy Gardens (Mudfield) Ltd (a company set up purely for name protection purposes), various loose tools and garden supplies, and a memory stick containing technical information such as details of plants which do well in local areas plus customer and contacts lists. Joan pays consideration of £10,000 with an agreed (and just and reasonable) allocation of £5,500 to tools and garden supplies, £4,400 to the memory stick and £100 to the shares. The tools, garden supplies and memory stick should all be regarded as 'goods, wares and merchandise' and may be ignored in assessing consideration for the overall transaction, which is therefore £100. Provided the stock transfer form transferring the shares contains the certificate of value set out above, no stamp duty will be payable on it and there will be no need to submit it to the Stamp Office.

Part of the amount allocated to the memory stick may be for goodwill and intellectual property, but the provisions which abolished stamp duty on these assets also provided for them to be left out of account in determining the overall level of consideration (*FA 2000, Sch 34, para 4*; *FA 2002, Sch 37, para 3*). However, if the assets had included, say, £1,200 of customer debts, the allocated consideration for which was agreed at £901, this would not be left out of account, even though no stamp duty would be due on the transfer of the debts themselves. The total consideration would then be £1,001 (£901 + £100) and it would not be possible to add a certificate of value. Stamp duty of 0.5% of £100, rounded up to £5, would be due in respect of the consideration correctly allocated to the share Transfer.

Sub-sales and successive transfers

8.12 Sometimes, perhaps most commonly in the course of a reorganisation, there is a need to transfer ownership of shares and securities several times in succession. In the interests of speed and efficiency, the parties may wish to rely on agreements for each transfer except the last, and then to execute a single Transfer of shares from the original owner to the final transferee. This is commonly referred to as a sub-sale. Provided the consideration paid by the final transferee is at least equal to the market value of the shares and securities, the Transfer will be liable to stamp duty only on that consideration. No stamp duty will be payable on the consideration paid by other parties under earlier agreements in the chain (*SA 1891, s 58(4)*).

However, if the shares and securities are within the charge to SDRT, any SDRT liability arising on those earlier agreements will remain chargeable, because no Transfer will be stamped in respect of those steps in order to cancel the SDRT (see **10.11** for further details). It will often be the case that the stamp duty charge on a transfer for some or all of the intermediate steps would be less than the SDRT charge, most commonly because a relief such as group relief (see **9.9**) could be claimed. Many reliefs apply only to stamp duty and not to SDRT. *In such a case, the sub-sale route should not be used.* Instead, a Transfer should be executed for each step in the series, and each Transfer should then be stamped.

8.13 Execution of a stock transfer form for each step may not be convenient, perhaps because it is considered that each such form should be stamped and registered before the next is executed. In that case, it may be simpler for the parties to execute a declaration of trust to act as the Transfer for each step, and to submit all of the declarations for stamping together. In this regard, see Example 9.3.

SCOPE – ASSETS

8.14 The legislative definitions of 'stock' and 'marketable security' are in *SA 1891, s 122*. They are not wholly enlightening, and the meaning of these terms is partly determined by judicial precedents, some of which are similarly ancient and difficult to interpret. The precise definition is not usually too important in practice, because most debt instruments which may fall within the definition are exempted under the 'loan capital' exemption (see next paragraph).

'Stock' includes shares (equity) of companies (UK and overseas) but also other 'instruments of a capital nature' issued by UK and overseas national and local Government and by companies and societies. This includes many debentures and may include instruments issued by incorporated partnerships such as UK LLPs. In many cases, such stock will also be a security.

The term 'security' encompasses a wide range of instruments evidencing indebtedness. 'Marketable' is defined by statute as meaning capable of being sold on any stock market in the UK. This is considered to exclude securities issued by UK private companies, partnerships and individuals and many overseas entities, which are therefore automatically outside the scope of stamp duty unless they also fall within the definition of stock.

Exempt loan capital

8.15 Although many debt instruments issued by companies, Governments and other organisations are within the definition of 'stock and marketable securities', they are mostly removed from the scope of stamp duty by the loan capital exemption in *FA 1986, ss 78–79*. For these purposes, loan capital includes:

- all Government stock and marketable securities,
- debt instruments or any other borrowed capital of companies,
- capital raised as 'alternative finance investment bonds' within *FA 2005, s 48A*, and
- loan capital raised by certain international organisations.

The last of these is completely exempt from stamp duty on transfer.

8.16 All other loan capital is exempt from stamp duty on transfer (*FA 1986, s 79(4)*) unless it has equity-like characteristics, such as rights to:

(1) conversion into shares or other securities,

(2) receipt of further or other shares or securities,

(3) interest which is dependent on the results of a business or the value of other assets,

(4) interest at a rate greater than a reasonable commercial return, or

(5) repayment at a premium greater than that generally available on similar quoted securities.

Point (3) is disapplied in relation to wholly commercial 'capital market' loans (so-called 'ratchet loans'), where the interest rate increases if business results worsen or decreases if they improve, or where interest reduces if the borrower does not have funds to pay.

Points (3) and (5) are disapplied if the interest and/or amount repayable vary in accordance with the UK Retail Price Index or Consumer Price Index.

Point (4) has led to dispute with HMRC in relation to so-called 'junk bonds', which carry a high interest rate to reflect greater risk; but HMRC have generally accepted that these are at a commercial rate where comparable publicly issued bonds have been identified.

Point (4) is disapplied in relation to alternative finance investment bonds (often referred to as Islamic bonds), and point (5) is modified to require that the total amount repaid should not exceed the amount originally subscribed plus a reasonable commercial return.

The risk of loan securities failing to qualify as exempt loan capital is considered in more detail at **11.3**. Care is needed when dealing with debt instruments which are not plain vanilla loans at interest.

Other financial assets outside the scope

8.17 Some debt instruments may not be loan capital, perhaps because they are too short term to be regarded as capital, or perhaps because they arise other than through the borrowing of money. Such instruments are unlikely to be stock and, in many cases, they will not be marketable and so will automatically fall outside the scope of stamp duty. Any which are marketable will often be exempt by virtue of *FA 1999, Sch 13, para 25(a)* because they are debentures. Overall, it is highly unlikely that a straightforward debt instrument bearing a commercial rate of interest will be within the stamp duty charge.

8.18 Transfers to recognised investment exchanges, clearing houses etc, are exempt, if the exchange or clearing house has entered into an appropriate arrangement with HMRC. This exemption was introduced specifically to facilitate reforms to the securities markets, and is not considered further in this book.

SCOPE – GEOGRAPHICAL

8.19 Stamp duty was introduced when Britain thought it ruled the world and, in principle, there is no territorial limit to the application of the tax. The lack of direct enforcement provisions means that this can be ignored for completely non-UK transactions. However, in theory at least, any document with a sufficient connection with the UK can be subject to stamp duty. In this regard, the scope is effectively defined by *SA 1891, s 14* as covering any document executed in the UK, or transferring any property located in the UK, or relating to any matter or thing to be done in the UK. For these purposes, shares of UK incorporated companies and shares of foreign companies which are recorded on a share register located in the UK are regarded as located in the UK.

8.20 As a general principle, a document is executed where the last action occurs to make it legally valid/effective – usually addition of a signature but, in the case of documents signed in escrow, it may be satisfaction of the escrow conditions followed by dating and release on behalf of the signatory.

8.21 The idea of any matter or thing to be done in the UK is very wide, and might include the payment of sale proceeds out of a UK bank account, for example (see *Faber v IRC* [1936] 1 All ER 617; *IRC v Maple & Co (Paris) Ltd* [1908] AC 22). So, in theory, a document transferring German shares from a French person to a Dutch person can be subject to UK stamp duty if signed in the UK, or even possibly if signed in Italy but paid for out of a UK bank account. Given the lack of enforceability, in most such cases stamp duty can safely be ignored. However, the existence of a theoretical but unenforceable liability can be difficult to explain to clients, and administrative difficulty can arise in multinational transactions involving both UK and overseas share transfers. HMRC do not appear to understand the point clearly – for example, the author has experience of the Stamp Office trying to reject a composite claim for group relief which included transfers of overseas shares because 'stamp duty is not payable on overseas shares'. This is, therefore, a piece of legislative nonsense well past its sensible abolition date.

CALCULATING THE CHARGE

Rates

8.22 For Transfers of stock and marketable securities, the normal rate of stamp duty is 0.5% of the amount or value of the consideration for the Transfer (*FA 1999, Sch 13, para 3*). A higher rate of 1.5% applies to certain transactions (see **8.53**). If application of the rate does not produce a precise multiple of £5, the charge is rounded up to the next £5 above (*FA 1999, s 112*). Restricting charges to multiples of £5 allows the stamping machines to be simpler than if they had to deal with lower denominations of duty; it also provides a small but useful increase in the tax take. The exemption for small transactions (consideration not exceeding £1,000) is mentioned at **8.8**, but apart from that, there is no 'zero rate band' and no variation in rate with consideration.

8.23 In principle, Transfers of interests in partnerships owning stock and marketable securities are subject to stamp duty at rates of up to 4%, depending on the amount of consideration. However, in practice, it is unlikely that such high rates would apply – see the explanation at **8.55**.

Consideration

8.24 In general, stamp duty is charged on the actual consideration given for a Transfer, irrespective of the value of the asset transferred. This principle is modified in some cases where the transfer is in satisfaction of a debt (see **8.32**). Only cash, securities, debt and the assumption, satisfaction or release of a pecuniary liability count as consideration. This is HMRC's long-established interpretation of words now in *FA 1999, Sch 13, para 2*: 'the amount or value of the consideration for the sale'; see STM1.11 for example. This contrasts with both SDRT and SDLT, where tax is chargeable by reference to any consideration 'in money or money's worth'. However, if relying on the restricted definition of consideration to escape or minimise stamp duty, care is needed in the wording of agreements, as shown in the examples below.

Example 8.2 – consideration which does not count

Pauline agrees to transfer her shares in Big plc, worth £1 million, to Robert in return for his collection of rare gemstones of similar value. The gemstones are not 'consideration' for stamp duty purposes. A stock transfer form may be completed showing 'nil' consideration. No stamp duty arises and there is no need for the document to be submitted to the Stamp Office for stamping.

Example 8.3 – satisfaction of a debt

Meanwhile, in an unrelated transaction, Pauline agrees to buy Sara's 100% shareholding in Tacky Ltd, an online jewellery retailer, for £1 on condition that Pauline also pays off Tacky's bank overdraft of £500,000 (thus releasing Sara from the guarantee she provided to the bank). The consideration for the Transfer of shares in Tacky is £500,001, and stamp duty at 0.5% rounded to the next £5 above is £2,505.

Example 8.4 – specified monetary value

The facts are as in Example 8.2 above, except that the agreement specifies that the consideration for the share transfer is £1 million, to be satisfied by transfer of the collection of gemstones. Although it may be subject to dispute, HMRC are likely to consider that stamp duty is payable on consideration of £1 million. This is on the grounds that the agreement creates a debt of £1 million (so the Transfer is for a debt) which is then satisfied by transfer of the gemstones.

When is a debt assumed?

8.25 The mere fact that a target company has outstanding debts does not mean that these debts are added to the consideration paid for the company. In Example 8.3 above, Pauline's agreement to pay off a debt counts as consideration. However, the debt is owed by Tacky Ltd, and Sara requires it to be paid off only because she needs to be released from her guarantee to the bank. Were it not for this, she might be happy to sell the shares leaving the debt in place, in which case the consideration would be £1 and it would be possible to certify the Transfer as a small transaction with no stamp duty liability.

8.26 Alternatively, if the debt must be paid off, it may be that a similar economic effect could be achieved without stamp duty cost. For example, Pauline could subscribe for further shares in Tacky Ltd, allowing Tacky Ltd itself to pay off the debt. No stamp duty should arise on the subscription. Other alternatives are less clear-cut – for example, Pauline might agree to ensure that Tacky Ltd pays off the debt. It may be open to dispute whether this amounts to the giving of consideration. Great care is needed in the wording of documents in such cases, and further specialist advice should be sought.

8.27 Shares are sometimes issued 'part paid' – that is, only part of the capital which the shares represent has been paid, and further amounts may become payable to the company at a later date. The liability to make such further payment falls on the shareholder who owns the shares when payment becomes due. When part-paid shares are transferred, provided payment of the further capital has not been called for (or if it has, it has been paid) at the date of the Transfer, stamp duty is chargeable only on the actual consideration given (STM4.375).

Distributions

8.28 In general, a distribution from a company to its shareholders is, by definition, for no consideration. The Stamp Office has occasionally claimed that a distribution of assets *in specie*, declared as a final dividend, should necessarily be re-characterised as the declaration of a dividend (creating a money debt) followed by the (stampable) transfer of the asset in satisfaction of the debt. It would doubtless be possible to create and satisfy a debt in this way. However, the idea that a distribution *in specie* should *necessarily* take this form appears to come from an over-enthusiastic application of an idea set out in STM4.404–4.408 and is probably not correct; STM4.49 is a more accurate statement of the position. To minimise the risk of dispute, it is worthwhile ensuring, where possible, that distributions *in specie* from UK companies are declared as interim dividends, as these do not create a debt between company and shareholder. Distributions from non-UK companies will be subject to the law of the country in which the distributing company is established – it would be worth checking whether declaration of the *in specie* distribution creates a money debt due to the shareholder under the governing law of the company concerned.

Valuation of consideration

8.29 Consideration expressed in a foreign currency must be translated into sterling. If the Transfer specifies the exchange rate, that rate is to be used – although HMRC would seek to set aside an unrealistic exchange rate inserted to reduce the stamp duty. Otherwise, the translation is to be at the appropriate market rate on the day the Transfer is executed; and, for this purpose, HMRC normally seek to use the closing spot exchange rate as listed in the Financial Times (STM4.23/24).

Stock and securities as consideration

8.30 If consideration includes stock or marketable securities, these are to be valued at market value on the date of execution of the stampable document (which will not necessarily be the same as the date on which the securities given in consideration are transferred).

For quoted securities, HMRC adopt the capital gains tax basis of valuation (STM4.28) – that is, the lower of:

- midway between the highest and lowest price of bargains on the day, and
- the lower closing price for the day plus one quarter of the difference between the lower and higher closing prices.

If securities given in consideration are marketable but not quoted, HMRC's share valuation division is likely to become involved in agreeing the value.

8.31 Where the consideration includes securities which are not marketable, their value is taken to be 'the amount due on the day of the date thereof for principal and interest' (*SA 1891, s 55(2)*). This curious phrase is taken to mean the stated principal plus any interest due but unpaid at the date of execution of the stampable document.

Transfer in satisfaction of debt

8.32 Where assets are transferred to a person in satisfaction of a debt, the consideration is taken to be the amount outstanding on the debt, including any interest due but unpaid at the date of Transfer. However, provided the Transfer is to the creditor, if the amount of debt is greater than the value of the assets transferred, the consideration is restricted to the value of the assets transferred (*FA 1980, s 102*; STM4.40). To take advantage of this relief, the Transfer must be adjudicated by HMRC (see **8.45**).

Consideration payable later or in instalments

8.33 If consideration is payable after the Transfer is executed, or in instalments, stamp duty is chargeable on the total amount, with no discount or postponement to allow for delay in payment. However, where the instalments take the form of an annuity which may last longer than 12 years but ceases on a death, only the first 12 years' instalments are taken into account. In other cases where the instalments will or may continue for more than 20 years, only the first 20 years are taken into account (*SA 1891, s 56*; STM4.112 et seq). The equivalent provision under SDLT only takes account of 12 years' instalments although, if these are variable, the highest 12 individual years are taken into account (see **2.26**).

VAT

8.34 Where consideration for a Transfer is subject to VAT, the VAT must be included in the amount on which stamp duty is chargeable (see *Glenthroes Development Corporation v IRC* [1994] STC 74). This will not normally be an issue in relation to Transfers of shares and securities, which do not normally give rise to VAT charges. It was widely regarded as unreasonable when stamp duty applied to Transfers of other assets, but the same principle has been carried into the SDLT regime (see **2.21**).

Unascertainable consideration

8.35 Stamp duty is only chargeable on consideration which is 'ascertainable' at the date of the Transfer. This principle is not overtly stated in the legislation, but see STM4.294 for confirmation of the HMRC view. Consideration is ascertainable if it is possible to deduce, with certainty, one or more specific figures for it from documents or facts extant at the time of execution of the Transfer. It does not matter whether payment of that particular amount is certain or contingent on future events. If more than one figure can be deduced, the consideration is assumed to be the highest of these, in accordance with the 'contingency principle' explained below. Where any amount of consideration is genuinely unascertainable at that date, it will not be subject to stamp duty. Note that the test is whether the amount is capable of being ascertained, not whether it has been ascertained.

Example 8.5 – unascertainable consideration

On 1 January 2011, Conglomerate plc agrees to buy all of the shares in Dan Ltd from Daniel for consideration equal to twice the pre-tax profits of Dan Ltd for the year to 28 February 2011 (with no upper or lower limit). The share Transfer is executed on 1 February 2011. The consideration is entirely unascertainable at the date of the Transfer, because it is based on events which will happen after that date, so there is no consideration on which stamp duty may be charged. There is no requirement to submit the Transfer to HMRC for stamping.

Example 8.6 – an ascertainable sum

The facts are as in Example 8.5, except that the consideration is specified to be at least £1 million. This is an ascertainable amount, and stamp duty will be chargeable on £1 million.

Example 8.7 – an ascertainable sum, variable up or down

The facts are as in Example 8.5, except that the consideration is specified to be £1 million, plus twice the amount by which the February 2011 profits exceed £500,000, or minus twice the amount by which they fall short of that figure. Stamp duty will again be charged on the £1 million, with no subsequent adjustment to the stamp duty if the consideration proves to be greater or less than £1 million.

Example 8.8 – ascertainable but not yet ascertained

The facts are as in Example 8.5, except that the share transfer is executed on 1 March 2011. The year has now ended, on the profits of which the consideration will be based. The profits are not yet likely to have been ascertained, but they are nonetheless ascertainable, because all events impacting on the profit figure have happened. Stamp duty will be chargeable on the actual consideration. Since it is unlikely this will be known when the deadline for payment of stamp duty arrives, Conglomerate plc may wish to apply for provisional stamping (see **8.44**).

8.36 The *LM Tenancies* case ([1996] STC 880) involved an attempt to render consideration unascertainable but limit the risk of change, by linking it to the value, a few days later, of a security with a very stable price. It was held that the consideration was not truly unascertainable and should be taken as the figure based on the value of the security at the date of the Transfer.

Contingency principle

8.37 The calculation of consideration is complicated by the application of the so-called 'contingency principle'. This principle, not explicit in the legislation, is based on case law, especially the *Underground Electric Railways* cases (STM4.291). The principle states that any sum stated to be payable by way of consideration on the happening of some contingency is subject to stamp duty as if certainly payable. The principle is subject to the question of whether the consideration is ascertainable, but generally means that the highest possible stamp duty is payable (STM4.295).

Example 8.9 – two or more ascertainable sums

The facts are as in Example 8.5, but the consideration is subject to a minimum of £500,000 and a maximum of £2 million. £500,000 and £2 million are both ascertainable sums, and the contingency principle requires the assumption that the higher amount of £2 million will be paid. Stamp duty is therefore chargeable on this sum, with no adjustment or refund if the actual consideration eventually proves to be less.

8.38 On occasion, when this principle has produced an unforeseen and manifestly unjust result, HMRC have been known to accept stamp duty based on actual consideration – but it would not be safe to rely on such largesse.

Different definitions of consideration for stamp duty and SDRT

8.39 The definition of consideration for SDRT purposes (see **10.4**) is wider than that for stamp duty purposes. As a result, the stamp duty on a Transfer may be less than the SDRT on the related agreement. In Example 8.6, SDRT would be chargeable on the actual consideration once finally ascertained. However, as explained at **10.11**, appropriate stamping of a Transfer within six years of the agreement to transfer the shares cancels the SDRT liability. Since, in that example, the stamp duty on a Transfer would be nil, it would clearly be a good idea to execute a Transfer (which, in this case, would immediately be deemed to be 'duly stamped'), in order to cancel the SDRT liability. This principle is widely relied on in order to mitigate stamp tax costs on share transactions (see Example 8.11 and **10.21**).

ADMINISTRATION

No need to stamp

8.40 If an exemption applies to eliminate any stamp duty charge, the Transfer is effectively deemed to be duly stamped, without any need to submit it to HMRC. As noted at **9.2**, it is possible for the availability of the exemption to be challenged, in which case the document may need to be submitted for adjudication, although in practice this rarely happens.

Routine stamping

8.41 Documents for routine stamping should be sent to the Birmingham Stamp Office (see **Appendix A**) with payment of the duty and, if necessary, a brief note setting out the calculation of the duty. Most importantly, in the author's experience, the documents must make clear to whom the stamped document must be returned, if necessary by including an addressed envelope.

8.42 In accordance with *SA 1891, s 5*, all facts and circumstances affecting liability must be set out in the Transfer. In practice, important facts may be in a separate agreement rather than on the stock transfer form. Where relevant, a copy of any such agreement should be sent with the stampable document. In the past, when consideration for a transfer included issue of new shares, it was sometimes necessary to have the agreement itself stamped 'not liable to any duty' in order to satisfy *Companies Acts* requirements; those requirements have now changed, so that this is no longer necessary.

8.43 The deadline is 30 days after the date of execution of the transfer, and late submission or payment will lead to penalties and/or interest being charged (see **8.47**). Payment may be by cheque, or by bank transfer to the HMRC stamp duty account (see **Appendix A**). If bank transfer is used, an appropriate reference must be given to the destination bank and repeated in the papers sent to Birmingham – for example, the name of the transferee. Unless there is manifestly an error, the documents will normally be stamped on the basis requested.

Provisional stamping and 'wait and see'

8.44 Where the consideration for a transfer is ascertainable at the date of the Transfer, but not yet ascertained when the due date arrives (see Example 8.8), delay in submission of the Transfer for stamping will lead to interest and penalty charges. It will also prevent any change of shareholder from being registered (see **8.4**). Penalties may be avoided by lodging the Transfer with the Stamp Office, either for them to keep until the duty can be determined ('wait and see') or for provisional stamping. Interest will still be charged on late paid stamp duty, but this may be minimised by paying an estimated amount, to be adjusted later. If the taxpayer needs the stamped Transfer, or if the delay in finalising figures will be more than a few weeks, provisional stamping should be requested. The Stamp Office will require a formal undertaking *from the person submitting the document*, confirming that they will return it for adjustment of the duty once figures are finalised. For this reason, advisers may ask clients to submit the documents in such cases, so that the client may give the necessary undertaking.

Adjudication

8.45 Technically, routine stamping is always provisional – that is, if the document is then required for an official purpose such as evidence in court, it would be open to any party to challenge whether it was adequately stamped. In practice, most documents are stamped in this way and no problems arise. To obtain complete certainty, the document must be submitted for HMRC to express their formal opinion as to the amount of duty (and, where appropriate, penalties) due – normally referred to as adjudication. Once the amount of duty has been adjudicated (and assuming no appeal is lodged against this within 30 days), it is no longer open to challenge apart from, possibly, on grounds of fraud.

8.46 There are certain cases where adjudication is compulsory, particularly in relation to claiming reliefs. It is rare for parties to request adjudication when it is not compulsory, but it is possible for all documents. HMRC takes adjudication seriously because of its finality. They will normally need to see all relevant documents and may seek further explanations; rarely, they may request assurances as to motives etc by way of formal statements (Statutory

Declarations) from individuals involved in the transaction. Adjudication is evidenced by impressing an 'adjudicated' stamp on the document alongside the duty stamps. As noted at **8.4**, there is no general compulsion to pay stamp duty. However, once the duty on a document has been adjudicated, if it is not paid within 30 days, a further penalty may be added to the duty when eventually paid.

Interest and penalties

8.47 Although there is no general compulsion to pay stamp duty, payment later than 30 days after the date of execution of the Transfer will lead to the addition of interest to the amount of stamp duty (*SA 1891, s 15A*). Interest is rounded down to the nearest £5 and, if the total is less than £25, it is not charged. Apart from this, however, interest charges are never mitigated, and the document will not be stamped unless any interest is paid in addition to the stamp duty itself. As with other taxes, the rates are set by regulation in accordance with *FA 1989, s 178*.

8.48 Penalties may be charged if a document is submitted for stamping after the deadline (*SA 1891, s 15B*). For a document executed in the UK, the deadline is the same as that for payment of duty: 30 days from execution. If the document is executed outside the UK, penalties do not arise unless it is submitted for stamping more than 30 days after first being brought into the UK. In practice, it will be rare for a Transfer of UK shares and securities to be executed and retained offshore, because of the SDRT implications (see **10.11**).

8.49 Provided the Transfer is submitted for stamping within one year of the deadline, the maximum penalty is the lesser of the amount of duty and £300. It follows that, where a relief is successfully claimed, reducing the stamp duty to zero, no penalty will be charged provided the Transfer is submitted within one year of the deadline. If a Transfer is submitted for stamping more than one year after the deadline, the maximum penalty becomes the greater of £300 and the duty. In such a case, therefore, a £300 penalty may be charged even if a relief reduces the duty to zero. However, in the experience of the author, penalties are not generally charged in these circumstances.

8.50 In other cases where substantial duty remains payable, penalties may be charged, but the maximum may be subject to mitigation, dependent on circumstances. A table of normal mitigated penalties is provided at STM3.32. It should be noted that reasonable excuse for late submission may lead to complete mitigation, but documents submitted more than two years late are likely to incur the maximum penalty.

Repayment of stamp duty

8.51 Occasionally, it may be discovered that too much stamp duty has been paid. This may occur, for example, where assets are subsequently found to be exempt, where an available relief has not been claimed, where consideration was incorrectly allocated to chargeable assets, or where a Transfer was inadvertently duplicated and both were stamped. The Stamp Office is empowered to consider claims for repayment (*Stamp Duties Management Act 1891, s 10*). The original stamped document must be submitted to Birmingham Stamp Office (see **Appendix A**) with a letter claiming repayment and setting out an explanation of the circumstances. In most cases, the claim must be made within two years of the date of execution of the document in question. However, where the claim relates to repayment of duty overpaid in the course of provisional stamping (see **8.44**) the two-year time limit does not apply. Interest may be payable in accordance with regulations under *FA 1999, s 110* and *FA 1989, s 178* on stamp duty repaid, although at the time of writing the official interest rate for these purposes is zero.

Higher rates on stock and marketable securities

8.52 Where stock or marketable securities are transferred to a clearance system or depository, any stamp duty charge is at the higher rate of 1.5% (*FA 1986, ss 67–72A*). In practice, such transfers are usually carried out electronically with no transfer document, so that the relevant tax is SDRT rather than stamp duty.

Bearer instruments

8.53 A 1.5% charge also arises on the *issue* of certain bearer instruments (*FA 1999, Sch 15*). In contrast with a registered security, a bearer instrument is a security or other financial asset which is transferable by delivery – that is, there is no need for a transfer document, but transfer is effected instead by giving the document which constitutes the asset to the transferee. Where stamp duty is due, it is charged on the market value of the security and is payable by the issuer. This is the one situation in which disclosure and payment of the stamp duty liability are compulsory.

8.54 If the stock, in registered form, would be exempt from stamp duty on transfer, no stamp duty is due on issue in bearer form. There are various other exemptions especially for stock expressed in a foreign currency. Issuers of bearer instruments will require specialist advice on compliance with stamp duty obligations. As far as holders of bearer instruments are concerned, a key point to note is that it is *possible* to transfer a bearer instrument by means of a transfer document rather than by delivery of the security itself, but if this is done, a stamp duty charge may arise.

Partnerships

8.55 With the introduction of SDLT, stamp duty charges were removed from most assets apart from stock and marketable securities. However, stamp duty remains chargeable on a Transfer of an interest in a partnership where the assets of the partnership include any stock or marketable securities (*FA 2003, Sch 15, paras 31–33*). The stamp duty charge is limited to the smaller of:

- the charge at 0.5% which would arise on a transfer of a proportion of the stock or marketable securities for market value consideration; the proportion is the same as the fractional share in the partnership which is transferred; and
- the charge at rates of up to 4% on the consideration actually given for the transfer of the partnership share; for these purposes, the consideration is reduced by a proportion of the 'net market value' of any UK land and buildings held by the partnership, and that proportion is the same as the fractional share in the partnership which is transferred. The 'net market value' is the actual market value less any debt secured solely on the property. The logic of this is that SDLT will often be charged by reference to the value of the UK land and buildings (see **5.25**). (When this provision was first enacted, it was expected that SDLT would always be charged. The SDLT provisions have subsequently been amended so that no charge will arise on many transfers of interests in property-owning partnerships, but the stamp duty provisions have been left unchanged. This possibly indicates that HMRC understand the limited effect of the retention of stamp duty on such transfers.)

8.56 In practice, it appears unlikely that stamp duty will be paid on many transfers of partnership shares. Most partnerships do not have substantial holdings of securities liable to stamp duty; many transfers will be left unstamped because, unless there is a dispute between the parties, it seems unlikely that a stamped transfer document will be required; the net consideration given is often very low; where necessary, it may be possible to construct a transfer of a partnership interest without creating a Transfer document. Where a Transfer is created, it should be noted that any attempt by the partners to agree contractually that they will not challenge the validity of the Transfer on the grounds it is not stamped is ineffective because of *SA 1891, s 117*. Where a stamped transfer document is required, it must be submitted for adjudication.

Stamp duty mitigation

8.57 There are three legitimate approaches to minimising the stamp duty cost when assets within the scope of the tax are transferred:

(1) Avoid creating a document which requires stamping. This approach was widely used when stamp duty applied to business assets such as goodwill, but is unlikely to be applicable in relation to transfers of stock and marketable securities because of the need to execute and stamp a document to cancel any SDRT charge (see **10.11**).

(2) Ensure the transfer is within the terms of a relief or exemption and claim the relief where appropriate – see **Chapter 9**. Where a relief or exemption may be available, care is needed to ensure the transaction qualifies; reliefs and exemptions are often subject to precise and detailed conditions, and it is often too easy accidentally to fall outside these.

(3) Minimise the amount which will be taken into account as consideration. Stamp duty is charged on the 'amount or value of the (actual) consideration'. There is no general requirement to substitute the market value of the assets transferred, even where the transaction is between connected persons and at an undervalue.

Example 8.10 – actual consideration below market value

Mustard plc is in the process of selling subsidiary Cress Ltd. Cress Ltd owns 50 shares in UK company Salad Ltd, with an historic cost of £10,000 but a current market value of £1 million. M always intended to keep the shares in S, but the process to sell C has now advanced far enough to create genuine doubt over whether M still has beneficial ownership of C. Therefore, it is not certain that group relief will be available for the transfer of S shares to M at full value. However, if C is able to transfer the S shares to M for payment of historic cost only, the stamp duty will be limited to £10,000 at 0.5%, which is £50, instead of the £5,000 which would apply to a transfer at market value.

Example 8.11 – minimising consideration

Non-UK company Cabbage SA owns UK company Sprout Ltd (current value £9 million) and non-UK company Broccoli Sarl (current value £1 million). Cabbage has agreed to sell both companies to Kale Pty Ltd for £10 million. A direct transfer of Sprout for £9 million would cost Kale £45,000 stamp duty. However, Cabbage first transfers Sprout to Broccoli in return for the issue of two shares by Broccoli. Broccoli already has 1,000 shares in issue, all held by Cabbage. Further (and this is very important), under the company law and constitution governing Broccoli, all shares are identical, giving shareholders identical rights in all respects. Cabbage then transfers Broccoli to Kale for £10 million.

For stamp duty purposes, the consideration given by Broccoli is simply the value of the two shares issued. This will be 2/1002ths of the £10 million value of Broccoli after the transfer of the Sprout shares, or £19,960. Most of the value of Sprout flows into the Broccoli shares already held by Cabbage, but this value shift does not count as consideration for stamp duty purposes. The stamp duty on this transfer will be £100 (after rounding). The SDRT, on the other hand, would probably be based on the increase in the value of Cabbage's holding of shares in Broccoli, ie £9 million. It is unlikely to be necessary to pay stamp duty on the Transfer of Broccoli to Kale because the shares of Broccoli are not UK registered.

Chapter 9

Stamp Duty Reliefs

INTRODUCTION

9.1 Perhaps the best-known stamp duty relief is that for transfers between group companies, commonly referred to as '*section 42* relief' because it is governed by *FA 1930, s 42*. This is modified by *FA 1967, s 27* and subject to HMRC guidance given in SP 3/98. The other main legislation on stamp duty reliefs and exemptions is in *FA 1986, ss 75–85*, but there are also relevant provisions at various points in other *Finance Acts*. References are given in the text below. Guidance on reliefs may be found in chapter 6 of the HMRC Stamp Tax Manual, available at www.hmrc.gov.uk/so/manual.htm.

9.2 To be consistent with the chapters on SDLT and SDRT, this book uses the term 'exemption' to refer to a measure which applies automatically to remove or reduce a stamp duty charge, and 'relief' to refer to a measure which requires a claim to be made. This is, in some ways, a false distinction. Even where a Transfer is considered to be exempt from stamp duty, it is possible for someone to challenge this. (In this book, the expression 'Transfer' is capitalised to make it clear that this is a reference to the potentially stampable document.) The only way to prove that the exemption applies is to ask HMRC to adjudicate the liability, as explained at **8.45**; this effectively amounts to making a claim for the exemption. However, it is not common for an apparently exempt document to be challenged in this way; so, in practice, it is rarely necessary to have the availability of an exemption settled by adjudication.

In contrast, where a relief applies, the relevant document is usually specifically stated not to be properly stamped unless it has been subject to adjudication (eg *FA 1930, s 42(1)*). If the document is not properly stamped, any SDRT liability which has arisen on the underlying agreement is not cancelled (see **10.11**) – so proper stamping is essential.

9.3 There is generally no theoretical time limit on claiming a relief. However, if stamp duty is paid on a document and it is subsequently realised that a claim to relief could have been made, the claim must be lodged within two years of the date of execution of the document, or the stamp duty will not be repaid (*Stamp Duties Management Act 1891, ss 9–10*; STM7.3 et seq). Where an SDRT charge has arisen, the Transfer must be executed and duly stamped within six years of the effective date of the agreement which gave rise to the SDRT charge, if that charge is to be cancelled (see **10.11**).

This has sometimes been a problem when subsidiaries have been moved around within a group on an informal basis. A typical scenario is as follows:

- parent company decides that ownership of a company should be transferred within the group, and instructs the relevant subsidiaries to take the necessary actions;
- the subsidiaries pass the necessary board resolutions, perhaps with consideration for the transfer being left outstanding on inter-company account;
- the resolutions, taken together, amount to an agreement to transfer the shares, so an SDRT charge arises at that point;
- however, no formal share Transfer is ever processed.

After six years have passed, the SDRT charge cannot be cancelled. HMRC are aware of the issue, and have made it clear that, where such situations come to light, they will pursue the SDRT charge.

9.4 Reliefs and exemptions may also apply to Transfers of interests in partnerships, although the absence of any SDRT charge means that, sometimes, documents are left unstamped rather than incurring the administrative costs of making claims (see **8.4**). Most of the reliefs described here also applied to property transactions before the introduction of SDLT in 2003, and most of them have been carried forward to the SDLT legislation (but often with more stringent anti-avoidance rules).

Exemptions

9.5 Exemptions are wide in scope, and are not limited to certain types of transaction or participant. They are listed here, but described in greater detail in **Chapter 8**:

(1) transfers which are not 'on sale';

(2) transfers for consideration not exceeding £1,000, if appropriately certified;

(3) transfers of exempt loan capital and other debt;

(4) transfers of units in a unit trust (see **10.3**); and

(5) transfers to recognised investment exchanges, clearing houses etc, where an appropriate arrangement has been entered into between the exchange etc and HMRC.

It must be remembered that the mere fact that a security is registered overseas or issued by a non-UK entity does not make a Transfer of that security exempt from stamp duty. However, no SDRT liability will normally arise on an agreement to transfer such a security, so there would not normally be any practical need to stamp the Transfer (see **10.5** and **10.11**).

Approved share incentive plans etc

9.6 No stamp duty is chargeable on a Transfer of shares to an employee under an approved share incentive plan (or an old employee share ownership plan) (*FA 2001, s 95*).

GROUP, RECONSTRUCTION AND ACQUISITION RELIEFS

9.7 Group, reconstruction and acquisition reliefs apply only to Transfers between companies. 'Company' is defined in the legislation for group relief as meaning body corporate, and so potentially encompasses all UK incorporated entities such as private and public companies, statutory corporations and limited liability partnerships. It also includes overseas entities, provided they have the necessary characteristics. This aspect is not defined in the legislation governing the reconstruction and acquisition reliefs, probably because those reliefs originally applied only if the acquiring company was UK registered. However, it was realised that this could cause difficulties in relation to European law, and *FA 2006, s 169* removed the requirement for UK registration. Nevertheless, a body corporate can only function as a subsidiary in a group if it has ordinary share capital, and can only participate in the other reliefs if it has non-redeemable share capital (STM6.123 et seq).

9.8 HMRC have already examined the characteristics of a range of overseas entities and expressed their view as to whether they qualify for the reliefs. A short list of 'approved' entities is at STM6.124, but this is out of date; so, for any other entity, it is worth asking HMRC whether they have already considered it (see **Appendix A** for contact details). If they have not done so, they will usually require details of the law under which the entity is formed, and a legal opinion (in English, or translated) setting out why the entity should be regarded as a body corporate.

Group relief – general description

9.9 According to the legislation, this should be referred to as 'associated companies relief'; it is widely called '*section 42* relief', after *FA 1930, s 42* which sets out the basic rules. In this book, it is referred to as group relief. Group relief is available to remove the stamp duty charge on a Transfer which transfers a beneficial interest in an asset between two associated companies.

9.10 The reference to beneficial interest sometimes causes confusion, because it is often considered that the *beneficial* interest in an asset passes to the purchaser as a result of payment of the consideration under an agreement, while the Transfer does no more than transfer *legal title*. However, HMRC interpret the legislation as requiring only that the Transfer be a formal step in the process of transferring a beneficial interest. On this understanding, a stock transfer form or other document giving effect to an agreement to transfer an asset on sale is able to qualify for group relief. However, there is a related point which does cause difficulties. If a beneficial interest is to be transferred, the transferor must hold that beneficial interest at the start of the process and the transferee must hold it (even if only briefly) at the end. If the asset is ultimately to be transferred to a third party, care must be taken to ensure that the group companies do nothing in relation to that disposal which may lead to loss of beneficial ownership, until the intra-group Transfer has been completed. Beneficial ownership may be lost, for example, as soon as there is a binding commitment to sell the asset to the third party, even though no payment has been made. See STM6.94 for HMRC's comments on the point.

9.11 Companies are associated if one is the parent of the other, or a third company is the parent of both. A company is the parent of another if it:

(1) is beneficial owner of at least 75% of the ordinary share capital of the other,

(2) is beneficially entitled to at least 75% of any profits available for distribution to equity holders, and

(3) would be beneficially entitled to at least 75% of assets available for distribution in a winding up.

'Ordinary share capital' means all share capital apart from fixed-rate preference shares. The rules in *Corporation Tax Act 2010, Pt 5, chapter 6* (previously *ICTA 1988, Sch 18*) apply in considering (2) and (3), but omitting the paragraphs taking account of potential future changes in rights. Where ownership is indirect, the usual algebraic rule applies to determine the effective percentage ownership – see Example 3.3 (SDLT group relief) for an illustration. The requirement for *beneficial* ownership/entitlement is important. As noted below (**9.15**), an arrangement to break the group relationship by disposal of the transferor does not prevent group relief on a prior intra-group

Transfer. However, if that arrangement has progressed too far, there may be a risk that the parent company has lost beneficial ownership of the transferor and that the group is therefore broken. Cases such as *Wood Preservation Ltd v Prior* ([1968] 2 All ER 849) provide guidance on this point. It is important that the necessary group relationship is intact at the time of execution of the Transfer – it is not enough for the companies to be associated only at the time of any agreement to transfer (see STM6.96).

Example 9.1 – group relief, associated companies

K LLP holds all of the shares in two UK companies, J Ltd and H Ltd. J Ltd also holds a portfolio of minority holdings of shares in key suppliers to K LLP. The partners of K LLP decide to transfer the shares of J Ltd into the ownership of H Ltd in return for an issue of H Ltd shares. They also decide J Ltd should transfer the shares of suppliers to H Ltd in settlement of an inter-company debt. K LLP, J Ltd and H Ltd are all associated companies for these purposes, so any Transfers between them are potentially eligible for relief. It should not matter whether the supplier shares are transferred before or after the Transfer of shares of J Ltd.

Group relief – anti-avoidance

9.12 Anti-avoidance rules are set out in *FA 1967, s 27*. Relief is denied if the Transfer is made in connection with any arrangements under which:

(1) any part of the consideration is to be provided or received by anyone other than another group company,

(2) the transferor and transferee are to cease to be associated by the transferee leaving the group, or

(3) the asset being transferred was previously conveyed by anyone other than a group company.

These rules have the potential to deny relief in a wide range of relatively innocent transactions, so HMRC have issued guidance on how they apply them (SP 3/98). The key points of this are as follows:

(1) 'Arrangement' is a very wide term, covering informal understandings as well as formal contracts; there are arrangements if there is an expectation that the event or series of events will happen and no likelihood in practice that it will not.

(2) Nevertheless, relief may be denied if it is found that there are arrangements even if, in the event, those arrangements do not come to fruition.

(3) Relief is not denied merely because the transferee obtains third party debt funding to buy the asset, but relief will be denied where the funding arrangement may lead to transfer of the economic risk and reward of ownership of the asset out of the group – for example, if the transferee borrows at an economically unsustainable level, or the lender has shareholder-type rights which could allow it to take control of the asset.

(4) The rule relating to 'previous conveyance' was intended to prevent a specific type of avoidance device which relied on the stamp duty version of sub-sale relief. This is unlikely to be of interest in relation to Transfers of shares and securities, because of the application of SDRT (see **8.12**). Relief will not be denied if the asset was previously transferred into the group from a third party under a Transfer on which stamp duty was paid.

(5) In any case of doubt, HMRC reserve the right to see relevant documents and to require formal statements of the facts by way of Statutory Declaration.

9.13 Until March 2000, HMRC routinely required group relief claims to be backed by a Statutory Declaration of the facts by an officer of the claimant company or its parent. It is now rare for this to be required, and claims are generally made by letter (see **9.16** et seq).

9.14 The most common point of doubt is whether there are offending arrangements, particularly where there is a possibility that the transferor and transferee companies will cease to be associated after the Transfer. It is generally accepted that mere uncommitted discussions with a third party potential purchaser do not cause there to be arrangements, unless perhaps it is economically inevitable that the relevant company will be sold. However, signature of heads of terms for the sale, even though not legally obliging the vendor to proceed, is likely to bring arrangements into existence (STM6.125; SP 3/98, para 6). To minimise risk, any intra-group Transfers should be done at the earliest possible stage, and certainly before any final decision is made as to whether the transferee company will leave the group.

9.15 The following matters often cause confusion:

(1) There is no question of stamp duty group relief being 'clawed back'. Clawback is a concept which applies only to SDLT. If stamp duty group relief is validly and successfully claimed on a Transfer, events thereafter have no impact on the claim. However, HMRC are entitled to have regard to subsequent events when considering claims, so it is wise to submit group relief claims quickly after the intra-group Transfer.

(2) Group relief will not usually be denied merely because there are plans for the asset itself to leave the group, provided that onward transfer of the asset is subject to stamp duty as normal – but, as noted above, care

is needed in relation to timing of that onward disposal (see SP 3/98, para 9).

(3) No problem is caused by plans to dispose of the transferor, because the legislation specifically refers to the ownership of the transferee, provided those plans have not progressed too far (see **9.11**).

(4) A company may repurchase its own shares from a shareholder. This repurchase may qualify for group relief, provided the companies are in the necessary group relationship, subject to the usual anti-avoidance rules (STM6.110).

Example 9.2 – group relief

Jersey plc owns 100% of Friesian Ltd, and Friesian Ltd in turn owns 100% of Galloway Ltd. It is decided to sell F but retain G. The group markets F, a preferred bidder is identified, and non-binding heads of terms are signed. Before there is any formal commitment to sell to that preferred bidder, G is transferred to J for cash. Assuming there are no other avoidance aspects, the Transfer of G should qualify for stamp duty group relief, even though there are certainly arrangements for F to leave the group. As noted at **9.10**, it is important that the group does not become committed to sell F before the group Transfer is finalised, or there may be a risk that J will have lost beneficial ownership of F, the companies thus ceasing to be associated for group relief purposes.

Example 9.3 – document essential for group relief

A multinational group headed by Dorian BV has a direct UK subsidiary Eve Ltd, which itself has a UK subsidiary Frank Ltd. It is decided that Frank Ltd should be sold. Eve Ltd agrees to transfer Frank Ltd to Dorian BV in satisfaction of a £10 million inter-company debt. In turn, Dorian BV agrees to sell Frank Ltd to a third party purchaser. Dorian BV then instructs Eve Ltd to transfer the shares of Frank Ltd directly to the purchaser.

An SDRT liability of £50,000 (£10 million at 0.5%) arises on the agreement to transfer Frank Ltd to Dorian BV. A further SDRT liability arises on the agreement to sell Frank Ltd to the third party purchaser. It is likely that a stock transfer form will be completed to transfer the shares from Eve Ltd to the third party purchaser. The purchaser will normally pay stamp duty on this, which will cancel the SDRT liability on the second step. However, no document is executed to transfer the shares from Eve Ltd to Dorian BV, so the SDRT liability on that step remains payable. If, instead, a document had been executed to transfer the shares from Eve Ltd to Dorian BV, stamp duty group relief could have been claimed on this under *FA 1930, s 42*, and a successful claim would have cancelled the SDRT charge. A separate document would then have been required to transfer the shares from Dorian BV to the third party purchaser.

A stock transfer form would not necessarily have been required for the transfer from Eve Ltd to Dorian BV; in appropriate circumstances, Eve could have executed a 'declaration of trust', declaring that it now held the shares of Frank Ltd on trust for the benefit of Dorian BV. This declaration of trust could have been submitted for stamping, without the need first to update the share register of Frank Ltd to show Dorian BV as the shareholder. In complex reorganisations, where shares of UK companies may be transferred several times in quick succession within a group, it is commonplace to effect Transfers by way of declarations of trust or similar documents, to avoid delays arising from the need to get documents stamped before share registers can be updated. As noted at **10.21**, where shares are held by a custodian, a 'letter of direction' fulfils a similar function. Appropriate legal advice should be taken where required, to establish what kind of documentation will be effective as a 'Transfer', which can then be submitted for stamping.

Group relief – claims process

9.16 Group relief is claimed by submission of documents to the Birmingham Stamp Office (see **Appendix A**) for adjudication. The outside of the envelope should be clearly marked 'Stamp duty claim under FA 1930, s 42' to ensure it is sent directly to the correct section. The following documents must be sent (STM6.166):

(1) the original, executed Transfer(s) (typically, for shares, a stock transfer form);

(2) certified* copies of the Transfer(s);

(3) copies* of any agreements governing the Transfer;

(4) where the parties to the transaction are indirectly associated, a family tree*;

(5) a certified* copy of the register of members of all subsidiary and intermediate companies;

(6) where the consideration was payable in cash, a copy of the latest accounts of the transferee company;

(7) copies of any other documents (eg board minutes) which help explain the transaction and the reasons for it;

(8) a letter of claim; and

(9) a self-addressed envelope for return of the document. This is not a requirement but, in the writer's experience, reduces the risk that the stamped document might be returned to a registered office address as shown on the stock transfer form, for example.

* Items marked thus either are required to be 'certified', or may require certification, so it may be as well to have them certified at the outset. 'Certified' means either the normal certification by a solicitor or other appropriate lawyer that the document is a true copy of an original, or an equivalent statement signed by a director or the company secretary of the company in question. It is not clear why the copy of the Transfer needs to be certified, since HMRC will also have the original in front of them, but this is a long-standing requirement. If any of the companies is non-UK incorporated, it may also be necessary to provide a copy of its incorporation documents or other information, to satisfy HMRC that it is indeed a body corporate with issued ordinary share capital (see **9.11**).

9.17 The precise format of the letter of claim is not specified, but HMRC do require it to make statements about particular matters. As a result, letters of claim tend to follow a fairly standard pattern. The letter must explicitly state (STM6.164):

- that a claim under *FA 1930, s 42*, as amended, is made in respect of the documents (which must be listed at this point);
- the authorised and issued share capitals of all companies in the group structure (or at least that part of it which includes the transferor, transferee and any intermediate companies up to a common parent) at the dates of all the documents. The reference to 'authorised' is probably redundant as UK companies are no longer required to have a specified level of authorised capital;
- what shares are held by each shareholder in each subsidiary company;
- that it is intended that the existing shareholder relationships are to be maintained (or give details of any change envisaged);
- that the group relationship between the companies meets the requirements of *Corporation Tax Act 2010, s 151(4)(a), (b)* and *Pt 5, chapter 6* (previously *ICTA 1988, s 413(7), Sch 18*);
- that none of the bodies corporate is in liquidation (or give further details if they are);
- that the transferee body corporate intends to keep the beneficial ownership of the asset (or give details of any intended transfer onwards);
- the amount of the consideration and whether it was paid in cash, by issue of shares or securities, through an inter-company loan or from a third party loan; and

- that none of the documents was executed in pursuance of, or in connection with, an arrangement as described in *FA 1967, s 27(3)* or *FA 1930, s 42(2)*, as appropriate.

9.18 Although some of these statements overlap and may seem unnecessary, HMRC does require them all to be made. The letter must be signed by an appropriate person with personal knowledge that the statements are correct: a director or other officer of the ultimate parent company, or of a company which is parent of a sub-group containing all of the other companies; a shareholder of the ultimate parent if that shareholder has a right to attend board meetings which discuss policy; a lawyer (in-house or external) acting for the parent company; or an administrator/receiver appointed to the parent company under insolvency law. For a long time, HMRC also readily accepted letters signed by other advisers (eg auditors and tax advisers) acting for the parent company, but recently they have been known to challenge whether these are based on personal knowledge, particularly of the intentions of the parties. It may, therefore, be safest for the letter to be signed by an appropriate officer of the parent company.

9.19 In major reorganisations, there may be numerous Transfers on which group relief is to be claimed, sometimes several transfers of the same shares. It is usually acceptable to combine all of the group relief claim letters into one, provided all relevant documents are made available for each Transfer. Where there are successive Transfers of the same shares, it is important that each step is completed by an appropriate Transfer document, in order to cancel any SDRT charge which would otherwise arise. However, there are possible company law difficulties in executing successive stock transfer forms before earlier forms have been stamped and the transfers registered. A solution may be for the original owner of the shares to execute a declaration of trust in respect of each successive transfer agreement, to confirm that it now holds the shares for the benefit of the new owner. Such a declaration acts as a Transfer and can be submitted for stamping.

9.20 Another potential issue, where there are successive transfers, concerns the question of beneficial ownership. If a company is committed to transfer shares onwards, even before it has acquired them, that company may never gain beneficial ownership; yet group relief is only available where beneficial ownership is transferred. Equally, if the transferor or transferee is itself to be transferred at a later stage in the reorganisation, there may be a risk that the necessary beneficial shareholding relationship does not exist when the earlier Transfer is made. Care should be taken in the timing of Transfers and the signature of agreements to minimise such risks. However, when dealing with purely internal group reorganisations, the writer has not known HMRC challenge the availability of group relief on these grounds. A challenge is perhaps more likely if the reorganisation is to be followed by disposal of some entities out of the group.

Reconstruction and acquisition reliefs – general description, common features

9.21 This section covers two reliefs (that is, reconstruction relief, and relief for insertion of a new holding company) which remove the stamp duty charge for certain Transfers which do not involve any change in ultimate ownership but which may not qualify for group relief. There is a third relief, which can properly be described as acquisition relief, which limits the stamp duty rate to 0.5%, even where there is a change in economic ownership; acquisition relief was useful when stamp duty applied to land and other assets but, because the normal stamp duty rate on transfers of stock and marketable securities is 0.5%, it is currently of very little practical use. The common feature of all three reliefs is that the consideration must include the issue of non-redeemable shares by the acquiring company, and either no other consideration, or only consideration from a very restricted list.

9.22 Reconstruction relief and relief for insertion of a new holding company are also subject to a general anti-avoidance condition, that the acquisition must be for bona fide commercial purposes and not as part of a scheme or arrangement which has avoidance of stamp duty, income tax, corporation tax or capital gains tax as a main purpose. In many cases, taxpayers will seek advance clearance from HMRC that the transaction will qualify as a reconstruction for direct tax purposes. Where such clearance is given, this is regarded as proving that this condition is satisfied. If no clearance is obtained, the relief may still be available, but it will be necessary to provide HMRC with further information to satisfy them on this point, as follows:

- a copy of the latest accounts of the 'target company' ('T' in the explanation below);
- full details of any scheme or arrangement of which this transaction forms part;
- confirmation that the 'acquiring company' ('A' in the explanation below) still holds the shares or undertaking of T, as appropriate; and
- a *detailed* (HMRC emphasis) note of the bona fide commercial reasons for the transaction.

Reconstruction relief

9.23 In the heading to the legislation (*FA 1986, s 75*), this is described as 'acquisition relief' but, because it applies only to schemes of reconstruction, it is widely known as 'reconstruction relief'. The relief reduces stamp duty to zero where, in pursuance of a scheme of reconstruction, a company

(A) acquires all or part of the undertaking of another company (T). The consideration for the acquisition must consist of or include the issue of non-redeemable shares by A to all of the shareholders of T (*not* to T itself). The only other consideration permitted is that A assumes or discharges debts of T. The general anti-avoidance condition applies, as mentioned above.

9.24 The other stated condition is that, after the acquisition, the shareholders of A must be the same as those of T, and the proportion of shares in A held by each shareholder must be the same as the proportion of shares in T held by that shareholder. Minor variations in proportions, as a result of the inability to allot fractional shares, for example, are permitted. HMRC insist that the shares be properly issued for these purposes – that is, all formalities to record the shareholders in the statutory books of A must be completed – and shares in A may only be issued to a nominee if the equivalent shares in T were held by the same nominee for the benefit of the same beneficial owner. In determining these proportions, any shares held in treasury by T itself are ignored.

9.25 In view of the limited application of stamp duty, clearly the relief is only applicable where the undertaking of T consists of or includes stock or marketable securities, or interests in partnerships which hold stock or marketable securities. There is no statutory definition of 'undertaking', but tax case precedents indicate that the mere passive holding of assets, as investments for example, does not amount to an undertaking. Furthermore, for the undertaking of T to be 'transferred', A must carry it on in much the same form as did T. So, if T holds a portfolio of shares as an investment, or if, after transfer to A, the shares are held as investments, relief is not likely to be available; however, if T carries on a share dealing business and, after the transfer, A also carries on a share dealing business, the Transfer could qualify for relief. HMRC also accept that acting as the holding company of controlling interests in one or more trading companies may amount to an undertaking, providing the holding company does in practice act as a parent company, taking an appropriate interest in the running of the subsidiary/ies. So, if T holds a controlling interest in trading company Z, this may amount to an undertaking and the relief may apply on transfer to A.

9.26 It is also the view of HMRC, again supported by precedent, that a transaction is not a reconstruction if there is any appreciable change in the ultimate ownership of the assets. The legislation does not explicitly require that the shares issued by A should be of the same class as each other or as the shares in T. However, if shares of different classes are issued and if these give the shareholders different economic rights, the transaction may not be a reconstruction and so may not qualify for relief. The following example is fairly complex, but illustrates many of the difficulties which can arise in relation to this relief.

Example 9.4 – reconstruction relief

Target Ltd is the parent company of a trading group, holding all of the shares of trading companies Yak Ltd and Zebra Ltd. The shareholders of T are two siblings, Rupert and Sandy, each holding 5,000 of the 10,000 £1 ordinary shares (all the same class) in issue. Rupert also holds 2,000 non-voting, non-cumulative 5% £1 redeemable preference shares, reflecting extra cash he put into the group many years ago. It is decided to separate Y and Z, with a view to the possibility that each sibling may wish to take a greater interest in a different company in future. It is proposed to liquidate T, transferring each of Y and Z under a new holding company (YH and ZH respectively) in return for an issue of shares to Rupert and Sandy. The following issues arise:

(1) The preference shares are a potential problem because they are redeemable, but all shares issued by YH and ZH must be non-redeemable. If YH and ZH issue non-redeemable preference shares to Rupert, their economic value may not be the same as redeemable shares. A solution would be for the redeemable shares to be either redeemed or converted to non-redeemable shares before the reconstruction proceeds.

(2) The preference would be to give Rupert a greater interest in Y, and Sandy a greater interest in Z, taking care to ensure that each ended up with the same overall commercial value as at the outset. They consider the following possibilities:

(a) YH issues 20 £1 preference shares and 70 £1 ordinary shares to Rupert, and 30 £1 ordinary shares to Sandy in return for the shares of Y. ZH issues 70 £1 ordinary shares to Sandy and 30 £1 ordinary shares to Rupert in return for the shares in Z. Neither the transfer of shares in Y to YH nor the transfer of Z to ZH would qualify for *s 75* relief, because at the end of the process Rupert and Sandy would not hold the same proportion of shares in either YH or ZH as they initially held in T.

(b) YH issues 20 £1 preference shares and 50 £1 class A ordinary shares to Rupert, and 50 £1 class B ordinary shares to Sandy in return for the transfer of Y. ZH issues 20 £1 preference shares and 50 £1 class B shares to Rupert, and 50 £1 class A shares to Sandy in return for the transfer of Z. This could qualify for *s 75* relief, as the proportions of shares in each company held by each of Rupert and Sandy at the end are the same as the proportions initially held in T. However, if the relative economic values of the three classes of shares in each company differ from the relative economic values of the shares in T, it is likely that the transaction will not amount to a 'reconstruction' within the terms of the relief, and relief will be denied. To avoid this problem, the rights and entitlements arising from the class A and class B shares in each company must be the same. In short, the siblings cannot skew the relative interests in the two businesses, so that one has a greater share of Y and the other a greater share of Z. If they wish to change this relative ownership, that must be done as a separate matter at a later date. The preference shares remain a particular problem. As shares in T, they give Rupert a reserves-dependent entitlement to a dividend of £100 per year. To achieve the same with 40 £1 shares in YH and XH (20 in each), the coupon rate would have to be 250% – and even that assumes the shares in YH and ZH are of equal worth. It really would be easier to get rid of the preference shares before commencing the reconstruction.

Relief for insertion of new holding company

9.27 In the heading to the legislation (*FA 1986, s 77*), this is also described as relief for acquisition, but the paragraph heading above is more accurate. No stamp duty is chargeable on a Transfer of shares in one company (T) to another company (A) where the Transfer forms part of an arrangement for A to acquire all of the shares in T, provided other conditions are satisfied. Again, the general anti-avoidance condition applies (as mentioned in **9.22**), and the information listed there will have to be supplied if direct tax clearance has not been obtained for the transaction. The other conditions are that:

(1) the only consideration is the issue of shares in A to shareholders of T;

(2) every shareholder of T immediately before the acquisition is a shareholder of A after the acquisition, and holds the same proportion of shares in A as previously held in T;

(3) if T has shares of different classes, the classes and relative proportions by number of each class are replicated in A; and

(4) the proportion of shares of A of any particular class, in issue or held by any particular shareholder, is the same as the proportion of shares of that class in T, in issue or held by that shareholder, immediately before the acquisition.

The reference to different share classes relates to the rights and characteristics of the shares, not particularly how they are labelled. So, if shares are labelled class A and class B purely to identify by which member of a consortium they are held and if they have identical rights etc, they will not be regarded as being of different classes. But shares which have different voting or dividend rights or different nominal values will be regarded as being of different classes.

9.28 The transaction must be part of the acquisition of all of the target company's share capital. If A already holds some shares in T (for example, after stake building in a quoted company) or if any shares of T remain with another shareholder (for example, a dissenting shareholder), the relief will not be available. In practice, therefore, the relief is only of use for insertion of a new holding company by a 100% shareholder or by agreement amongst a group of shareholders with 100% between them. This is most commonly done as a first step in a further reconstruction or reorganisation, or perhaps to put a 'clean' company at the top of a group prior to a stock market initial public offering.

Example 9.5 – insertion of holding company

In Example 9.4, it is possible that the proposed reconstruction would be easier if, as a first step, a new holding company H Ltd was inserted between T and the shareholders, Rupert and Sandy. This might, for example, allow T to be liquidated first, thus removing any difficulty arising from an accumulated deficit on reserves. To this end, Rupert might establish H, taking one £1 ordinary share as founder subscriber. Rupert, Sandy and H would then agree that the shares in T be transferred to H in return for H issuing 2,000 £1 non-redeemable preference shares and 4,999 £1 ordinary shares to Rupert and 5,000 £1 ordinary shares to Sandy. Note the same comments apply as in the original example with regard to the redeemable preference shares. Note also that the key requirement is that numbers/ proportions of shares held in H after the transaction are the same as those in T before. Since Rupert starts with one share in H, he must agree to be issued with one share less than expected, to ensure the final numbers are correct. In the original form of this relief, precise replication of proportions was vitally important, and real claims failed because the subscriber share was overlooked. However, an amendment inserted by *FA 2006* relaxed this requirement, and now proportional shareholding must be replicated 'as nearly as may be'. This relaxation was intended to allow for the inability to issue fractional shares, and still may not cover overlooking subscriber shares so, to be safe, they should be taken into account as suggested here.

Acquisition Relief Mk II

9.29 This relief, in *FA 1986, s 76*, limits the rate of stamp duty on a Transfer to 0.5% if relevant conditions are met. The relief is available where a company (A) acquires all or part of the undertaking of another company (T) for consideration which includes the issue of non-redeemable shares of A to T or any or all of the shareholders of T. The only other consideration permitted is the assumption or discharge of debts of T and/or cash not exceeding 10% of the nominal value of the shares issued. The general anti-avoidance condition which applies to the two reliefs described in the previous paragraphs does not apply to this relief, and there is no need for replication of proportionate shareholdings. Therefore, in principle, this relief may apply when there is a change in overall economic ownership – the SDLT version of this relief is still useful in such a situation (see **3.21**).

9.30 The relief only applies to the Transfer of an undertaking or part, and the comments at **9.25** are relevant here too. It is currently likely to be of use only in relation to a Transfer of an interest in a partnership which holds stock and marketable securities which themselves are within the charge to stamp duty. Stamp duty could be charged on a Transfer of such a partnership interest at rates of up to 4%, so in principle this relief may be of use. However, stamp duty on such a Transfer is already limited to 0.5% of the market value of any chargeable stock and marketable securities, multiplied by the fractional share in the partnership which is transferred. It seems unlikely that this will often exceed 0.5% of the consideration for the Transfer of the partnership interest, so in practice it is not likely to be necessary or worthwhile to claim relief under *s 76*.

Acquisition reliefs – claims process

9.31 Each of the three reliefs just described is claimed by submission of documents to the Birmingham Stamp Office (see **Appendix A**) for adjudication. The outside of the envelope should be clearly marked 'Stamp duty claim under FA 1986, s [75/76/77, as appropriate]' to ensure it is sent directly to the correct section. The following documents must be sent:

Item	**s 75**	**s 76**	**s 77**
The original, executed Transfer(s) (typically, for shares, a stock transfer form)	✓	✓	✓
Certified* copies of the Transfer(s)	✓	✓	✓
Copies* of any agreements governing the Transfer	✓	✓	✓
Certified* copy of the register of members of the target company immediately before the Transfer	✓		✓
Certified* copy of the register of members of the acquiring company after the Transfer	✓		✓
Copies of any other documents (eg board minutes) which help explain the transaction and the reasons for it	✓	✓	✓
A letter of claim	✓	✓	✓
A self-addressed envelope for return of the stamped document #	✓	✓	✓

* Items marked thus either are required to be 'certified', or may require certification, so it may be as well to have them certified at the outset. 'Certified' means either the normal certification by a solicitor or other appropriate lawyer that the document is a true copy of an original, or an equivalent statement signed by a director or the company secretary of the company in question.

This is not a requirement but, in the writer's experience, reduces the risk that the stamped document might be returned to a registered office address, as shown on the stock transfer form, for example, rather than the postal address of the appropriate individual.

9.32 HMRC provide model letters of claim for these reliefs but, unfortunately, they are only available as hard copies. Appropriate pro-forma letters are reproduced in **Appendix B**.

Charities relief

9.33 This is a simple relief – any Transfer to a charity or charitable trust is relieved from stamp duty (*FA 1982, s 129*) – and HMRC are keen to ensure that charities benefit from the relief where appropriate. Provided the Transfer is clearly to a registered charity, the transferee normally only needs to submit the Transfer to HMRC with a note of the charity's registration number and a request that the Transfer be adjudicated exempt under the charities exemption. If the charity is not registered, it may also be necessary to submit the deed or other document establishing the charity, and perhaps engage in correspondence to satisfy HMRC that the entity is indeed established for charitable purposes. It is, however, expected that HMRC will have regard to the updated definition of a charity for tax purposes in *FA 2010, s 30* and *Sch 6*. In future, HMRC may challenge the availability of relief where they do not believe the charity is managed by 'fit and proper' persons.

Relief for transfer to new LLP

9.34 No stamp duty is chargeable on a Transfer to a limited liability partnership within one year of formation of that LLP, provided the Transfer is, effectively, a step in the incorporation of some other form of partnership (such as a UK general or limited partnership) with no change in overall economic ownership (*Limited Liability Partnership Act 2000, s 12*). The partners in the LLP immediately after the Transfer must be the same as the partners in the old partnership immediately before, and the proportionate interest of each in the assets transferred must remain unchanged. The relief is available whether the assets were previously owned directly by the 'old' partnership or by a partner or other person holding as nominee for some or all of the partners. The Transfer must be submitted for adjudication for the relief to apply.

Recognised intermediary exemption etc

9.35 Any Transfer to a recognised intermediary (RI) is relieved from stamp duty (*FA 1986, s 80A*). An RI is a person who carries on a bona fide business of dealing in stock (or certain other financial instruments) and has been recognised for these purposes. Adjudication is required to take advantage of this relief, but the same recognition also exempts such Transfers from SDRT and, in practice, most such Transfers are electronic and so only within the SDRT net; further details about this exemption are provided at **10.22**. Other reliefs are provided specifically to facilitate financial market activity in the form of repurchases and stock lending, where in practice recognised intermediaries are normally involved (*FA 1986, ss 80C–84*).

Demutualisation of insurance companies

9.36 A Transfer executed in connection with the demutualisation of a mutual insurance company is relieved from stamp duty. This allows the transfer of investments from the mutual insurer to the new company taking over the insurance business, without stamp duty cost, provided the Transfer is submitted for adjudication (*FA 1997, s 96*).

Mergers of unit trusts and related transactions

9.37 Transfers executed in connection with the merger of authorised unit trusts, conversion of an authorised unit trust into an open ended investment company (OEIC), or merger of an authorised unit trust into an OEIC, are relieved from stamp duty (*FA 1997, s 95*; *SI 1997/1156*).

Chapter 10

Stamp Duty Reserve Tax (SDRT)

INTRODUCTION

10.1 SDRT was introduced by *FA 1986, ss 86–99*, in response to market developments under which the paperless transfer of beneficial ownership of shares became more common. Because no Transfer document is produced, a paperless transfer does not give rise to stamp duty; SDRT is designed to collect the same amount of tax as stamp duty, even where there is no document. (In this book, the expression 'Transfer' is capitalised to make it clear that this is a reference to the potentially stampable document.) At that time, the London Stock Exchange was trying to develop an electronic trading platform ('Taurus'). The Government of the day was eventually persuaded that charging stamp duty or SDRT would inhibit trading on this new platform, and *FA 1990, Pt III* was enacted to abolish both taxes on transfers of securities, from a date to be fixed by statutory instrument (the 'abolition day'). This date was intended to coincide with the launch of Taurus. Unfortunately, technical difficulties meant that Taurus was abandoned before completion. By the time the current electronic trading system was introduced in 1996, the Government view had changed. *FA 1990, Pt III*, although still on the statute book, has not been activated, and both SDRT and stamp duty remain potentially chargeable on securities transactions.

10.2 SDRT is potentially within the rules for disclosure of tax avoidance schemes (DOTAS) but, at the time of writing, regulations had not yet been made to activate this.

10.3 In practice, virtually all SDRT is paid on electronic stock market transactions (where it is collected automatically) and under the special SDRT regime which applies to trustees and managers of UK unit trust schemes. A general explanation of those arrangements is set out below, but detailed consideration of them is beyond the scope of this book. Outside these special areas of commerce, the main need is for taxpayers and advisers to understand how SDRT may arise on ordinary transactions in shares and securities, and how to ensure any such SDRT charge is appropriately dealt with. This chapter aims to provide that appreciation and understanding. In most cases, 'appropriately dealt with' means cancelled by execution of a Transfer document and ensuring it is 'duly stamped'. The interaction with stamp duty and the actions necessary to ensure cancellation of any SDRT charge are outlined below at **10.11**.

BASIC RULES

What gives rise to an SDRT charge?

10.4 SDRT arises when there is an unconditional agreement to transfer 'chargeable securities' for consideration in money or money's worth (*FA 1986, s 87*). The tax is chargeable whether the agreement is documented or not; in principle, it remains chargeable even if the transaction is subsequently abandoned, unless it can be argued that abandonment is evidence that the original agreement was not in reality unconditional. The normal rate is 0.5% of the consideration (*FA 1986, s 87(6)*), which is the same rate as stamp duty. As with stamp duty, a higher rate of 1.5% is chargeable in certain circumstances, but this is only likely to impact financial market transactions. However, the definition of consideration – anything which is money or money's worth – is far wider than for stamp duty (see **8.24**). As a result, an ordinary transaction may give rise to an SDRT liability which is greater than any stamp duty liability on the same transaction.

Example 10.1 – contrast between SDRT and stamp duty

Abigale agrees to transfer 500 shares in UK company Brian Ltd to Carol, a professional decorator. In consideration, Carol agrees to redecorate Abigale's house (a job for which Carol would normally charge £6,000). The agreement gives rise to an SDRT liability of £30 (£6,000 × 0.5%), subject to possible debate over the 'value' of the decorating work. However, the 'consideration' simply does not count for stamp duty purposes, so no stamp duty is payable on any document transferring the shares. As noted below (**10.11**), if a document of transfer is executed and 'duly stamped' within the period allowed, this will cancel the SDRT charge.

Chargeable securities

10.5 Chargeable securities are defined in *FA 1986, s 99(3)–(12)*. These subsections begin with a blanket definition to include stocks, shares and loan capital, various interests in and options over such assets, and units in unit trust schemes. This definition is then restricted by excluding:

(1) securities which are neither UK registered nor paired with securities which are so registered. (It is uncommon for UK and non-UK securities

to be paired. This particular provision was enacted to deal with the company formed to build the Channel Tunnel, which issued paired UK and French shares.);

(2) securities issued by an SE (a 'European company' formed under EC Council Regulation 2157/2001) unless its registered office is in the UK;

(3) units in a unit trust if all of the trustees are resident, and the registered office is maintained, outside the UK, or if it can only invest in assets which are themselves not within the charge to stamp duty, SDRT or SDLT;

(4) interests in depositary receipts; and

(5) stock or marketable securities, the transfer of which is exempt from all stamp duties.

In practice, the main categories which remain within the definition of chargeable securities are UK registered shares and UK registered corporate debt with equity-like characteristics (for example, convertible debt). Most debt securities are not chargeable as a result of (5) above, because they are exempt from stamp duty on transfer in accordance with the exemption for 'loan capital' in *FA 1986, s 79* (see **8.15**). However, this exemption may not apply if the debt has equity-like characteristics such as convertibility, a return which depends on business results or asset values, the potential for repayment at a premium, or a coupon which exceeds a reasonable commercial return. The last of these restrictions has caused many disputes in relation to so-called 'junk bonds', which carry a high interest rate in recognition of a high risk of default by the borrower. Where there is a transfer of a UK corporate debt, the terms of the debt should be checked carefully to ensure that they do not contain features which may disapply the *s 79* exemption.

10.6 The scope of stamp duty was restricted in association with the introduction of SDLT in 2003. At that time, the rules excluding stock etc which is exempt from stamp duty were amended, presumably in an attempt to fit in with the new stamp duty rules. The result is a highly convoluted definition, written in such a way as to suggest that there may be securities which are, in practice, outside the stamp duty charge, but which may still be subject to SDRT. There are indeed such securities – units in a UK unit trust; it would have been simpler for the definition to say so.

10.7 Although not specifically excluding the securities from being 'chargeable securities', *FA 1986, s 90* lists a number of cases when no SDRT is chargeable, as follows:

- various agreements relating to unit trust schemes (see **10.30** for the special arrangements for unit trusts);

- agreement to transfer a non-UK bearer instrument, or many UK bearer instruments (but the exemption for UK instruments does not apply in certain cases, mainly where no stamp tax was payable on original issue of the instrument and it would be subject to stamp tax on transfer in registered form);
- agreement to transfer securities to a charity or charitable trust or to certain bodies established for national purposes; and
- agreement to transfer shares held in treasury by the company which issued them.

10.8 No SDRT liability arises on a conditional agreement until such time as it becomes unconditional.

Administration and compliance

10.9 Liability to SDRT should be notified to HMRC and the tax paid by the 'accountable date' (*SDRT Regulations 1986, SI 1986/1711, regs 3, 4*). For financial market transactions, the accountable date is fixed by agreement between HMRC and the operators of the electronic transfer systems used on those markets; it is generally 14 days from the date of the transaction. In the rare cases where SDRT remains payable on non-financial market transactions, the accountable date is the seventh day of the month following that in which the agreement is made or becomes unconditional. So, if an agreement to transfer shares is entered into on the last day of a month, SDRT obligations arise just seven days later.

10.10 Responsibility for notification and payment rests with the 'accountable person'. When a broker or other market professional acts in the transaction, that broker or other professional is the accountable person. When more than one such person is involved, the rules specify which one has the responsibility. The broker then normally adds the SDRT to the amount charged to the client; the client has no direct responsibility to HMRC, but is still liable for the tax, and this fact gives the market professional the right to recover the tax from the client.

In non-financial market transactions, the accountable person is normally the purchaser (*SI 1986/1711, reg 2*). No standard return form is specified; liability must be notified by sending appropriate information to the SDRT Unit at Birmingham Stamp Office (see **Appendix A**). The information required is a full description of the securities (including number/amount), amount of consideration, when the SDRT is due, and the fact that this is a private or off-market transaction. Payment may be made by any of the normal methods but, for any form of direct bank transfer, it will be important to check with HMRC to ensure the correct current destination bank account details are used.

These are set out on the HMRC website at www.hmrc.gov.uk/payinghmrc/stamp-reserve.htm.

Interaction between SDRT and stamp duty

10.11 Chargeable securities are usually also 'stock or marketable securities'. Stamp duty is chargeable on Transfers of these types of asset, so clearly both stamp duty and SDRT can apply to the same transaction. To avoid a double charge, any SDRT charge is automatically cancelled (and any tax paid can be reclaimed) if a document giving effect to the transaction (usually a stock transfer form) is executed and 'duly stamped' within six years of the agreement (*FA 1986, s 92*). Private transactions in securities are almost invariably documented and any stamp duty paid. As noted at **10.14**, there are several reasons why it is often best to arrange to fall within the stamp duty regime.

10.12 In some circumstances, Transfers are automatically deemed to be 'duly stamped' (**8.40**), so that mere execution of the Transfer is sufficient to cancel the SDRT charge. In some other cases, especially where a relief is claimed, the Transfer is not duly stamped unless the liability has been adjudicated (see **8.45**). In yet other cases, adjudication is not required, and simple stamping with the correct duty is sufficient to render the Transfer duly stamped unless and until the adequacy of stamping is challenged. Thus, no SDRT is normally paid on such transactions; the main risk is that the parties fail to execute a suitable document and ensure it is 'duly stamped' before the six-year deadline. HMRC have made it clear that, where such cases come to light, they will pursue the outstanding SDRT.

10.13 Often, the execution and stamping of a Transfer will not happen until after the SDRT has technically become due and payable. In recognition of this, HMRC do not in practice seek to collect SDRT on private, non-financial market transactions, or pursue penalties for failure to notify liability, where it is expected that the liability will be cancelled within a few weeks. This delay effectively amounts to an interest-free deferral of payment of the tax. However, should the liability eventually prove payable, interest will be charged from the accountable date, and a penalty may be charged for failure to notify liability.

Issues in non-financial market transactions

10.14 In relation to non-financial market transactions, it is normally best to ensure that the stamp duty rules apply and that any SDRT liability is automatically cancelled for the following reasons:

- Stamp duty reliefs such as group transfer relief (*FA 1930, s 42*) and the reorganisation reliefs (*FA 1986, ss 75* and *77*) do not apply directly to SDRT. An appropriate document must be executed and submitted for stamping in order to claim the relief under the stamp duty rules and cancel any SDRT liability at the same time.
- The definition of 'consideration' for stamp duty purposes is more restricted than that for SDRT purposes. So, the tax bill is often less under stamp duty than under SDRT, but payment of the correct tax under the stamp duty rules is still sufficient to cancel a potentially larger SDRT liability.

10.15 Note that the document of transfer must transfer the securities to the person who was the original transferee under the agreement (or their nominee) – *FA 1986, s 92(1A)*. If A agrees to transfer to B, and B agrees to transfer to C, but there is a single stock transfer form from A to C, this does *not* cancel the SDRT charge on the A to B transfer agreement. In practice, this can be a particular problem where a relief is to be claimed on the A to B transfer. It is usually necessary to ensure that a transfer document is produced for each individual transfer step, to avoid incurring multiple SDRT charges (see Example 9.3).

10.16 In general, shares and securities issued by companies not registered in the UK are outside the scope of SDRT. The exception is where those shares are held on a share register in the UK. Some non-UK registered companies, especially those registered in the Channel Islands and the Isle of Man, maintain copies of their share registers in the UK – often for administrative convenience where, for example, the shareholders are in the UK. In these situations, care must be taken to ensure that the UK copy truly is no more than a copy of the main register kept in the country of registration. It is not unknown for HMRC to allege that the UK 'copy' is in fact a main share register, bringing the shares within the UK SDRT net.

10.17 *FA 1986, s 88* specifies a few situations in which execution (and stamping, where necessary) of a Transfer does not cancel the SDRT charge. These are mostly anti-avoidance provisions to prevent exploitation of exemptions such as those for financial market operators. There are two cases of potential interest to ordinary investors – although, even here, a financial market professional will normally be involved and will deal with the SDRT obligations:

- units in a UK unit trust are exempt from stamp duty on transfer, but may still be liable to SDRT on agreement to transfer to anyone other than the managers of the scheme; execution of a Transfer does not cancel any SDRT charge; and
- when a company issues bonus shares or makes a rights issue, the right to receive the shares may be in 'renounceable letters of allotment' issued

to the existing shareholders. Entitlement to the shares may be passed to others by transferring the renounceable letters. A Transfer is normally automatically exempt from stamp duty, but execution of a Transfer does not cancel any SDRT liability which may arise.

SDRT AND FINANCIAL MARKETS

10.18 The vast majority of quoted UK securities are held in electronic systems such as CREST (see below) and traded electronically, without production of any document of transfer. When a client buys quoted chargeable securities in this way, SDRT remains the final tax. The securities are usually purchased through market operators such as stockbrokers and banks; these are normally members of the relevant stock exchange (or 'qualified dealers'), and the SDRT regulations make them responsible for collecting and paying any SDRT which arises (*SI 1986/1711, reg* 2). When such an operator buys securities on behalf of a client, the SDRT is normally automatically added to the client bill by the electronic system and passed directly to HMRC. The client has no responsibility for notifying liability or making payment to HMRC.

10.19 Quoted securities are usually purchased for monetary consideration, and the liability under stamp duty would not be any less than under SDRT, so no disadvantage arises to the client from suffering SDRT. In fact, the SDRT liability is often slightly lower, because stamp duty is generally rounded to the next £5 above, whereas SDRT is only rounded to the nearest penny. The one exception is where the total consideration does not exceed £1,000, in which case stamp duty would be nil but SDRT is still charged.

CREST

10.20 Buying or selling securities generally involves two distinct stages: first, an agreement or contract; then a transfer in settlement of the contract. CREST is an electronic settlement system for quoted securities, originally established by a consortium of banks in the mid 1990s but now owned by the Euroclear Group. It formed a key part of the 1996 transition from paper-based transfers to electronic transfers on the London Stock Exchange. This transition was part of the general deregulation or freeing up of the market, colloquially referred to as 'Big Bang'. Stock market transactions are mostly processed within CREST without the need for paper documents. When the sale and purchase of securities within CREST is agreed, the brokers or other market operators acting on behalf of vendor and purchaser enter details of the transaction into the CREST system. Provided the details entered on behalf of vendor and purchaser agree, CREST matches them and processes the transfer. At the same time, CREST transfers the purchase/ sale price between the accounts of the parties. Finally, CREST also collects (from the purchaser's broker's account) any SDRT due on the transaction and pays this to HMRC. As part of the compliance arrangement, each evening CREST sends details of that day's trades to HMRC.

Letters of direction

10.21 As explained above (at **10.14**), an SDRT charge may arise on certain agreements to transfer securities when no stamp duty would arise on a paper transfer, because the consideration for the transfer does not count for stamp duty purposes. In the financial sector, this commonly occurs in relation to large holdings of quoted securities in connection with mergers and consolidations – for example, certain mergers of pension funds. In theory, it would be possible to remove all of the quoted securities in question from CREST, carry out a paper transfer, then put them all back into CREST – but this would be an administrative nightmare, where hundreds of different securities might be involved. The securities are typically held on behalf of the pension fund or similar owner by custodians (often special purpose subsidiaries of banks). The transferor can effectively create a transfer document by issuing a letter of direction to the custodian, directing him to hold the shares for the benefit of the transferee. This is known as a letter of direction. It may be submitted for stamping if necessary and, once 'duly stamped', is sufficient to cancel any SDRT charge which would otherwise arise.

The 'recognised intermediary' exemption

10.22 The efficient operation of the securities market depends on the existence of traders who 'make a market' by offering to buy and sell securities from/to all comers. The profit on such trading, as a proportion of price, is often very small, and the imposition of SDRT would inhibit the market. An exemption is, therefore, available for purchase of securities by appropriate market operators, generally referred to as 'recognised intermediaries' (RIs) (*FA 1986, s 88A*).

10.23 Initially, the exemption was restricted to persons (individuals, companies or other entities) which were members of the London Stock Exchange, although it was gradually expanded to include other exchanges. However, in order to comply with the requirements of the EU Markets in Financial Instruments Directive (MiFID), the scope of the exemption was considerably widened from November 2007 to include non-members of stock exchanges carrying on share trading who are authorised by a state in the European Economic Area to provide investment services or activities as set out in the Directive.

10.24 Note the use of the word 'recognised' – the relief does not apply unless the trader has applied for and gained HMRC recognition for the purpose.

10.25 An RI must not carry on any 'excluded business'. Excluded businesses encompass those which involve making or managing investments (for example, insurance or running unit trusts) as well as the provision of services to related companies. In practice, financial services groups often also carry on excluded businesses, and so carry on their RI business through a separate company. However, a few have negotiated arrangements with HMRC under which they 'ring fence' their RI business within a greater company, and treat movements of stock between parts of the company as if they were sales and purchases.

Example 10.2 – SDRT on market transactions

Harry instructs his broker, Irena Associates, to buy up to 10,000 shares in Jeremiah plc. Meanwhile, Karen instructs her bank Liam Corporation to sell her holding of 3,000 shares in Jeremiah plc. Irena Associates agrees to buy Karen's shares, initially on its own account. Because Irena Associates is a recognised intermediary, no SDRT arises on the purchase. Once Irena Associates has purchased a further 7,000 shares, it transfers all 10,000 to its client account, for the benefit of Harry. At the moment of transfer, CREST charges Irena Associates SDRT on the price which Harry is paying for the shares. As regards the 3,000 shares originally owned by Karen, one lot of SDRT is paid, just as if Karen had sold them directly to Harry (and the same is true in principle for the other 7,000 shares).

Contracts for differences (CFDs)

10.26 The relief is available to prevent double charges when a trader buys shares and sells them onwards to a customer. However, it applies to all purchases of chargeable securities by the intermediary and, in practice, one of the biggest uses is to allow traders to buy shares free of SDRT to hedge 'contracts for differences' (CFDs). Under a CFD, a customer gains the economic effect of having bought shares without actually buying them.

Example 10.3 – Contracts for differences

Moira believes shares of quoted UK company Nick plc will increase in value over the next six weeks. Broker Olive Ltd agrees to write a CFD for 5,000 shares in Nick plc. Under the CFD, Moira immediately pays Olive Ltd an amount equal to the current price of 5,000 shares in Nick plc (plus a small commission). In return, Olive Ltd agrees that, in six weeks' time, it will pay Moira the value of 5,000 Nick plc shares at that time. Moira, therefore, is in the same economic position as if she had invested in 5,000 Nick plc shares for a fixed six-week period. However, writing the CFD does not involve any agreement to transfer securities, so no liability to SDRT arises for either party. Meanwhile, Olive Ltd does not wish to suffer the risk that Nick plc shares will rise in value, so it goes into the market and buys 5,000 Nick plc shares for its own account. Because Olive Ltd is a recognised intermediary, it does not pay SDRT on this purchase. In six weeks' time, it will sell the Nick plc shares and use the proceeds to pay Moira under the CFD.

It is thought that up to half of all UK stock market transactions relate to use of CFDs. HMRC do not generally seek to impose SDRT on such transactions, provided they are implemented with due care; there would probably be no point in trying to do so, as most such transactions would simply not happen if there was an SDRT cost.

Depositories and clearing systems

10.27 Overseas investors often prefer to buy UK securities through a clearance system operating in their home country or in the form of depository receipts. The rate of SDRT is increased to 1.5% where there is an agreement to transfer securities to a depository receipt issuer or clearance system. The justification for this is that, while the shares remain within the clearance system or depository, subsequent transfers occur without imposition of SDRT. The higher rate is also charged where new shares are *issued* to a non-European clearance system or depository receipt issuer. Until October 2009, the charge was also applied when shares were issued to a European clearance system or depository. However, a European Court case (*HSBC & Vidacos v HMRC*) decided this was contrary to EU law and the charge is no longer applied in these cases. An anti avoidance rule was introduced by *FA 2010, s 54* to prevent tax-free transfers to non-European clearance systems via a European system.

The 1.5% charge is sometimes referred to as a 'season ticket'. There is at least anecdotal evidence that, on average, such shares are transferred fewer than three times within the system before being transferred out of the clearance or depository system, so the 1.5% charge is probably punitive. Clearing systems can avoid the 1.5% charge by agreeing with HMRC to charge SDRT as normal on transfers (*FA 1986, s 97*).

Public issues

10.28 When there is a public issue of shares, the underwriters typically take temporary ownership of any shares not immediately taken up, and then sell them in the market over the next few weeks. There is normally no SDRT or stamp duty on the issue of shares, but this process would give rise to an SDRT charge on the subsequent sale, which would add to the costs of the share issue. A relief (*FA 1986, s 89A*) therefore applies to stop this charge arising, provided the strict conditions are complied with.

Stocklending

10.29 In origin, stocklending was a process by which institutional investors 'lent' their investments to traders to allow them to sell shares they had not yet bought, all in the interests of maintaining market liquidity. However, this is not a true loan – rather, it is a sale and repurchase agreement which could have given rise to SDRT. So, to maintain liquidity, subject to stringent conditions, there is a relief (*FA 1986, s 89AA*). The process gained notoriety in 2008, as speculators borrowed huge numbers of bank shares, flooding the market with them, thus driving the share price down, in turn allowing them to buy back at a reduced price and return the loan – and all helped by an SDRT relief!

Unit trusts

10.30 Units in unit trusts are specifically exempted from stamp duty. If units in a UK unit trust are transferred directly between investors, the usual SDRT charge applies, and this cannot be cancelled by execution of a document of transfer. However, in practice, such units in publicly listed unit trusts are not usually transferred, they are surrendered to the manager (who then cancels them or reissues them to a new investor). No charge arises on the investor when this happens; but, under a special regime in *FA 1999, Sch 19*, the manager has to pay a composite SDRT charge which takes account of numbers of surrenders and issues, and the composition of the unit trust investment portfolio. The manager recoups the SDRT cost through the margin between the prices at which he issues and repurchases units. The *Sch 19* regime is widely regarded as burdensome and unduly complex. It has proved a fruitful area for investigation by HMRC auditors.

Chapter 11

Planning, Pitfalls and Legacy Liabilities

INTRODUCTION

11.1 The complexity and illogicality of stamp tax rules have often been exploited through contrived avoidance arrangements. However, increasing volumes of general and specific anti-avoidance legislation, including the requirement in the case of SDLT to disclose novel planning arrangements, have dramatically reduced the scope for tax mitigation. Planning now is often as much a matter of avoiding unintended and unexpected additional liabilities as reducing the headline tax cost of a transaction.

This chapter draws together thoughts on planning, both to minimise costs and to avoid potential pitfalls arising from all three stamp taxes. It also considers situations in which current liabilities may arise or increase as a consequence of disturbing transactions carried out, or structures adopted, long ago.

References to particular arrangements or structures are included in this chapter purely for illustrative purposes. Their appearance should not be taken as advising that they succeed in reducing liabilities. Some of the arrangements described are believed to have been effective under previous legislation but have subsequently been blocked. It is essential that expert advice be taken before entering into any arrangement to mitigate tax, and no responsibility is accepted for the consequences of any persons acting or failing to act on the basis of the comments or examples in this book.

STAMP DUTY LAND TAX

Planning

11.2 SDLT mitigation has generally involved one or more of four general approaches:

(1) Arrange to have the benefit of a relief or exemption, or a combination of two or more reliefs or exemptions.

Example 11.1 – combining relief and exemption

Charles wishes to buy a house at a cost of £600,000 to give to his nephew Dan. Charles contracts to buy the house, paying the usual deposit. He then agrees to sell it to Dan for £1,000. The two purchases (by Charles and by Dan) are substantially performed and completed at the same time. If the arrangement were effective, the purchase by Charles would be ignored and only the onward sale to Dan would be subject to SDLT. The consideration for this is below the SDLT threshold, so no tax would be payable. Note that, even if this arrangement might once have worked, it is undoubtedly now blocked by *FA 2003, s 75A*.

---

(2) Transfer something other than land.

Example 11.2 – transfer land-owning company

Dale Group plc owns a subsidiary company Hill Ltd which owns a number of valuable properties. It is decided to sell one property. The other properties are transferred out of Hill Ltd to sister company Valley Ltd for cash, and surplus cash is paid out of Hill Ltd to Dale Group plc as a dividend. The value of Hill Ltd is now the same as the value of the one remaining property which it holds. Hill Ltd is then sold. The purchaser has to pay stamp duty at 0.5% on the price paid for the shares, rather than SDLT at 4% on a land purchase. Note that versions of this planning have been widely used in the past and, in principle, HMRC do not appear to have regarded it as objectionable. However, the specific circumstances of each transaction must be examined in detail to establish whether a version of the planning could be of use.

---

(3) Reduce the value of the land transferred (with most of the consideration paid for something else) – see Example 7.2 for an explanation of a type of planning which may have been used until blocked by *FA 2003, s 75A*.

(4) Arrange to fall within a specific statutory treatment which gives rise to a low or zero SDLT charge.

Example 11.3 – PFI relief

Litebuild plc is negotiating with Marsh Education Authority (MEA) to buy a disused school site for housing development. MEA intends to use the sale proceeds to pay part of the cost of rebuilding a college. It is agreed that MEA will grant to Litebuild a 30-year lease of the college site, and Litebuild will grant an underlease back to MEA for two days short of 30 years. Litebuild will rebuild the college, or procure its rebuilding, and will maintain the grounds and fabric of the building during the lease. In return, MEA will transfer the disused school site to Litebuild in part-payment for the rebuilding of the college, will make a one-off initial payment to cover the balance of the rebuilding cost, and will make yearly payments under the lease for the maintenance services. On the face of it, this arrangement could fall within the terms of *FA 2003, Sch 4, para 17* (PFI relief), so that no SDLT would be payable. The facts outlined here appear readily to fall within the terms of this treatment. The treatment could be available for a transaction starting from a less favourable fact pattern, but it would be important to examine the precise circumstances of the parties and the proposed transactions before there could be any confidence that this would be the case.

11.3 Specific anti-avoidance legislation and *FA 2003, ss 75A–75C* make it difficult to find 'off the shelf' combinations of these approaches which can be applied to a range of transactions to reduce the SDLT liability below the expected level. New versions of old ideas emerge from time to time, but the recently extended DOTAS rules will allow HMRC to block them quickly with new legislation when necessary.

11.4 The best approach is probably to have the fullest possible knowledge of the various statutory reliefs, exemptions and treatments which are available, so that these can be applied to each individual transaction in the most favourable way. In virtually every case, it remains essential to consider carefully whether the combination of steps required to complete the transaction bring it within the scope of *FA 2003, ss 75A–75C* (see **7.5** et seq) and whether any disclosure responsibility arises under the DOTAS rules (see **7.26**).

Pitfalls

11.5 At least as important is the need to be aware of the pitfalls waiting to trap the unwary. In relation to SDLT, these arise from current legislation and are listed here, but are mostly dealt with in more detail elsewhere, as indicated:

- clawback of relief previously claimed, where there is a change of control of a company (**3.23** et seq);
- transfer to a company which is connected with the transferor, but not in a group together with the transferor (**2.27**);
- informal arrangements for occupation of a property, which continue for long enough to give rise to a tenancy on which SDLT arises (**4.8** et seq);
- execution of a lease after substantial performance of the related agreement, so that the first rent review falls less than five years after the date of execution (**4.38**);

- transfer of a lease, when relief was claimed on grant (**4.15**);
- transfer of property by operation of law, especially in non-UK mergers etc (**2.4**); and
- withdrawal of cash or other value from a partnership after transfer of property to the partnership from a partner or connected person (**5.17**).

11.6 In the context of transactions in land as well as other assets, there are also stamp duty pitfalls which arise from legacy structures – that is, structures and arrangements which were put in place in the course of previous tax planning, often many years ago. These may give rise to current liabilities if not dealt with in the correct manner. Examples are described at **11.26** et seq.

STAMP DUTY AND SDRT

11.7 There are no general anti-avoidance rules for stamp duty and SDRT equivalent to *FA 2003, ss 75A–75C* for SDLT. There are specific anti-avoidance rules relating to particular assets and transactions. SDRT is potentially within the DOTAS rules but, at the time of writing (September 2010), no regulations had been issued to activate this. Stamp duty is not within the DOTAS rules, presumably reflecting the fact that it is not strictly speaking a 'tax'.

SDRT planning

11.8 SDRT is only payable on an agreement to transfer chargeable securities. 'Planning' to minimise SDRT usually takes one of three forms, or a combination of them:

(1) minimising the amount of consideration which is subject to tax;

(2) transferring something which is not a chargeable security; or

(3) cancelling the SDRT charge by ensuring a Transfer document is executed and duly stamped (see **10.11**). (In this book, the expression 'Transfer' is capitalised to make it clear that this is a reference to the potentially stampable document.)

11.9 The first approach is mostly of interest for financial market transactions. It commonly involves the use of options and other financial instruments, detailed consideration of which is beyond the scope of this book. However, SDRT is only charged by reference to the value of consideration given in money or money's worth. Therefore, a transfer of valuable securities which is genuinely for zero or low consideration (for example, between family or group members) will attract zero or low SDRT, the market value of the securities themselves being irrelevant.

11.10 The second approach is also mainly of interest to financial and capital markets, although the risk of transferring securities which are *unintentionally* within the charge to SDRT is a pitfall described at **11.13**. Outside financial and capital markets, it may be possible to achieve SDRT-free transfer of chargeable securities by placing them in some kind of 'wrapper'.

Example 11.4 – chargeable securities in a wrapper

Serena owns 100% of the shares in a valuable company T Ltd, which she intends to sell to Vera. Serena arranges to set up a Jersey-registered company U Ltd, and she subscribes £100 for 100 shares in the company. Once all formalities for formation of the company and issue of the shares have been completed, Serena sets up a Jersey-registered limited partnership, W LP, with herself and U Ltd as partners. Serena contributes the shares of T Ltd to W LP as partnership capital. This is a transfer for no consideration for stamp duty purposes, and execution of a stock transfer form by Serena is sufficient to cancel any SDRT charge which might otherwise arise. Serena then sells the shares of U Ltd and her interest in W LP to Vera for full value (the same as the value of T Ltd). Although this effectively transfers the shares of T Ltd to Vera, none of the assets actually transferred is within the charge to SDRT. Theoretically, the transfers may be subject to stamp duty but, as none of the assets is located in the UK, it is unlikely to be necessary to stamp the related documents. The benefit is shared with Serena through a price adjustment.

11.11 Alternatively, the nature of the security itself may be chosen to be outside the scope of SDRT.

Example 11.5 – securities outside the scope of SDRT

Yorrick intends to set up a company to manufacture better mousetraps. He anticipates that, within five years, he will be able to sell the successful company to a major manufacturer for a large sum. He therefore chooses to set up a company registered in the Isle of Man but managed and controlled in the UK. For other tax purposes, this is treated in the same way as a UK incorporated company. But, provided Yorrick does not make the mistake of keeping the company's principal share register in the UK, its shares will remain outside the SDRT net when the time comes to sell.

11.12 In practice, for non-stock market transactions, the third approach is normally what automatically happens, and any planning is directed at minimising the stamp duty (see **11.17**).

Example 11.6 – rely on stamp duty definition of consideration

On 1 April 2011, Raj agrees to sell his minority holding of shares in unquoted UK company Courgette Ltd to Petra in exchange for Petra's collection of rare books, valued at £120,000. This agreement gives rise to an SDRT liability of £600 which is technically payable by 7 May 2011. However, the consideration does not count for stamp duty purposes (see **8.22** et seq) so, provided a stock transfer form is completed no later than 31 March 2017, the SDRT charge will be cancelled. Because there is *no* consideration for stamp duty purposes, the stock transfer form is deemed to be 'duly stamped' as soon as it is executed (see **8.38**). If there is consideration which counts for stamp duty purposes such that a liability arises, the form would have to be executed and presented for stamping no later than 31 March 2017 in order to cancel the SDRT charge. It would generally be desirable to do this as soon as possible after 1 April 2011.

SDRT pitfalls

11.13 The main pitfall to be wary of is the risk of a security unintentionally being or becoming a 'chargeable security' and therefore within the SDRT net. The commonest category of chargeable security consists of shares in UK companies. Most loan capital and debt instruments, such as corporate bonds, as well as most shares of non-UK companies are outside the scope of SDRT (see **10.5**). However, bonds and other loan capital may be within the SDRT net if they have certain 'equity-like' characteristics. In particular, any of the four following factors may bring the security into the SDRT net:

(1) A high coupon/interest rate. If the interest rate exceeds 'a reasonable commercial return on the nominal amount of the capital', the security will not qualify for the loan capital exemption from SDRT (although it may still escape under other exemptions). This is often a problem in relation to so-called 'junk bonds', which have a high interest rate to reflect risk. It may be necessary to gather evidence that the interest rate is comparable to that on other publicly traded securities with a similar risk profile, to convince HMRC that the interest rate does not exceed a reasonable commercial return.

Example 11.7 – high coupon bond

Ralph and Simon are brothers. Ralph owns all of the shares of travel agent Timeout plc, a UK company. Timeout needs additional funds, and Simon agrees to lend £2 million at an annual interest rate of 18%, reflecting perceived risk. The debt is formalised as a two-year bond. After six months, Ralph agrees to buy the bond from Simon for face value. The high interest rate means that the bond may not qualify for the loan capital exemption from SDRT, and the agreement to transfer may give rise to an SDRT charge of £10,000 (£2 million at 0.5%). The problem may be avoided if Ralph makes a new loan to Timeout, allowing it to prepay the original bond – assuming the terms of the bond allow this.

---

(2) A variable interest rate, where the issuer of a debt security has the right to vary the interest rate, including the right to cancel or withhold a payment, or the interest varies in the light of business results or asset values. Note. however. that so-called 'ratchet loans', where the interest rate goes up to reflect increased risk when business results or asset values deteriorate (and/or goes down when values or results improve) may still qualify for exemption. Equally, no problem is caused by the fact that the interest or amount repayable on repayment may vary by reference to the UK Retail Price Index or a similar index.

Example 11.8 – variable interest rate bond

UK company Zebra plc borrows from a private equity firm P (which is also a shareholder) and issues a loan note which pays monthly interest at an annual rate 3% above Bank of England base rate. The loan note provides that the interest rate will fall to base rate for the year following any year in which Zebra makes a loss, but will increase to 6% above base rate for the year following any year in which Zebra makes a pre-tax profit of more than £1 million. No stamp tax consequences arise from the issue of the note. However, two years later, P agrees to sell the loan note to Q, a wealthy individual. The loan note will not qualify for the loan capital exemption and is a 'chargeable security', so the sale will be subject to SDRT on the sale price. Assuming it has no features which prevent it from being 'stock or (a) marketable security', a Transfer document will be subject to stamp duty on the sale price.

---

(3) Right of conversion into shares or other securities, or right to receive shares or securities, for example in lieu of interest. These are often called PIK notes, because interest is or may be 'paid in kind' – that is, paid by the issue of further debt instruments. However, if the security bears interest at an acceptable rate, but the *issuer* has a unilateral right to make payment in the form of further securities, the security is not thereby prevented from qualifying as loan capital until the issuer exercises that right and commits to making an interest payment in kind.

Example 11.9 – right to further securities, PIK notes

Yak plc issues five-year loan notes to a consortium of investors. The loan notes provide for yearly payment of interest at 6%, which is considered to be a normal commercial rate, and repayment at par at the end of the term. However, they also give Yak plc the right to make up to two interest payments by issuing further loan notes with a face value equal to the amount of interest due, an interest rate of 10% per year and redeemable at par at the same time as the original notes (a PIK payment). Yak must give three months' notice of intention to make each PIK payment. The 10% notes only provide for payment of interest in cash. In all other respects, both kinds of note qualify as exempt loan capital.

No SDRT arises on the issue of the notes. Unless and until Yak gives notice to make a PIK payment, the securities qualify for the loan capital exemption, and transfers in that period should not give rise to any SDRT. However, from the time Yak gives notice until after the PIK payment is actually made, the original securities cease to qualify for the loan capital exemption, and any transfers of those notes will be subject to SDRT. Once the PIK payment is made, the notes again qualify as exempt loan capital, unless or until notice of a further PIK payment is given.

The notes issued in lieu of interest do not carry any PIK option, and so should qualify for the loan capital exemption on any transfers after they are issued, assuming the interest rate is not regarded as excessive.

(4) A high premium on repayment – for example, a bond with a face value of £100 is issued at a price of £100 but, at the end of its five-year life, the amount repayable is £160, being the face value plus a premium of £60. Remarkably, the same economic effect may be achieved without risk of falling within the SDRT net, by issuing the bond with a £160 face value but at a £60 discount, so that the amount paid at issue is £100. However, this may affect the treatment of the bond for other purposes.

Any of these characteristics may lead to denial of the loan capital exemption. This is a complex area, and specialist advice is likely to be needed to determine whether SDRT applies to any transfer if these characteristics are present.

11.14 The other main risk is that shares of a non-UK incorporated company, normally outside the SDRT net, will become chargeable securities if they are 'registered in a register kept in the UK' (*FA 1986, s 99(4)(a)*). As suggested at Example 11.5, non-UK incorporated companies (often incorporated in the Channel Islands or the Isle of Man) are widely and validly used by UK-based individuals and businesses. The share register of such a company is normally kept in the territory of incorporation, but a copy may be maintained in the UK for administrative convenience. Care must be taken to ensure that the UK document (or electronic record) is no more than a copy, and that the overseas register is the definitive document for determining the identity of the shareholders. HMRC have been known to examine this matter very closely, with a view to showing that the UK record is a definitive register so that the shares become chargeable securities.

Stamp duty planning

11.15 Stamp duty is currently chargeable only on documents effecting transfers of 'stock and marketable securities' and interests in partnerships owning stock and marketable securities.

11.16 In relation to transfers of partnership interests, the simplest planning is to choose not to present any transfer document for stamping. This is effective provided the parties are satisfied that there is no need for a stamped document. A stamped document is normally only required if it is to be produced in evidence or used for other official purposes. Therefore, the most likely occasions on which a stamped document may be needed are in relation to a dispute between the parties or in order to prove to HMRC that the transfer has taken place. In practice, it appears to be rare for transfers of partnership interests to be stamped. An alternative approach is to structure the transaction so that there is no Transfer document which may require to be stamped. For example, an effective transfer of a partnership interest might be achieved by the outgoing partner withdrawing capital from the partnership, and the incoming partner introducing the same amount of capital. This may be regarded as a transfer for some purposes (including SDLT, where relevant). However, it should not be necessary to execute a Transfer and no stamp duty liability should arise.

11.17 It is usually only necessary to stamp a transfer document for stock and marketable securities, if they are chargeable securities, so that the SDRT charge is cancelled (see **10.11**) and any registration formalities may be completed. The simplest form of planning is, therefore, to transfer securities which are not chargeable – for example, shares in a non-UK incorporated company – and then choose not to present the Transfer for stamping (but beware the risk of making them chargeable by keeping the register in the UK). Alternatively, it may be possible either to arrange to fall within the terms of a relief (see **Chapter 9**) or to minimise the consideration which is taken into account, as set out below.

11.18 See **8.24** et seq for discussion of the measurement of consideration for stamp duty purposes. Some planning has taken the form of attempting to make the consideration wholly unascertainable (see **8.35**), but there are risks. In particular, in the case of *L M Tenancies 1 plc v IRC* ([1996] STC 880), HMRC succeeded in arguing that linking consideration to the price of a publicly traded security, when that price was not likely to change much, did not make the consideration wholly unascertainable. It is safer to make the consideration ascertainable but low (see **8.55** et seq).

Stamp duty pitfalls

11.19 A major risk in relation to stamp duty is linked with the SDRT risk identified at **11.13**. Transfers of many shares and securities may theoretically be within the charge to stamp duty but, if the securities are outside the charge to SDRT, there is normally no imperative to stamp the Transfers. If shares or debt instruments unintentionally become chargeable securities, an SDRT charge will arise on an agreement to transfer for valuable consideration. This may be cancelled by stamping a Transfer, but that in itself will require payment of stamp duty unless the Transfer qualifies for a relief.

11.20 A related difficulty arises where different assets are transferred by means of the same Transfer. This is unlikely to be a problem where UK shares are transferred by means of a stock transfer form, because that form is normally only valid to transfer UK shares. However, where the Transfer takes the form of a declaration of trust (see Example 9.3), it would be possible for a single document to transfer UK and non-UK shares. This should generally be avoided!

Example 11.10 – mixed assets in a single Transfer

Reptile plc, a UK company, agrees to pay market value to buy the shares of two companies, Lizard Ltd and Gecko Ltd, from Reptile's 51% shareholder, Zoo Inc. Lizard is a UK company worth £100,000, Gecko is a Cayman-registered company worth £1 million. The agreement gives rise to an SDRT liability of £500. Reptile intends immediately to carry out a reorganisation which will involve further transfers of the shares of these companies, so it is agreed that Zoo Inc will execute a declaration of trust in favour of Reptile in relation to the shares. Zoo Inc will then eventually transfer the shares to the final shareholder within Reptile's group. Because Reptile is a UK company and makes payment out of a UK bank account, it is likely that any Transfer will relate to 'any matter or thing to be done' in the UK and so will be liable to stamp duty (see **8.17** et seq). If a single declaration of trust is executed, it will be necessary to pay stamp duty in relation to both the Lizard and the Gecko shares – a total of £5,500 – before the Transfer can be regarded as 'duly stamped' thus cancelling the SDRT charge. To avoid the problem, separate declarations of trust should be completed for the two companies, allowing Reptile to stamp only the one relating to the Lizard shares. Alternatively, the

SDRT could be paid on the Lizard shares and the declaration of trust could be left unstamped, but only if Reptile is happy it will never be necessary to produce the declaration of trust for any UK official purpose (see **8.3**).

11.21 Many other risk areas relate to specific reliefs (especially group and reconstruction reliefs), and these are described in relation to those reliefs in **Chapter 9**. It is important to note that the restrictions which may lead to denial of these reliefs only apply at the time of the transaction in respect of which relief is claimed. There is no question of stamp duty reliefs being clawed back as a result of subsequent events, although relief may be denied if there were arrangements for those subsequent events at the time of the original transaction. This is in contrast to the equivalent reliefs under SDLT, where a change in control too soon after the original transaction, even if unrelated to that original transaction, may lead to retrospective disallowance of the relief.

11.22 The other major pitfall in relation to stamp duty concerns the measurement of consideration and, more specifically, the impact of the contingency principle. As noted at **8.37**, under this principle any ascertainable consideration which may be payable on the happening of a particular contingency is regarded as payable and subject to stamp duty. There is no relief or adjustment if the consideration eventually proves not to be payable.

Example 11.11 – contingency principle

David buys the shares of a trading company from Goliath for consideration of £1 million payable now, plus further consideration equal to 20% of the company's trading profits for the next two years. The further payment is subject to a ceiling of £2 million. Meanwhile, Saul buys a similar company from Goliath for consideration of £1 million, plus 20% of the company's trading profits for the next two years with no ceiling specified. David will have to pay stamp duty of £15,000 (£1 million certain plus £2 million contingent, at 0.5%) but Saul will only have to pay £5,000, because the further consideration is wholly unascertainable.

Unfortunately, there is often a conflict between the desire to minimise stamp duty and the commercial need to limit the contingent consideration. As a result, David's fact pattern is perhaps seen more often than Saul's.

LEGACY LIABILITIES

11.23 When a company or other entity is bought, there is always a risk that the purchased entity has failed to comply with tax obligations and may harbour undisclosed liabilities, including stamp taxes. The purchaser will doubtless minimise the risk by a combination of due diligence investigation and warranties or indemnities. However, unexpected stamp tax liabilities may also arise on purchase of shares or assets, even though the vendor or purchased entity has fully complied with past obligations. This section seeks to highlight the liabilities which may arise.

SDLT

11.24 The acquisition of a company which has claimed group, reconstruction or acquisition reliefs from SDLT may lead to clawback of that group relief, as described at **3.23** et seq.

11.25 Apart from the normal SDLT charge, the only SDLT liabilities which may arise on direct acquisition of an interest in land relate to leases. The acquisition of an existing lease may be treated as the grant of a new lease if certain reliefs were claimed on original grant of the lease – see **4.15** for details of this. If the SDLT liability was not determined when the lease was granted (normally because the rent was variable or not finalised at that point), a new tenant taking on the lease may inherit ongoing obligations and liabilities – see **4.37** for details.

Stamp duty

11.26 In past years, stamp duty has been payable on Transfers of many different categories of assets, such as goodwill, intellectual property and, of course, land and buildings. Various structures and strategies were adopted to reduce or avoid this charge. These strategies and structures often merely defer the crystallisation of the charge, until such time as another event occurs. Stamp duty has been abolished on Transfers of these categories of assets, but that abolition generally only applies to subsequent transactions. Stamp duty is likely to remain potentially payable on documents relating to transactions entered into before the time of abolition. It is, therefore, important to understand the old transactions when dealing with the assets in question, in order to avoid having to pay the old stamp duty charges.

Documents executed and retained offshore

11.27 A Transfer of UK situs assets which are within the charge to stamp duty is liable to stamp duty, no matter where executed. However, if the document is executed and retained offshore, payment of any stamp duty may be deferred. This deferral is potentially permanent if the document is never brought to the UK. Alternatively, if it becomes necessary to stamp the document (for example, in order to produce it in evidence in a civil court case), no late stamping penalty will be incurred, provided the document is presented for stamping within 30 days of first arrival in the UK. For documents executed before 1 October 1999, no late payment interest is incurred, provided the duty is paid within 30 days of the first arrival of the document in the UK.

For this reason, many transfers of certain types of asset (but not generally shares or registered land) have been executed and retained outside the UK (typically in the Channel Islands or the Isle of Man). Although stamp duty no longer applies to Transfers of such assets, those Transfers executed under the old rules remain subject to whatever stamp duty charge applied at the time of execution. To retain the benefit of not incurring interest and penalties should it eventually be necessary to stamp them, it is important that the documents are not brought to the UK in the meantime.

Shares and land

11.28 Offshore execution has not been widely used in relation to transfers of shares and securities. This is because a duly stamped Transfer is required (a) for registration of the new owner in the company's books, and (b) since 1986, to cancel the related SDRT charge. For registered land, a duly stamped transfer is also required to change the owner at the Land Registry, so offshore execution was not appropriate. The alternative approach adopted for land transfers was generally known as 'resting on (or in) contract' or, less commonly, 'split title planning'. It was widely considered that this planning could not be used in Scotland because of differences in land law, although some lawyers maintained that these could be overcome. In an attempt to curtail the planning, any contracts for purchase of land for consideration exceeding £10 million executed after 24 July 2002 were treated as stampable Transfers.

Resting on contract

11.29 Bare legal title to the land was transferred to a nominee who held the land for the benefit of the beneficial owner (for reasons of land law, generally this would be two 'special purpose companies' or SPVs holding as joint trustees). With care, especially in relation to one anti-avoidance provision, such a transfer was liable only to a fixed stamp duty of £5 (50p prior to *FA 1999*). The vendor then entered into a contract to sell to the purchaser. The contract entitled the purchaser to call for a Transfer of the land. The purchaser paid the consideration (which gained him a beneficial interest in the land), and the vendor transferred the shares of the SPVs to the purchaser. The purchaser now had a beneficial interest in the land and control of the legal title through ownership of the SPVs which held title. This was generally accepted as equivalent to full legal and beneficial ownership. However, because no Transfer had been executed to transfer title to the purchaser, the purchase contract remained technically uncompleted and virtually no stamp duty had been paid.

If necessary, the purchaser could subsequently require the SPVs to transfer legal title to him. This Transfer would complete the purchase contract and so would crystallise the stamp duty charge on the original purchase. However, the charge would only crystallise at the date of the Transfer, so interest- and penalty-free deferral would have been achieved. In most cases, title was left in the hands of the SPVs, no Transfer was ever executed, and the stamp duty charge was not crystallised. When the time came for the purchaser to sell the land, the process could be repeated, leaving title in the hands of the same SPVs and transferring the shares in those companies. At that point, it became clear that the first sale and purchase would never be technically completed (because title to the land would never be transferred to the original purchaser), so the deferral of stamp duty on that original purchase would become permanent. This could be repeated many times on successive sales and purchases of the land. However, it would always be the case that the stamp duty on the latest sale and purchase in the sequence was merely deferred. That latest stamp duty charge would become payable if the latest purchase was completed by Transfer of legal title from the SPVs to the current beneficial owner.

Therein lies the danger. There are many properties still held in this 'split title' structure. If the structure is collapsed by transferring title from the SPVs to the beneficial owner, any deferred stamp duty on acquisition by the current beneficial owner will become payable. To avoid this problem, the structure must be maintained at least until the next time ownership of the land is transferred. The structure is not effective for saving SDLT, and so may as well be collapsed when a sale is entered into which is subject to SDLT, provided this can be done without also crystallising any old stamp duty charges. To achieve this, it is important that title is transferred directly from the SPVs to the purchaser under the contract which is subject to SDLT. Title must not first be transferred to the vendor under this latest contract.

Example 11.12 – completion of 'resting on contract' transaction

In 1971, Oldmoney Ltd purchased a prime city centre site from Armateur Ltd for £2 million. The purchase was effected by the 'resting on contract' scheme – so the parties entered into a sale and purchase contract, Oldmoney paid the purchase price and Armateur transferred to Oldmoney the shares of two Jersey-registered SPVs (S1 and S2) which jointly held legal title to the land. No Transfer was completed in conformity with the contract and no stamp duty was paid. At the time, the rate of stamp duty was 2%, so duty of £40,000 was effectively deferred.

On 1 April 2011, Oldmoney contracts to sell the property to Newrich Ltd for £80 million. Newrich will pay SDLT of £320,000 (£80 million at 4%) on the purchase. The contract provides that Oldmoney will convey the property to Newrich, and Newrich refuses to accept a conveyance from S1 and S2. The property is therefore first conveyed from S1 and S2 to Oldmoney. This crystallises the stamp duty charge deferred in 1971, and Oldmoney has to pay this before completing the onward conveyance to Newrich. Had Newrich accepted the conveyance direct from S1 and S2, the 1971 deferral of stamp duty would have become permanent and Oldmoney would have been spared the need to pay it. Under either scenario, beneficial and legal ownership of the property are reunited, whether in the hands of Oldmoney or directly in Newrich.

A potentially interesting subsidiary point arises. Stamp duty rates have increased since 1997 to a current maximum of 4% (soon to be 5% for residential property) but, at each increase, the old rates have been retained for contracts already signed but uncompleted. So, there should be no risk of the increased rates applying on completion of Oldmoney's original purchase. For a brief period between 1 August 1972 and 30 April 1974, rates were reduced, and the reduction also applied to any contracts signed but uncompleted at the start of the period. In the author's view, this means that, if the original Oldmoney purchase is completed as noted above, the stamp duty payable should be reduced to £20,000 (£2 million at 1%, being the rate introduced from 1972). HMRC may not agree.

Avoiding a document; the memorandum rule

11.30 The practice of 'resting on contract' described above was really just a specific example of this general principle: because stamp duty is chargeable on certain documents, no stamp duty is payable if no Transfer document (or document which is deemed to be a Transfer) is created. It was the development of share transfers without a Transfer document which led to the introduction of SDRT. SDLT was introduced because avoidance of stamp duty on property transactions was widespread, much of it historically by resting on contract. It was also often possible to avoid a liability on transfers of other assets such as goodwill, intellectual property and interests in partnerships by avoiding creation of the wrong type of document. For such assets, there is generally no legal requirement for a Transfer document in a particular form; compliance with the terms of the contract itself (eg making payment) usually gives effect to the transfer. This means the contract itself was usually the document liable to stamp duty. To avoid stamp duty, it was necessary to avoid creating a written contract. The normal approach was for the vendor to make a written offer to sell to the purchaser. The purchaser accepted the offer by his action – paying the purchase price to the vendor's solicitors, for example – and not by anything in writing. In some cases, the purchaser accepted orally, the acceptance being video-recorded and given in front of reliable witnesses!

11.31 In relation to transactions of this kind, HMRC (relying on cases such as *Associated British Engineering Ltd v IRC* ([1941] 1 KB 15) considered that any document which recorded the agreement in such a way as to become a primary record of the contract was subject to stamp duty. On this basis, any memorandum which the purchaser prepared to record the terms could be subject to stamp duty, even if prepared purely for internal purposes and a long time after the original transaction. Of course, this was only relevant if there was a need to produce such documents for official purposes – but that included proving the terms of the contract to HMRC for other tax purposes!

As time passes, it becomes less likely that any such memoranda will be created or required for official purposes. However, taxpayers who were purchasers under such undocumented contracts should continue to think carefully before 'tidying up' old arrangements by creating written records for posterity.

Last word

11.32 The idea of countering 'tax avoidance' has great popular appeal. However, in relation to stamp taxes as other taxes, much 'planning' consists of trying to ensure complex rules do not give rise to commercially damaging liabilities. Stamp taxes are very different from taxes on income and profits, and are often encountered only occasionally. As a result, the risk of accidental and unforeseen liabilities is high. It is hoped that this book may help reduce that risk.

Appendix A

Addresses, contact details etc

SDLT RETURNS

If SDLT returns are not filed electronically, original paper returns and any accompanying cheques should be sent to the HMRC Data Capture Centre at:

HM Revenue & Customs
Stamp Taxes/SDLT
Comben House
Farriers Way
NETHERTON
Merseyside
L30 4RN

Alternatively, they can be sent via the DX system to:

Rapid Data Capture Centre
DX 725593
Bootle 9

Returns should not be folded and therefore require an A4 or larger size envelope. Only forms SDLT1 to 4, plus plans if provided and cheques if that payment method is used, should be included – correspondence should be sent to Birmingham Stamp Office as noted below (see **6.8**).

DOTAS FORMS

Paper copies of forms relating to DOTAS (see **7.26**) may be ordered from the Anti-Avoidance Group on 08459 000404, but they may be more conveniently downloaded from www.hmrc.gov.uk/aiu/index.htm, or completed online following links from that webpage. If not completed and submitted online, completed DOTAS forms must be sent to:

Anti Avoidance Group
HM Revenue and Customs
1st Floor South
22 Kingsway
London WC2B 6NR

OTHER FORMS AND LEAFLETS

Paper copies of other forms and explanatory leaflets may be ordered from the HMRC publications department. The postal address is PO Box 37, St Austell

PL25 5YN, but HMRC strongly prefer requests to be made online using the form at www.hmrc.gov.uk/contactus/staustellform.htm or by phone to 0845 302 1472. St Austell do not appear to be aware of some of the very old stamp duty forms and leaflets (eg forms ADJ473 – ADJ475, listing the required information and setting out pro-forma letters for stamp duty reliefs under *FA 1986, ss 75–77*; see **9.31**), and it may be necessary to call the stamp taxes enquiry line (0845 603 0135) to request them.

SCOTTISH TRANSACTIONS

Scottish transactions requiring rapid delivery of SDLT forms or stamping of documents may be referred directly to Edinburgh Stamp Office, located at:

HM Revenue & Customs
Edinburgh Stamp Office
68 Queen Street
Edinburgh
EH2 4NF

Telephone 0131 528 3833

Where same-day stamping/adjudication is required, or immediate issue of a paper SDLT5 certificate is to be requested, the Stamp Office should be contacted in advance to obtain their agreement.

OTHER CORRESPONDENCE

All other stamp tax correspondence for HMRC must be sent to the Birmingham Stamp Office. The address is:

Birmingham Stamp Office
[Reference]
9th Floor, City Centre House
30 Union Street
Birmingham B2 4AR

Telephone 0121 616 4513

Alternatively the DX system may be used; the address is:

Birmingham Stamp Office
[Reference]
DX 15001
Birmingham 1

An appropriate reference or other description should be inserted in place of '[Reference]', as noted in the table below, to ensure that the correspondence is directed to the right section:

Purpose of correspondence	[Reference]	Paragraphs in this book; notes
Submission of further information at same time as SDLT return is submitted*	SDLT (return, further information)	**6.48**
Amendment of SDLT return; submission of further return after ordinary return was submitted for original transaction*	SDLT amended/further return	**6.17**
Advice on format of schedules listing multiple properties	Complex Transactions Unit	**6.27**
Application for deferment of SDLT	SDLT Deferment Application	**6.34**
Claim for relief from excessive SDLT assessment, after normal period to amend return has expired*	SDLT Excessive Assessment claim	**6.52**
Submission of documents for routine stamping, including provisional stamping or 'wait and see' cases	Stamp Duty section	**8.41–8.44** If same-day stamping required, call 0121 616 4513 first
Submission of documents for adjudication, including claims to relief where adjudication is compulsory	Stamp Duty section (adjudication, *insert reference to the relief, eg Group Relief*)	**8.45**; **9.7**
Claim for repayment of stamp duty	Stamp Duty section (repayment claim)	**8.51**
Payment of bearer instrument duty	Stamp Duty Section (bearer instruments)	**8.53**
Enquiry as to status of foreign entity; enquiry/ claim to be recognised as an Intermediary	Stamp Duty Section (Technical)	**9.8**; **9.35**; **10.22**
Notifying and paying SDRT (other than Financial Markets transactions)	SDRT	**10.9**

* UTRN of original return must be quoted in the heading to the letter; see **6.7**.

THE STAMP TAX ENQUIRY LINE

HMRC assert that answers to most stamp tax questions can be found on their website, starting from www.hmrc.gov.uk/so. Although most information probably is on the website, it can be frustratingly difficult to find; where possible, this book gives addresses of appropriate pages. Furthermore, the website does not (and realistically cannot) deal with all technical nuances arising from real-life transactions. A telephone enquiry line is provided at 0845 603 0135. This is not manned by technical experts and, therefore, is unlikely to provide definitive answers to difficult questions. However, with persistence, it is possible to have questions referred to such experts who, in the author's experience, are generally helpful. If you obtain a name, it is possible to contact the person by email – HMRC email addresses are in the form firstname.lastname@hmrc.gsi.gov.uk.

TAX PAYMENTS

Cheques should be payable to HMRC (*insert name of tax, eg SDLT*). For SDLT, the UTRN of the return to which the payment relates should be added to the payee line. However, for all three taxes, HMRC prefer electronic payment, either by direct bank transfer or by online card payment. HMRC maintain different bank accounts for the different taxes. Bank account details (including SWIFT codes and IBAN numbers for payments from outside the UK) may be found via links at www.hmrc.gov.uk/payinghmrc. The bank accounts have changed in recent years, so it is worth checking to ensure that current details are used (to avoid possibly being out of date, the details are deliberately not reproduced here). If payments are made electronically, it is important to quote an appropriate reference. For SDLT, this is the UTRN which appears on the paper return and payslip (see **6.7**) or on the electronic SDLT5 issued where returns are submitted online (see **6.11**). For stamp duty and SDRT, taxpayers may create their own reference numbers, but these should be quoted on the physical documents submitted for stamping or other correspondence, so that HMRC can easily link the payment to the document.

THE TRIBUNAL SERVICE

It is unlikely to be necessary to contact the Tribunal Service unless a matter is already in dispute with HMRC and under appeal – in which case, HMRC should provide appropriate contact details. The general address for correspondence is:

Tribunals Service (Tax)
2nd Floor
54 Hagley Road
Birmingham B16 8PE

Telephone 0845 223 8080

Email: taxappeals@tribunals.gsi.gov.uk

Website: www.tribunals.gov.uk/tax

Appendix B

Sample forms etc

PART 1 – SDLT RETURN FORMS

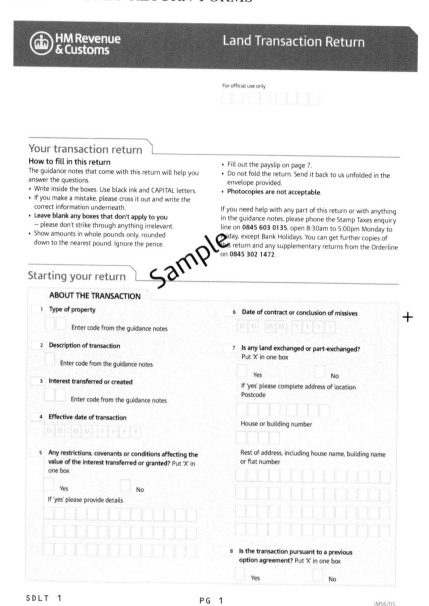

HM Revenue & Customs

Land Transaction Return

For official use only

Your transaction return

How to fill in this return

The guidance notes that come with this return will help you answer the questions.

- Write inside the boxes. Use black ink and CAPITAL letters.
- If you make a mistake, please cross it out and write the correct information underneath.
- **Leave blank any boxes that don't apply to you** – please don't strike through anything irrelevant.
- Show amounts in whole pounds only, rounded down to the nearest pound. Ignore the pence.
- Fill out the payslip on page 7.
- Do not fold the return. Send it back to us unfolded in the envelope provided.
- **Photocopies are not acceptable.**

If you need help with any part of this return or with anything in the guidance notes, please phone the Stamp Taxes enquiry line on **0845 603 0135**, open 8:30am to 5:00pm Monday to Friday, except Bank Holidays. You can get further copies of this return and any supplementary returns from the Orderline on **0845 302 1472**.

Starting your return

ABOUT THE TRANSACTION

1 **Type of property**

Enter code from the guidance notes

2 **Description of transaction**

Enter code from the guidance notes

3 **Interest transferred or created**

Enter code from the guidance notes

4 **Effective date of transaction**

D D M M Y Y Y Y

5 **Any restrictions, covenants or conditions affecting the value of the interest transferred or granted?** Put 'X' in one box

Yes No

If 'yes' please provide details

6 **Date of contract or conclusion of missives**

D D M M Y Y Y Y

7 **Is any land exchanged or part-exchanged?** Put 'X' in one box

Yes No

If 'yes' please complete address of location

Postcode

House or building number

Rest of address, including house name, building name or flat number

8 **Is the transaction pursuant to a previous option agreement?** Put 'X' in one box

Yes No

SDLT 1 PG 1 IMS6/05

ABOUT THE TAX CALCULATION

9 Are you claiming relief? Put 'X' in one box

Yes ☐ No ☐

If 'yes' please show the reason

Enter code from the guidance notes

Enter the charity's registered number, if available, or the company's CIS number

For relief claimed on part of the property only, please enter the amount remaining chargeable

£ . 0 0

10 What is the total consideration in money or money's worth, including any VAT actually payable for the transaction notified?

£ . 0 0

11 If the total consideration for the transaction includes VAT, please state the amount

£ . 0 0

12 What form does the consideration take?
Enter the relevant codes from the guidance notes

13 Is this transaction linked to any other(s)?
Put 'X' in one box

Yes ☐ No ☐

Total consideration or value in money or money's worth, including VAT paid for all of the linked transactions

£ . 0 0

14 Total amount of tax due for this transaction

£ . 0 0

15 Total amount paid or enclosed with this notification

£ . 0 0

Does the amount paid include payment of any penalties and any interest due? Put 'X' in one box

Yes ☐ No ☐

ABOUT LEASES

If this doesn't apply, go straight to box 26 on page 3

16 Type of lease

Enter code from the guidance notes

17 Start date as specified in lease

D D M M Y Y Y Y

18 End date as specified in lease

D D M M Y Y Y Y

19 Rent-free period
Number of months

20 Annual starting rent inclusive of VAT (actually) payable

£ . 0 0

End date for starting rent

D D M M Y Y Y Y

Later rent known? Put 'X' in one box

Yes ☐ No ☐

21 What is the amount of VAT, if any?

£ . 0 0

22 Total premium payable

£ . 0 0

23 Net present value upon which tax is calculated

£ . 0 0

24 Total amount of tax due – premium

£ . 0 0

25 Total amount of tax due – NPV

£ . 0 0

Check the guidance notes to see if you will need to complete supplementary return 'Additional details about the transaction, including leases', SDLT4.

SDLT 1 PG 2

ABOUT THE LAND including buildings

Where more than one piece of land is being sold or you cannot complete the address field in the space provided, please complete the supplementary return 'Additional details about the land', SDLT3.

26 **Number of properties included**

27 **Where more than one property is involved, do you want a certificate for each property?** Put 'X' in one box

Yes No

28 **Address or situation of land**
Postcode

House or building number

Rest of address, including house name, building name or flat number

Is the rest of the address on the supplementary return 'Additional details about the land', SDLT3?
Put 'X' in one box

Yes No

29 **Local authority number**

30 **Title number, if any**

31 **NLPG UPRN**

32 **If agricultural or development land, what is the area (if known)?** Put 'X' in one box

Hectares Square metres

Area

33 **Is a plan attached?** Please note that the form reference number should be written/displayed on map. Put 'X' in one box

Yes No

ABOUT THE VENDOR including transferor, lessor

34 **Number of vendors included** (Note: if more than one vendor, complete boxes 45 to 48)

35 **Title** Enter MR, MRS, MISS, MS or other title
Note: only complete for an individual

36 **Vendor (1) surname or company name**

37 **Vendor (1) first name(s)** Note: only complete for an individual

38 **Vendor (1) address**
Postcode

House or building number

Rest of address, including house name, building name or flat number

ABOUT THE VENDOR CONTINUED

39 **Agent's name**

40 **Agent's address**
Postcode

Building number

Rest of address, including building name

41 **Agent's DX number and exchange**

42 **Agent's e-mail address**

43 **Agent's reference**

44 **Agent's telephone number**

ADDITIONAL VENDOR

Details of other people involved (including transferor, lessor), other than vendor (1). If more than one additional vendor please complete supplementary return 'Land Transaction Return – Additional vendor/purchaser details', SDLT2.

45 **Title** Enter MR, MRS, MISS, MS or other title
Note: only complete for an individual

46 **Vendor (2) surname or company name**

47 **Vendor (2) first name(s)**
Note: only complete for an individual

48 **Vendor (2) address**

Put 'X' in this box if the same as box 38.

If not, please give address below
Postcode

House or building number

Rest of address, including house name, building name or flat number

ABOUT THE PURCHASER including transferee, lessee

49 **Number of purchasers included** (Note: if more than one purchaser is involved, complete boxes 65 to 69)

50 **National Insurance number (purchaser 1), if you have one.** Note: only complete for an individual

51 **Title** Enter MR, MRS, MISS, MS or other title
Note: only complete for an individual

52 **Purchaser (1) surname or company name**

53 **Purchaser (1) first name(s)**
Note: only complete for an individual

54 **Purchaser (1) address**

Put 'X' in this box if the same address as box 28.

If not, please give address below

Postcode

House or building number

Rest of address, including house name, building name or flat number

55 **Is the purchaser acting as a trustee?** Put 'X' in one box

Yes No

56 **Please give a daytime telephone number** - this will help us if we need to contact you about your return

57 **Are the purchaser and vendor connected?**
Put 'X' in one box

Yes No

58 **To which address shall we send the certificate?**
Put 'X' in one box

Property (box 28) Purchaser's (box 54)

Agent's (box 61)

59 **I authorise my agent to handle correspondence on my behalf.** Put 'X' in one box

Yes No

60 **Agent's name**

61 **Agent's address**

Postcode

Building number

Rest of address, including building name

62 **Agent's DX number and exchange**

63 **Agent's reference**

64 **Agent's telephone number**

SDLT 1 PG 5

ADDITIONAL PURCHASER

Details of other people involved (including transferee, lessee), other than purchaser (1). If more than one additional purchaser, please complete supplementary return 'Land Transaction Return - Additional vendor/purchaser details', SDLT2.

65 **Title** Enter MR, MRS, MISS, MS or other title
Note: only complete for an individual

66 **Purchaser (2) surname or company name**

67 **Purchaser (2) first name(s)**
Note: only complete for an individual

68 **Purchaser (2) address**

Put 'X' in this box if the same as purchaser (1) (box 54).

If not, please give address below

Postcode

House or building number

Rest of address, including house name, building name or flat number

69 **Is purchaser (2) acting as a trustee?** Put 'X' in one box

Yes No

ADDITIONAL SUPPLEMENTARY RETURNS

70 **How many supplementary returns have you enclosed with this return?** Write the number in each box. If none, please put '0'.

Additional vendor/purchaser details, SDLT2

Additional details about the land, SDLT3

Additional details about the transaction, including leases, SDLT4

DECLARATION

71 **The purchaser(s) must sign this return.** Read the guidance notes in booklet SDLT6, in particular the section headed *'Who should complete and sign the Land Transaction Return?'*.

If you give false information, you may face financial penalties and prosecution.
The information I have given on this return is correct and complete to the best of my knowledge and belief.

Signature of purchaser 1

Signature of purchaser 2

Please keep a copy of this return and a note of the unique transaction reference number, which is in the 'Reference' box on the payslip.

Finally, please send your completed return to:
HM Revenue & Customs, Stamp Taxes/SDLT, Comben House, Farriers Way, NETHERTON, Merseyside, Great Britain, L30 4RN, or the DX address is: Rapid Data Capture Centre, DX725593, Bootle 9

Please don't fold it - keep it flat and use the envelope provided. Fill out the payslip on the next page and pay in accordance with the 'How to pay' instructions.

SDLT 1 PG 6

How to pay

Please allow enough time for payment to reach us by the due date. We suggest you allow at least 3 working days for this.

MOST SECURE AND EFFICIENT

We recommend the following payment methods. These are the most secure and efficient.

1. Direct Payment
Use the Internet or telephone to make payment. Provide your bank or building society with the following information
- payment account
- sort code 10-50-41
- account number 23456000
- your reference as shown on the payslip.

2. BillPay
You can pay by Debit Card over the Internet. Visit **www.billpayment.co.uk/hmrc** and follow the guidance.

3. At your bank
Take this form with payment to **your** bank and where possible to **your own** branch. Other banks may refuse to accept payment. If paying by cheque, make your cheque payable to 'HM REVENUE & CUSTOMS ONLY'.

4. At a Post Office
Take this form with your payment to any Post Office. If paying by cheque, make your cheque payable to 'POST OFFICE LTD'. The Post Office also accept payment by Debit Card.

5. Alliance & Leicester Commercial Bank Account
Alliance & Leicester Commercial Bank customers can instruct their bank to arrange payment.

OTHER PAYMENT METHODS

By post
If you use this method
- Make your cheque payable to 'HM REVENUE & CUSTOMS ONLY'.
- Write your payslip reference after 'HM REVENUE & CUSTOMS ONLY'.
- Send the payslip and your cheque, **both unfolded**, in the envelope provided to
  HM Revenue & Customs SDLT
  Netherton
  Merseyside
  L30 4RN

By DX
As above, but send to
Rapid Data Capture Centre
DX725593
Bootle 9

FURTHER PAYMENT INFORMATION

You can find further payment information at **www.hmrc.gov.uk/howtopay**

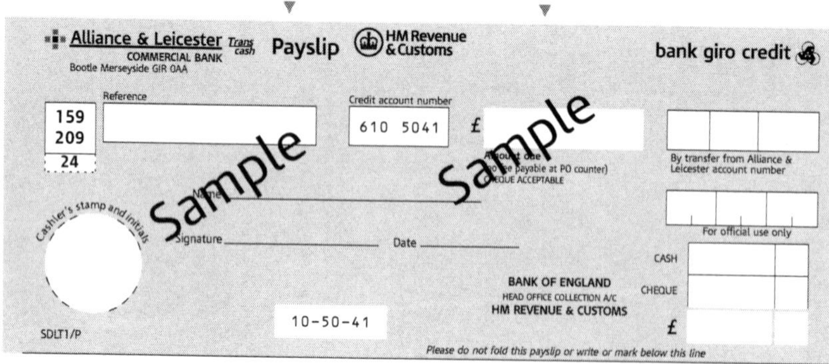

Alliance & Leicester COMMERCIAL BANK Bootle Merseyside GIR 0AA Transcash | Payslip | HM Revenue & Customs | bank giro credit

159
209
24

Reference

Credit account number 610 5041

£

Amount due (to be payable at PO counter) CHEQUE ACCEPTABLE

By transfer from Alliance & Leicester account number

For official use only

Cashier's stamp and initials

Name

Signature ______ Date ______

CASH

CHEQUE

£

BANK OF ENGLAND
HEAD OFFICE COLLECTION A/C
HM REVENUE & CUSTOMS

10-50-41

SDLT1/P

Please do not fold this payslip or write or mark below this line

Please do not write or mark below this perforation

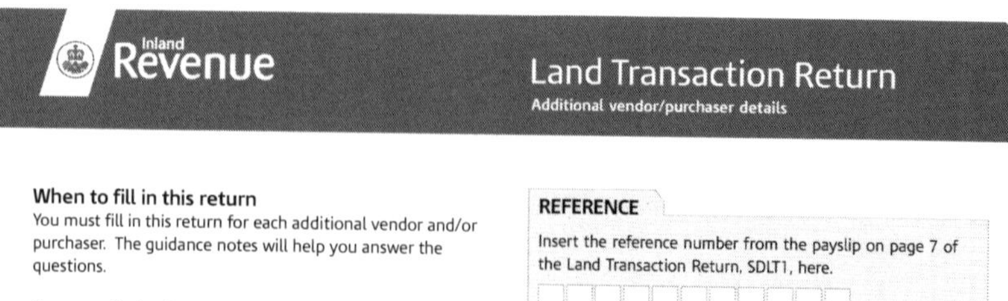

Inland
Revenue
Land Transaction Return
Additional vendor/purchaser details

When to fill in this return

You must fill in this return for each additional vendor and/or purchaser. The guidance notes will help you answer the questions.

If you need help with any part of this return or with anything in the guidance notes, please phone the Stamp Taxes enquiry line on **0845 603 0135**, open 8:30am to 5:00pm Monday to Friday, except Bank Holidays. Calls are charged at local rates. You can get further copies of this return from the Orderline on **0845 302 1472**.

REFERENCE

Insert the reference number from the payslip on page 7 of the Land Transaction Return, SDLT1, here.

For official use only

VENDOR OR PURCHASER

1 **Please indicate if this return is for an additional vendor or an additional purchaser.** Put 'X' in one box

Vendor Complete section below only

Purchaser Complete section below and the section over the page

COMPLETE IN ALL CASES

2 **Title** Enter MR, MRS, MISS, MS or other title
Note: only complete for an individual

3 **Surname or company name**

4 **First name(s)**
Note: only complete for an individual

5 **Address**
Postcode

House or building number

Rest of address, including house name, building name or flat number

Please turn over for additional purchaser details

SDLT 2 PG 1 BS09/03

+

ADDITIONAL PURCHASER DETAILS

Only complete this section if this return is for an additional purchaser.

6 **Are the purchaser and vendor connected?**
Put 'X' in one box

☐ Yes ☐ No

7 **Is the purchaser acting as a trustee?** Put 'X' in one box

☐ Yes ☐ No

8 **Declaration**
The purchaser(s) must sign this return.
Read the notes in Section 1 of the guidance notes, SDLT6 'Who should complete the Land Transaction Return?'

If you give false information, you may face financial penalties and prosecution.

The information I have given on this form is correct and complete to the best of my knowledge and belief.

Signature of purchaser

+

SDLT 2 PG 2

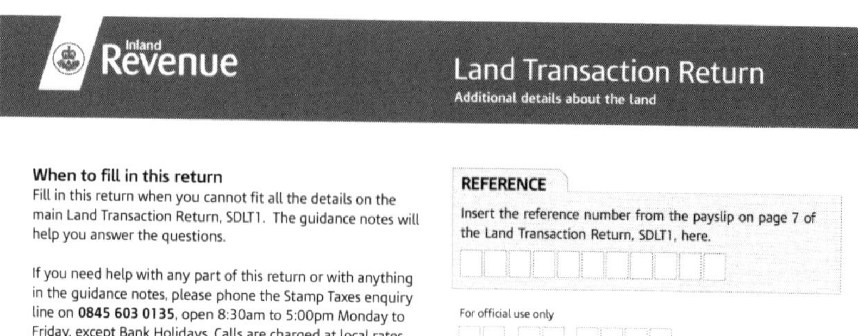

Inland Revenue
Land Transaction Return
Additional details about the land

When to fill in this return

Fill in this return when you cannot fit all the details on the main Land Transaction Return, SDLT1. The guidance notes will help you answer the questions.

If you need help with any part of this return or with anything in the guidance notes, please phone the Stamp Taxes enquiry line on **0845 603 0135**, open 8:30am to 5:00pm Monday to Friday, except Bank Holidays. Calls are charged at local rates. You can get further copies of this return from the Orderline on **0845 302 1472**.

REFERENCE

Insert the reference number from the payslip on page 7 of the Land Transaction Return, SDLT1, here.

For official use only

sample

ABOUT THE LAND

1 **Type of property**

Enter code from the guidance notes

2 **Local authority number**

3 **Title number, if any**

4 **NLPG UPRN**

5 **Address or situation of land**

Postcode

House or building number

Rest of address, including house name, building name, flat number or continuation from the SDLT1

Please turn over

SDLT 3 PG 1 BS09/03)

ABOUT THE LAND CONTINUED

6 **If agricultural or development land, what is the area (if known)?**

Hectares Square metres

Area

7 **If there are any minerals or mineral rights reserved enter the code below**

Enter code from the guidance notes

8 **Is a plan attached?** Please note that the form reference number should be written/displayed on map. Put 'X' in one box

Yes No

9 **Interest transferred or created**

Enter code from the guidance notes

SDLT 3 PG 2

Land Transaction Return

Additional details about the transaction, including leases

When to fill in this return

You must fill in this return where additional information about the transaction and/or lease can be provided.
The guidance notes will help you answer the questions.

If you need help with any part of this return or with anything in the guidance notes, please phone the Stamp Taxes enquiry line on **0845 603 0135**, open 8:30am to 5:00pm Monday to Friday, except Bank Holidays. Calls are charged at local rates. You can get further copies of this return from the Orderline on **0845 302 1472**.

REFERENCE

Insert the reference number from the payslip on page 7 of the Land Transaction Return, SDLT1, here.

For official use only

ABOUT THE TRANSACTION

1 **If this transaction is part of the sale of business, please say if the sale includes** Put 'X' in relevant boxes

Stock | Goodwill

Other | Chattels and moveables

What is the total amount of the consideration for the sale of the business apportioned to these items?

£ . 0 0

2 **If the property is for commercial use, what is it?** Put 'X' in the appropriate box(es)

Office | Hotel

Shop | Warehouse

Factory | Other

Other industrial unit

3 **Have you applied for and received a post transaction ruling in accordance with Code of Practice 10, or asked us for advice on the application of the law to this transaction?** Put 'X' in one box

Yes | No

If 'yes' have you followed it when completing this return? Put 'X' in one box

Yes | No

Ruling not received

4 **Is any part of the consideration contingent or dependent on uncertain future events?**

Yes | No

5 **Have you agreed with the Inland Revenue that you will pay on a deferred basis?**

Yes | No

6 **If there are any minerals or mineral rights reserved enter the code below**

Enter code from the guidance notes

7 **If the purchaser is VAT registered, give their VAT reference number**

8 **If the purchaser is a company please give the following details**

Tax reference number

Company registration number

If registered abroad, give its place of registration

SDLT4 V2

PG 1

Please turn over

BS11/04

ABOUT THE TRANSACTION CONTINUED

9 Give a description of the purchaser
Enter code from the guidance notes

ABOUT LEASES

Complete if the transaction notified on SDLT1 is for the grant of more than one lease

10 Type of property
Enter code from the guidance notes

11 Address or situation of land
Put 'X' in this box if the same as box 28 on SDLT1
If not, please give address below
Postcode

House or building number

Rest of address, including house name, building name, flat number or continuation from the SDLT1

continued at the top of the next column

12 Local authority number

13 Title number, if any

14 NLPG UPRN

15 If the transaction is for land, what is the unit and area of measurement? Put 'X' in one box
Hectares
Square metres
Area

16 Is a plan attached? Please note that the form reference number should be written/displayed on the map.
Put X in one box
Yes
No

17 Interest transferred or created
Enter code from the guidance notes

18 Type of lease
Enter code from the guidance notes

SDLT 4 V2 PG 2

ABOUT LEASES CONTINUED

19 **Start date as specified in lease**

D D M M Y Y Y Y

20 **End date as specified in lease**

D D M M Y Y Y Y

21 **Rent free period**
Number of months

22 **Annual starting rent inclusive of VAT (actually) payable**

£ . 0 0

End date for starting rent

D D M M Y Y Y Y

Later rent known? Put 'X' in one box

Yes No

23 **What is the amount of VAT, if any?**

£ . 0 0

24 **Total premium payable**

£ . 0 0

25 **Net present value upon which tax is calculated**

£ . 0 0

26 **Total amount of tax due - premium**

£ . 0 0

27 **Total amount of tax due - NPV**

£ . 0 0

28 **Any terms surrendered**

29 **Break clause type** Put 'X' in one box

Landlord Tenant only

Either

30 **What is the date of the break clause?**

D D M M Y Y Y Y

31 **Which of the following relate to this lease?**
Put 'X' in relevant boxes. If none, leave blank

Option to renew

Market rent

Turnover rent

Unascertainable rent

Contingent reserved rent

32 **Rent review frequency**

33 **Date of first review**

D D M M Y Y Y Y

34 **Rent review clause (type)** Put 'X' in one box

Open market RPI

Other

35 **If Schedule 17A para 7FA 2003 has been used in calculating the NPV, what is the date of the rent change?**

D D M M Y Y Y Y

Please turn over

ABOUT LEASES CONTINUED

36 **Service charge amount if known**

£ . 0 0

37 **Service charge frequency** Put 'X' in one box

Monthly

Annually

Quarterly

Other

38 **Other consideration – tenant to landlord**
(for example, services, building works)
Enter the relevant codes from the guidance notes

39 **Other consideration – landlord to tenant**
(for example, services, building works)
Enter the relevant codes from the guidance notes

SDLT 4 V2 PG 4

PART 2 – DOTAS FORMS

Disclosure of avoidance scheme
(Notification by scheme promoter)

Scheme reference number

(for HMRC official use only)

Who should use this form?

This form is for use by a scheme promoter notifying under:

- Section 308, Finance Act 2004; and/or
- Regulation 7 of the National Insurance Contributions (Application of Part 7 of the Finance Act 2004) Regulations 2007 (SI 2007, Number 785).

Guidance on making a disclosure is available on our website, go to **www.hmrc.gov.uk**

Scheme promoter's details

Name of promoter

Email address of promoter (if any)

Address of promoter

Address

Postcode

Phone number of promoter

Internal reference number of promoter (if any)

Scheme details

Title of the arrangements (if any)

Specify the provision under which the disclosure is being made.

SDLT Avoidance (Prescribed Description of Arrangements) Regulations (SI 2005, Number 1868). *Tick one box only*

Residential property with a market value of £1 million and over ☐

Non-residential property with a market value of £5 million and over ☐

Use of property not known or mixed ☐

Other avoidance *Tick any box that applies*

NIC Avoidance (SI 2007 Number 785) ☐

IT, CT, and CGT Avoidance (Prescribed Description of Arrangements) Regulations (SI 2006 Number 1543) ☐

For IT, CT, CGT and NIC avoidance only, tick the regulation below that applies. Where more than one regulation applies, please specify only the main applicable regulation.

Regulation 6 Confidentiality ☐

Regulation 8 Premium fee ☐

Regulation 9 Off market terms ☐

Regulation 10 Standardised tax products ☐

Regulation 12 Loss schemes ☐

Regulation 13 Leasing arrangements ☐

Regulation 17A Pensions ☐

Summary of proposal or arrangements

AAG1 Page 1 HMRC 03/10

Explanation of each element in the proposal or arrangements from which the expected tax and/or NICs advantage arises

If you need more space continue on form AAG5 (continuation sheet)

Statutory provisions relevant to those elements of the proposal or arrangements from which the expected tax and/or NICs advantage arises

If you need more space continue on form AAG5 (continuation sheet)

Declaration

The information I have given on this form, and any continuation sheets, is correct and complete to the best of my knowledge and belief.

Signature

Date *DD MM YYYY*

Name of signatory (use capital letters)

Capacity in which signed

Number of forms AAG5 (continuation sheet) used

You should send this form to the:
Anti-Avoidance Group (Intelligence)
First Floor
22 Kingsway
London
WC2B 6NR

Page 2

Disclosure of avoidance scheme (Notification by scheme user where offshore promoter does not notify)

Scheme reference number

(for HMRC official use only)

Who should use this form?

This form is for use by a scheme promoter notifying under:

- Section 308, Finance Act 2004; and/or
- Regulation 8 of the National Insurance Contributions (Application of Part 7 of the Finance Act 2004) Regulations 2007 (SI 2007, Number 785).

Guidance on making a disclosure is available on our website, go to **www.hmrc.gov.uk**

Scheme user's and promoter's details

Name of scheme user making disclosure

Address of scheme user making disclosure

Address

Postcode

Email address of scheme user making disclosure

Phone number of scheme user making disclosure

Scheme user's internal reference number (if any)

Name of promoter

Address of promoter

Address

Postcode

Scheme details

Title of the arrangements (if any)

Specify the provision under which the disclosure is being made.

SDLT Avoidance (Prescribed Description of Arrangements) Regulations (SI 2005, Number 1868). *Tick one box only*

Residential property with a market value of £1 million and over ☐

Non-residential property with a market value of £5 million and over ☐

Use of property not known or mixed ☐

Other avoidance *Tick one box only*

NIC avoidance (SI 2007 Number 785) ☐

IT, CT, and CGT avoidance (Prescribed Description of Arrangements) Regulations (SI 2006, Number 1543) ☐

For IT, CT, CGT and NIC avoidance, tick the regulation below that applies. Where more than one regulation applies, please specify only the main applicable regulation.

Regulation 6 Confidentiality ☐

Regulation 8 Premium fee ☐

Regulation 9 Off market terms ☐

Regulation 10 Standardised tax products ☐

Regulation 12 Loss schemes ☐

Regulation 13 Leasing arrangements ☐

Regulation 17A Pensions ☐

AAG2 Page 1 HMRC 03/10

Summary of proposal or arrangements

Explanation of each element in the proposal or arrangements from which the expected tax and/or NICs advantage arises

Statutory provisions relevant to those elements of the proposal or arrangements from which the expected tax and/or NICs advantage arises

Number of continuation sheets used

Declaration

The information I have given on this form, and any continuation sheets, is correct and complete to the best of my knowledge and belief.

Signature

Date *DD MM YYYY*

Name of signatory (*use capital letters*)

Capacity in which signed

Number of forms AAG5 (continuation sheet) used

You should send this form to the:
Anti-Avoidance Group (Intelligence)
First Floor
22 Kingsway
London
WC2B 6NR

Page 2

Disclosure of avoidance scheme

(Notification by scheme user where no promoter, or promoted by lawyer unable to make full notification)

Scheme reference number

(*for HMRC official use only*)

Who should use this form?

This form is for use by a scheme user notifying under:

- Section 310, Finance Act 2004; and/or
- Regulation 9 of the National Insurance Contributions (Application of Part 7 of the Finance Act 2004) Regulations 2007 (SI 2007, Number 785).

Guidance on making a disclosure is available on our website, go to **www.hmrc.gov.uk**

Scheme user's details

Name of scheme user making disclosure

Address of scheme user making disclosure

Address

Postcode

Unique taxpayer reference (UTR)

Email address of scheme user making disclosure

Phone number of scheme user making disclosure

Scheme user's internal reference number (if any)

Scheme details

Title of the arrangements (if any)

Specify the provision under which the disclosure is being made.

SDLT Tax Avoidance (Prescribed Description of Arrangements) Regulations (SI 2005, Number 1868) *Tick one box only*

- Residential property with a market value of £1 million and over ☐
- Non-residential property with a market value of £5 million and over ☐
- Use of property not known or mixed ☐

Other avoidance *Tick any box that applies*

- NIC Avoidance (SI 2007 Number 785) ☐
- IT, CT and CGT Tax Avoidance (Prescribed Description of Arrangements) Regulations (SI 2006, Number 1543) ☐

For IT, CT, CGT and NIC avoidance, tick the regulation below that applies. Where more than one regulation applies, please specify only the main applicable regulation.

- Regulation 6 Confidentiality (Promoter) ☐
- Regulation 7 Confidentiality (No promoter) ☐
- Regulation 8 Premium fee ☐
- Regulation 9 Off market terms ☐
- Regulation 10 Standardised tax products ☐
- Regulation 12 Loss schemes ☐
- Regulation 13 Leasing arrangements ☐
- Regulation 17A Pensions ☐

AAG3 | Page 1 | HMRC 03/10

Summary of proposal or arrangements

Explanation of each element in the proposal or arrangements from which the expected tax and/or NICs advantage arises

Statutory provisions relevant to those elements of the proposal or arrangements from which the expected tax and/or NICs advantage arises

Number of continuation sheets used

Declaration

The information I have given on this form, and any continuation sheets, is correct and complete to the best of my knowledge and belief.

Signature

Date *DD MM YYYY*

Name of signatory (*use capital letters*)

Capacity in which signed

Number of forms AAG5 (continuation sheet) used

You should send this form to the:
Anti-Avoidance Group (Intelligence)
First Floor
22 Kingsway
London
WC2B 6NR

Disclosure of SDLT avoidance scheme – notification of scheme reference number

Scheme details

Name of scheme user

Address of scheme user

Address

Postcode

Phone number of scheme user

Unique transaction reference number (UTRN) (if allocated)

Scheme reference number

Title number of the relevant property (if allocated)

Address of the relevant property

Address

Postcode

Market value of the relevant property

Date of first land transaction *DD MM YYYY*

Who should use this form?

You should use this form if you have received an 8-digit scheme reference number (SRN) from HM Revenue & Customs (HMRC), a scheme promoter, or the client of a scheme promoter, and you expect to obtain a Stamp Duty Land Tax (SDLT) advantage. This will usually be because you are the purchaser of a property.

If you are a partner in a partnership, read the notes about 'How to complete this form' on page 2.

Declaration

The information I have given on this form, and any continuation sheets, is correct and complete to the best of my knowledge and belief.

Signature

Date *DD MM YYYY*

Name of signatory (*use capital letters*)

Capacity in which signed

If the scheme user named above is also notifying as the representative partner on behalf of other partners in a partnership to which he belongs, indicate here the number of additional partners who are liable to notify, and list them separately

For guidance on completing this form please see the notes overleaf or go to **www.hmrc.gov.uk**

AAG4 (SDLT) Page 1 HMRC 04/10

Notes

Background

Details of certain SDLT avoidance schemes must be notified to HMRC, usually by the scheme promoter. The user of the scheme must make the notification where the scheme is devised 'in-house', the promoter is outside the UK and no promoter notifies, or the information is to be covered by legal professional privilege.

When a SDLT scheme is notified, HMRC may issue a SRN to the person making the notification. A promoter to whom a SRN is issued must provide it to each client who implements the scheme. If there are other users of the scheme the client must provide the SRN to them.

If you have received a SRN, whether from HMRC, the scheme promoter, or a client of the promoter, you are required to declare the use of the scheme to HMRC. This is done by entering the SRN and certain other information on this form.

How to complete this form

Partnerships

If you are a partner in a partnership, you should consider any expected SDLT advantages from the perspective of your own liabilities to SDLT, notwithstanding that the partnership may be regarded as a legal person or body corporate under the law of the country or territory under which it is formed.

If you and other members of the partnership have a duty to notify the SRN, a representative partner may make a single notification on behalf of the others provided that the names of all of those with a duty to notify are scheduled and attached to this form.

Title number of the relevant property

Enter the title number of the property forming the subject of the arrangements, if any is allocated.

Address of relevant property

Enter the address of the property forming the subject of the arrangements.

Unique transaction reference number (UTRN)

Enter the UTRN for the land transaction return relating to the transaction on which you expect to obtain an SDLT advantage. The UTRN can be found either on the submission receipt (called the Submission Receipt and Electronic SDLT5 certificate) if you have filed your return online, or at the bottom of page 2 and on the payslip on page 7 of your paper SDLT return.

Open market price of the relevant property

Enter the price which the property might reasonably be expected to fetch if on sale on the open market. If a formal valuation has not been obtained this should be a reasoned estimate.

Scheme reference number (SRN)

Enter in the boxes the 8-digit SRN provided to you.

Date of first land transaction

Enter the effective date of the first land transaction which forms part of the scheme.

When to send in this form

You must send in this form within 30 days of the first land transaction which forms part of the scheme or receipt of the SRN, whichever is later. Submission should not be delayed if for example a formal valuation of the property has not been obtained.

Where to send this form

You should send this form to:
Anti-Avoidance Group (Intelligence)
First Floor
22 Kingsway
London WC2B 6NR

Any SDLT return due to be submitted should not accompany this form and should be sent to HMRC in the normal way.

Page 2

Disclosure of SDLT avoidance scheme – notification of scheme reference number

Details to be completed by the promoter

Scheme reference number (SRN)

Brief description or name of the scheme

Promoter's name

Promoter's address

Postcode

Date form issued *DD MM YYYY*

Scheme reference numbers and your obligations

You have been given this form because you have been provided with an avoidance scheme which is intended to produce a Stamp Duty Land Tax advantage. The scheme promoter has disclosed it to HM Revenue & Customs (HMRC) as required by law and it has been given the scheme reference number (SRN) shown above.

If you use the scheme and you expect to obtain a Stamp Duty Land Tax advantage, you must notify the SRN to HMRC - see 'How do I notify the SRN to HMRC?' in the next column. You may be liable to a penalty if you do not report the SRN correctly. You may have to pass the SRN to another person - see 'When do I have to pass the SRN to another person?' in the next column.

You can find more detailed guidance on our website, go to **www.hmrc.gov.uk/aiu/guidance.htm**

Note: Issuing a SRN does not mean that HMRC accepts that the scheme achieves any intended Stamp Duty Land Tax advantage. However, it does mean that you have some obligations and we explain them on this form.

How do I notify the SRN to HMRC?

You need to report it to HMRC on form AAG4 (SDLT). You can find more details below.

Report it on AAG4(SDLT)

A SRN for Stamp Duty Land Tax can only be notified to HMRC using form AAG4 (SDLT). It cannot be notified on a SDLT return or any other tax return. You may be liable to a penalty if form AAG4 (SDLT) is not used.

When do I have to submit form AAG4 (SDLT)?

In general, you should submit form AAG4 (SDLT) within 30 days of entering into the first land transaction in connection with the scheme.

You can get form AAG4 (SDLT) and further guidance about filling it in and when it must be submitted from our website, go to **www.hmrc.gov.uk/aiu/forms-tax-schemes.htm** or you can order it from the HMRC order line on **08459 000 404**.

When do I have to pass the SRN to another person?

If you have been given the SRN by a scheme promoter but you are not the person who actually uses the scheme or you do not expect to get a Stamp Duty Land Tax advantage from it, then you should pass it on. Pass the SRN on to any other person you know who is, or is likely to be, party to the scheme and who might reasonably be expected to get the Stamp Duty Land Tax advantage.

Pass on the SRN as soon as you receive this form. You can do this by passing on a copy of this form or downloading a new copy. Complete the date box below to show the date on which you passed on the SRN.

Date SRN passed on *DD MM YYYY*

For more detailed guidance go to **www.hmrc.gov.uk/aiu/guidance.htm**

AAG6(SDLT) Page 1 HMRC 03/10

PART 3 – PRECEDENT LETTERS FOR STAMP DUTY CLAIMS UNDER *FA 1986, SS 75* AND *77*

These letters are based on HMRC leaflets ADJ473 and 475. Although they are similar, there are sufficient differences to make it worthwhile to reproduce them separately. They are written on the assumption that all companies are UK registered, that certain details are set out in an agreement governing the transaction, and that the letter is submitted by an adviser acting for the claimant. They have been slightly adapted to recognise changes in the UK Companies Acts, for example removing the concept of authorised share capital. They may require adapting further to accommodate characteristics of overseas companies or to reflect the precise form of the agreement. Where words may or may not be required, depending on circumstances, they are enclosed in square brackets. Information to be inserted is indicated in [square brackets] and in italics. In places the language used is quaint, but it is as well to use the approved wording so far as it fits the facts. It is also worth reviewing the draft agreement between the parties before execution, to ensure its provisions accord with the statements which must be made in the letter of claim.

(a) Section 75 claim

Dear Sir

[name of claimant company]

1. We act for *[name of claimant company]* ("the Acquiring Company").

2. In connection with the transactions referred to below we hereby apply on behalf of the Acquiring Company for exemption from transfer duty under Section 75 Finance Act 1986.

3. The Acquiring Company, whose registered office is at *[address]* was incorporated in *[country]* on *[date]* under *[name of law]* with number *[registered number]*. A copy of the certificate of incorporation [and of certificate(s) of change of name] is enclosed marked "A".

4. *[Name of target company]*, ("the Target Company"), whose registered office is at *[address]* was incorporated in *[country]* on *[date]* under *[name of law]* with number *[registered number]*. A copy of the certificate of incorporation [and of certificate(s) of change of name] is enclosed marked "B". A list of all the members of the Target Company immediately prior to *[date of transaction]* certified by the [Registrars] [Company Secretary] of the Target Company, is enclosed marked "C".

[Note – a computer print-out of the Register of Members may be used as "C" and need not be certified]

5. The Acquiring Company has acquired [the whole][part] of the undertaking of the Target Company in pursuance of a scheme for the reconstruction of the Target Company in order that *[set out brief reasons for/explanation of the transaction]*.

6. By an agreement dated *[date]* and made between the Target Company and the Acquiring Company ("the Agreement"), it was provided that the Target Company should sell and the Acquiring Company should purchase [the whole][part] of the undertaking of the Target Company as described in *[refer to appropriate part of the Agreement]* ("the Business") in pursuance of a scheme for the reconstruction of the Target Company and that as consideration for such sale the Acquiring Company should allot credited as fully paid to all the shareholders of the Target Company the respective numbers of shares of the Acquiring Company as specified in *[refer to schedule or other part of the Agreement setting out the numbers and classes of shares to be allotted to each shareholder of the Target Company]* ("the Consideration Shares"). A copy of the Agreement is enclosed marked "D".

7. The said sale was duly completed on *[date]* when the Target Company transferred the business to the Acquiring Company.

8. At a meeting of [the Directors]*[or specify committee or similar]* of the Acquiring Company held on *[date]* the consideration shares were duly allotted to the shareholders of the Target Company pursuant to the provisions of the Agreement. We enclose marked "E" [and "F" respectively] a certified copy of the resolution of the Directors of the Acquiring Company passed on *[date]* [appointing the said committee and of the Resolution of the said Committee] making such allotment. We also enclose marked "G" a certificate under the hand of [the senior official of the Registrars][the company secretary] of the Acquiring Company, confirming that the names of the respective allottees of the Consideration Shares have been entered in the Register of Members of the Acquiring Company in respect of the Consideration Shares, together with a list of all members of the Acquiring Company immediately following the allotment, certified by the [Registrars][company secretary] of the Acquiring Company and marked ["H"].

[Note – as in (4) above, a computer printout may be substituted and need not be certified]

9. It is confirmed that no part of the consideration for the acquisition consisted of the issue of redeemable shares in the Acquiring Company.

10. It is confirmed that, immediately after the acquisition:

    a. Each shareholder of the Target Company was also a shareholder of the Acquiring Company;

b. Each shareholder of the Acquiring Company was also a shareholder of the Target Company;

c. Each shareholder held the same proportion (or as nearly as may be the same proportion) of shares in the Target Company as that shareholder held in the Acquiring Company.

11. [No application for clearance under the relevant direct tax provisions] [An application for clearance under [section numbers]] was made by the Acquiring Company. [A copy of the application together with copies of the correspondence with HMRC is enclosed marked ["I"]].

[Note – if no clearance application was made, the information listed below must be supplied]

12. It is submitted that the acquisition was effected for bona fide commercial reasons and did not form part of a scheme or arrangement of which the main purpose or one of the main purposes is the avoidance of liability to stamp duty, income tax, corporation tax or capital gains tax and that the appropriate conditions of Section 75 of the Finance Act 1986 have been complied with, and accordingly exemption from ad valorem stamp duty under the head "Transfer on Sale" is claimed in respect of the Transfers executed pursuant thereto.

13. We enclose for adjudication [give adequate list or description of the documents enclosed] together with certified copies.

Further information to be provided if no clearance application was made as set out in (11) above:

1. A copy of the latest accounts of the Target Company;
2. Full details of any scheme, arrangement or overall transaction of which this transaction forms part;
3. Confirmation that the Acquiring Company still holds the Business;
4. A detailed note of the bona fide commercial reasons for the acquisition.

(b) Section 77 claim

Dear Sir

[name of claimant company]

We act for *[name of claimant company]* ("the Acquiring Company").

1. In connection with the transactions referred to below we hereby apply on behalf of the Acquiring Company for exemption from transfer duty under Section 77 Finance Act 1986.

2. The Acquiring Company, whose registered office is at *[address]* was incorporated in *[country]* on *[date]* under *[name of law]* with number *[registered number]* and immediately prior to *[date of transaction]* the issued share capital of the Acquiring Company was *[amount]* divided into *[give details of the classes, denominations and numbers of shares]* such shares being fully paid up *[or give details if shares were part paid]*. A copy of the certificate of incorporation [and of certificate(s) of change of name] is enclosed marked "A".

3. *[Name of target company]*, ("the Target Company"), whose registered office is at *[address]* was incorporated in *[country]* on *[date]* under *[name of law]* with number *[registered number]* and immediately prior to *[date of transaction]* the issued share capital of the Target Company was *[amount]* divided into *[give details of the classes, denominations and numbers of shares]* such shares being fully paid up *[or give details if shares were part paid]*. A copy of the certificate of incorporation [and of certificate(s) of change of name] is enclosed marked "B". A list of all the members of the Target Company immediately prior to *[date of transaction]* certified by the [Registrars][Company Secretary] of the Target Company, is enclosed marked "C".

[Note – a computer print-out of the Register of Members may be used as "C" and need not be certified]

4. The transactions referred to below were carried out in order that [set out reasons for the transactions. If no direct tax advance clearance was obtained, give a detailed explanation of the bona fide commercial reasons for the overall transaction].

5. By an agreement dated [date] and made between [names of shareholders of the Target company] ("the Shareholders"), the Target Company and the Acquiring Company ("the Agreement") it was provided that the Shareholders should sell and the Acquiring Company should purchase the respective numbers of shares of the Target Company as described in [refer to appropriate part of the Agreement] (such shares amounting in aggregate to the whole of the issued share capital of the Target Company and that as consideration for such sale the Acquiring Company should allot credited as fully paid to the Shareholders (being all the shareholders of the Target Company) the respective numbers of shares of the Acquiring Company as specified in [refer to schedule or other part of the Agreement setting out the numbers and classes of shares to be allotted to each shareholder of the Target Company] ("the Consideration Shares"). A copy of the Agreement is enclosed marked "D".

6. The said sale was duly completed on [date] when the Shareholders delivered to and in favour of the Acquiring Company duly executed transfers of the whole of the issued shares, together with relevant Share Certificates, of the Target Company. [Immediately following such

delivery one Ordinary Share of the Target Company was transferred to [name] as nominee of the Acquiring Company.]

7. At a meeting of [the Directors][or specify committee or similar] of the Acquiring Company held on [date] the consideration shares were duly allotted to the shareholders of the Target Company pursuant to the provisions of the Agreement. We enclose marked "E" [and "F" respectively] a certified copy of the resolution of the Directors of the Acquiring Company passed on [date] [appointing the said committee and of the Resolution of the said Committee] making such allotment. We also enclose marked "G" a certificate under the hand of [the senior official of the Registrars][the company secretary] of the Acquiring Company, confirming that the names of the respective allottees of the Consideration Shares have been entered in the Register of Members of the Acquiring Company in respect of the Consideration Shares, together with a list of all members of the Acquiring Company immediately following the allotment, certified by the [Registrars][company secretary] of the Acquiring Company and marked ["H"].

[Note – as in (4) above, a computer printout may be substituted and need not be certified]

8. Immediately after the acquisition the issued share capital of the Acquiring Company was *[give details of classes, denominations and numbers of shares]* such shares being fully paid up *[or give details if not]*.

9. It is confirmed that immediately after the acquisition the classes of shares in the Acquiring Company were in the same proportions (or as nearly as may be the same proportions) as they had been in the Target Company.

10. It is confirmed that, immediately after the acquisition the proportion of shares of any particular class in the Acquiring Company held by each respective shareholder was the same (or as nearly as may be the same) as the proportion of shares of that class in the Target Company held by that shareholder immediately before the acquisition was made.

11. [No application for clearance under the relevant direct tax provisions] [An application for clearance under *[section numbers]*] was made by the Acquiring Company. [A copy of the application together with copies of the correspondence with HMRC is enclosed marked ["I"].

[Note – if no clearance application was made, the information listed below must be supplied]

12. It is submitted that the acquisition was effected for bona fide commercial reasons and did not form part of a scheme or arrangement of which the main purpose or one of the main purposes is the avoidance of liability to stamp duty, income tax, corporation tax or capital gains tax and that the

appropriate conditions of Section 75 of the Finance Act 1986 have been complied with, and accordingly exemption from ad valorem stamp duty under the head "Transfer on Sale" is claimed in respect of the Transfers executed pursuant thereto.

13. We enclose for adjudication *[give adequate list or description of the documents enclosed]* together with certified copies.

Further information to be provided if no clearance application was made as set out in (11) above:

1. A copy of the latest accounts of the Target Company;
2. Full details of any scheme, arrangement or overall transaction of which this transaction forms part;
3. Confirmation that the Acquiring Company still holds the shares of the Target Company and that there is no intention to dispose of them (or give details if disposal will occur in the course of a greater overall transaction);
4. A detailed note of the bona fide commercial reasons for the acquisition.

Index

[*References are to paragraph number and appendices*]

R